Innovation, Technology, and Knowledge Management

Series Editor
Elias G. Carayannis, George Washington University, Washington, DC, USA

For further volumes:
http://www.springer.com/series/8124

Elias G. Carayannis • George M. Korres

Editors

European Socio-Economic Integration

Challenges, Opportunities and Lessons Learned

Editors
Elias G. Carayannis
School of Business
George Washington University
Washington, DC, USA

George M. Korres
University of Newcastle
Centre of Urban and Regional Development
    Studies (CURDS)
Newcastle, UK
and
University of the Aegean
Department of Geography
Athens, Greece

ISBN 978-1-4614-5253-9   ISBN 978-1-4614-5254-6 (eBook)
DOI 10.1007/978-1-4614-5254-6
Springer New York Heidelberg Dordrecht London

Library of Congress Control Number: 2012952285

Printed on acid-free paper

Springer is part of Springer Science+Business Media (www.springer.com)

Series Foreword

The Springer book series *Innovation, Technology, and Knowledge Management* was launched in March 2008 as a forum and intellectual, scholarly "podium" for global/local, transdisciplinary, transsectoral, public–private, and leading/"bleeding"-edge ideas, theories, and perspectives on these topics.

The book series is accompanied by the Springer *Journal of the Knowledge Economy*, which was launched in 2009 with the same editorial leadership.

The series showcases provocative views that diverge from the current "conventional wisdom," that are properly grounded in theory and practice, and that consider the concepts of *robust competitiveness*,[1] *sustainable entrepreneurship*,[2] and *democratic capitalism*,[3] central to its philosophy and objectives. More specifically, the aim of this series is to highlight emerging research and practice at the dynamic intersection of these fields, where individuals, organizations, industries, regions, and nations are harnessing creativity and invention to achieve and sustain growth.

Books that are part of the series explore the impact of innovation at the "macro" (economies, markets), "meso" (industries, firms), and "micro" levels (teams, individuals),

---

[1] We define *sustainable entrepreneurship* as the creation of viable, profitable, and scalable firms. Such firms engender the formation of self-replicating and mutually enhancing innovation networks and knowledge clusters (innovation ecosystems), leading toward robust competitiveness (E.G. Carayannis, *International Journal of Innovation and Regional Development* 1(3), 235–254, 2009).

[2] We understand *robust competitiveness* to be a state of economic being and becoming that avails systematic and defensible "unfair advantages" to the entities that are part of the economy. Such competitiveness is built on mutually complementary and reinforcing low-, medium- and hightechnology and public and private sector entities (government agencies, private firms, universities, and nongovernmental organizations) (E.G. Carayannis, *International Journal of Innovation and Regional Development* 1(3), 235–254, 2009).

[3] The concepts of *robust competitiveness* and *sustainable entrepreneurship* are pillars of a regime that we call " *democratic capitalism* " (as opposed to "popular or casino capitalism"), in which real opportunities for education and economic prosperity are available to all, especially—but not only—younger people. These are the direct derivative of a collection of top-down policies as well as bottom-up initiatives (including strong research and development policies and funding, but going beyond these to include the development of innovation networks and knowledge clusters across regions and sectors) (E.G. Carayannis and A. Kaloudis, *Japan Economic Currents*, p. 6–10 January 2009).

drawing from such related disciplines as fi nance, organizational psychology, research and development, science policy, information systems, and strategy, with the underlying theme that for innovation to be useful it must involve the sharing and application of knowledge.

Some of the key anchoring concepts of the series are outlined in the fi gure below and the defi nitions that follow (all defi nitions are from E.G. Carayannis and D.F.J. Campbell, *International Journal of Technology Management*, 46, 3–4, 2009).

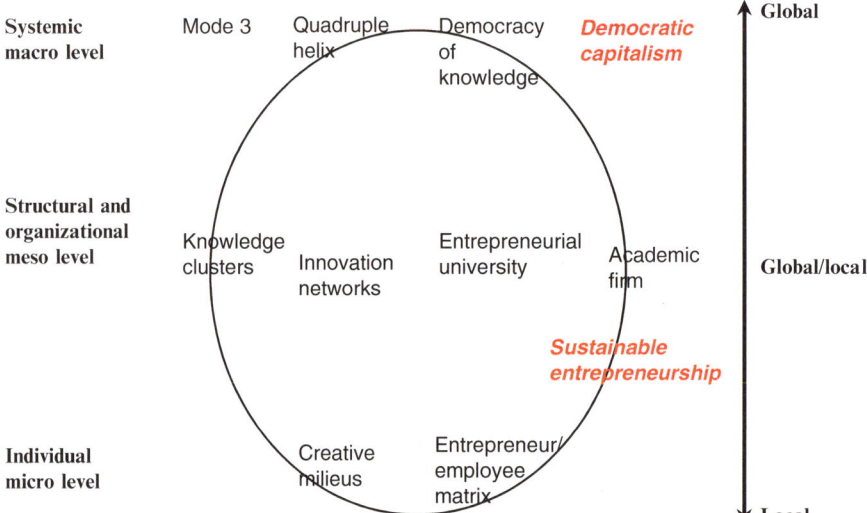

Conceptual profile of the series *Innovation, Technology, and Knowledge Management*

- The "Mode 3" Systems Approach for Knowledge Creation, Diffusion, and Use: "Mode 3" is a multilateral, multinodal, multimodal, and multilevel systems approach to the conceptualization, design, and management of real and virtual, "knowledge-stock" and "knowledge-fl ow," modalities that catalyze, accelerate, and support the creation, diffusion, sharing, absorption, and use of cospecialized knowledge assets. "Mode 3" is based on a system-theoretic perspective of socio-economic, political, technological, and cultural trends and conditions that shape the coevolution of knowledge with the "knowledge-based and knowledge-driven, global/local economy and society."
- Quadruple Helix: Quadruple helix, in this context, means to add to the triple helix of government, university, and industry a "fourth helix" that we identify as the "media-based and culture-based public." This fourth helix associates with "media," "creative industries," "culture," "values," "life styles," "art," and perhaps also the notion of the "creative class."
- Innovation Networks: Innovation networks are real and virtual infrastructures and infratechnologies that serve to nurture creativity, trigger invention, and catalyze innovation in a public and/or private domain context (for instance, government–university–industry public–private research and technology development coopetitive partnerships).

- Knowledge Clusters: Knowledge clusters are agglomerations of cospecialized, mutually complementary, and reinforcing knowledge assets in the form of "knowledge stocks" and "knowledge fl ows" that exhibit self-organizing, learning-driven, dynamically adaptive competences and trends in the context of an open systems perspective.
- Twenty-First Century Innovation Ecosystem: A twenty-fi rst century innovation ecosystem is a multilevel, multimodal, multinodal, and multiagent system of systems. The constituent systems consist of innovation metanetworks (networks of innovation networks and knowledge clusters) and knowledge metaclusters (clusters of innovation networks and knowledge clusters) as building blocks and organized in a self-referential or chaotic fractal knowledge and innovation architecture[4], which in turn constitute agglomerations of human, social, intellectual, and fi nancial capital stocks and fl ows as well as cultural and technological artifacts and modalities, continually coevolving, cospecializing, and cooperating.These innovation networks and knowledge clusters also form, reform, and dissolve within diverse institutional, political, technological, and socioeconomic domains, including government, university, industry, and nongovernmental organizations and involving information and communication technologies, biotechnologies, advanced materials, nanotechnologies, and next-Generation energy technologies.

Who is this book series published for? The book series addresses a diversity of audiences in different settings:

1. *Academic communities*. Academic communities worldwide represent a core group of readers. This follows from the theoretical/conceptual interest of the book series to infl uence academic discourses in the fi elds of knowledge, also carried by the claim of a certain saturation of academia with the current concepts and the postulate of a window of opportunity for new or at least additional concepts. Thus, it represents a key challenge for the series to exercise a certain impact on discourses in academia. In principle, all academic communities that are interested in knowledge (knowledge and innovation) could be tackled by the book series. The interdisciplinary (transdisciplinary) nature of the book series underscores that the scope of the book series is not limited a priori to a specific basket of disciplines. From a radical viewpoint, one could create the hypothesis that there is no discipline where knowledge is of no importance.
2. *Decision makers—private/academic entrepreneurs and public (governmental, subgovernmental) actors*. Two different groups of decision makers are being addressed simultaneously: (1) private entrepreneurs (fi rms, commercial fi rms, academic fi rms) and academic entrepreneurs (universities), interested in optimizing knowledge management and in developing heterogeneously composed knowledge-based research networks; and (2) public (governmental, subgovernmental) actors that are interested in optimizing and further developing their

---

[4]E.G. Carayannis, *Strategic Management of Technological Learning*, CRC Press, 2000.

policies and policy strategies that target knowledge and innovation. One purpose of public *knowledge and innovation policy* is to enhance the performance and competitiveness of advanced economies.

3. *Decision makers in general.* Decision makers are systematically being supplied with crucial information, for how to optimize knowledge-referring and knowledge-enhancing decision-making. The nature of this "crucial information" is conceptual as well as empirical (case-study-based). Empirical information highlights practical examples and points toward practical solutions (perhaps remedies), conceptual information offers the advantage of further-driving and further-carrying tools of understanding. Different groups of addressed decision makers could be decision makers in private fi rms and multinational corporations, responsible for the knowledge portfolio of companies; knowledge and knowledge management consultants; globalization experts, focusing on the internationalization of research and development, science and technology, and innovation; experts in university/business research networks; and political scientists, economists, and business professionals.

4. *Interested global readership.* Finally, the Springer book series addresses a whole global readership, composed of members who are generally interested in knowledge and innovation. The global readership could partially coincide with the communities as described above ("academic communities," "decision makers"), but could also refer to other constituencies and groups.

Elias G. Carayannis
Series Editor

Preface

Economic integration is the most noteworthy issue in international economic policy at the end of the twentieth century. The recent successful examples of the European Union (EU) and the North American Free Trade Association (NAFTA) have raised some important questions about the economic integration process and the possible establishment of economic unions in other parts of the world. This book makes an important contribution to the investigation of this topic.

The book is intended to provide a basic understanding of the current issues in and the problems of economic integration and it examines many aspects and consequences of this integration that are obscure or as yet unexplored. After addressing general issues in the field of economic integration, the discussion turns to empirical and theoretical aspects of monetary union, social policy reform and social union, public finance, and technology policy. In particular, with its wide range of topics, methodologies, and perspectives, the book offers stimulating and wide-ranging analyses that will be of interest to students, economic theorists, empirical social scientists, policy makers, and the informed general reader.

The volume comprises from two main parts. Part I is devoted to economic integration, macroeconomic issues, and the problems and process of economic integration. The chapters in this part contain theoretical and empirical analyses of economic integration, the European Union and the integration process. Part II investigates the social policy and integration process and deals with institutional matters and the policies of integration, the challenges for an integrated Europe, with emphasis on social policy, the welfare state, and political reforms.

The book argues that national or regional economic development depends mainly on technical change, social and human capital, and knowledge creation and diffusion. The book is intended to provide a basic understanding of the current issues and the problems of knowledge economy, technical change, and innovation activities; the book also examines many aspects and consequences of regional integration that are obscure or yet to be explored. In particular, with its wide range of topics, methodologies, and perspectives, the book offers stimulating and wide-ranging analyses that will be of interest to students, economic theorists, empirical and social scientists, policy makers, as well as the informed general reader.

The book consists of nine main chapters. In particular, the structure of this book includes the following:

- The first chapter attempts to analyze the inflation convergence n Europe. A new technique for the convergence is analyzed through a common factor framework which is implemented using principal components analysis that is applied to a dataset of monthly inflation rates of the European Monetary Union (EMU) members and of the Eastern European New Member Countries (NMC) over 1996–2007.
- The second chapter attempts to investigate the behavior of fiscal variables and the current account after joining the EU and the euro. Euro membership is preceded by fiscal consolidation but followed by fiscal expansion, while the current account balance worsens both before and after the euro is adopted.
- The third chapter contributes significantly to the development of analytical and critical thinking of mathematics as well as of rationalism. This chapter introduces the concept of individual and social mathematical capital and focuses on its economic value. It also provides a framework of hypotheses and open problems for theoretical and empirical research, which can lead to the economic and social evaluation of investments and policies on mathematical research, education, as well as to the optimization of planning in these areas.
- The fourth chapter attempts to examine the decision theory that is closely related with game theory and especially uncertainty, rationality, and optimal decision. We aim to study and analyze the various conflict situations, using game theory, where rational agents take action which leads to a particular purpose and is independent regarding the selection of the decisions but dependent on the results. This chapter attempts to analyze and examine the constraints and the rules in a political decision problem and furthermore attempts to construct and adopt an appropriate model for the political decision problems using a game theory approach. Finally, it attempts to examine the impact and the possible effects in a political decision problem.
- The fifth chapter attempts to analyze the theoretical framework regarding the effects of economic integration and their measurement. It deals with the literature on economic integration and small states and provides the methodology used for the analysis and also presents the results of the research conducted in Malta and Cyprus.
- The sixth chapter examines and analyses the role of mobile payment, the info-communication industry, the "*Code of Digital Transactions*" (*CO.D.TRA*) and the *Global Info-Cash* (*GIC*) in the recent cultural and economic crisis. It outlines the mobile payments methods and the role of digital transactions in the info-communication globalization. Finally, it introduces actions programs for switch on the digital form of money as an alternative way of physical payment in free market economy after the Greek elections of 2012.
- The seventh chapter explores the prospects for regional cooperation through e-governance by SAARC in South Asia and the limits of social integration due to sociopolitical complexities in the region.

- The eighth chapter focuses on education policy, economic growth, and convergence in the European Union. This chapter aims to analyze the European educational policy and also to examine the effects and the role of human capital in economic growth and regional socioeconomic convergence in Europe.
- The ninth chapter attempts to examine the new trends related to globalization, imply the increase of social and economic complexity, as well as higher rates of change and competitiveness. It also attempts to focus on the European Space Policy and the Galileo Project.
- The tenth chapter attempts to analyze, in a benchmarking study, the effects of human capital in European regional growth and competiveness. It also attempts to provide a clear understudying of the main related questions of economic growth and social development and regional cohesion in Europe.
- The eleventh chapter attempts to review the social and public policy and the effects for European member states. Within this analytical framework, this chapter aims to provide a clear understudying of main questions related to socioeconomic integration in Europe.
- The twelfth chapter attempts to analyze the East European public administration reform in search of socioeconomic development. This chapter reports on the findings collected during 56 conversations with civil servants and politicians in Estonia, Lithuania, Czech Republic, and Poland.
- The thirteenth chapter attempts to examine the Job Requirement Assessment in a research study through questionnaire carried out by a project of OECD, and it attempts to measure the implications and the effects in Greece.
- The fourteenth chapter attempts to analyze a critical evaluation of the Greek tourism policy and the effects of socioeconomic growth and integration process.

We would also like to thank the contributors for this volume, also the anonymous reviewer of the volume, and above all, our publisher for the great encouragement and support.

Washington, DC, USA   Elias G. Carayannis
Athens, Greece   George M. Korres

Contents

Contributors

Gloria Pirzio Ammassari Department of Political Sciences, Sapienza University of Rome, Rome, Italy

Rose Marie Azzopardi University of Malta, San Gwann, Malta

Bettina Becker School of Business and Economics, Loughborough University, Loughborough, UK

George K. Gantzias Department of Cultural Technology and Communication, University of the Aegean, Lesvos, Greece

Panagiotis Giavrimis Department of Sociology, University of the Aegean, Mytilene, Lesbos, Greece

Stephen G. Hall Department of Economics, University of Leicester, Leicester, UK

Georgios Karras Department of Economics, University of Illinois at Chicago, Chicago, IL, USA

Roswitha M. King Østfold University College, Halden, Norway

Centre for European and Transition Studies, University of Latvia, Riga, Latvia

Aikaterini Kokkinou Department of Economics, University of Glasgow, Glasgow, Scotland, UK

George M. Korres Centre of Urban and Regional Development Studies (CURDS), University of Newcastle, Newcastle, UK

Department of Geography, University of Aegean, Mytilene, Greece

Dimitrios G. Lagos Department of Business Administration, University of the Aegean, Chios, Greece

Panagiotis Liargovas Department of Economics, School of Economics and Management, University of Peloponnese, Tripolis, Greece

Maria Cristina Marchetti Department of Political Sciences, Sapienza University of Rome, Rome, Italy

Efstratios Papanis Department of Sociology, University of the Aegean, Mytilene, Lesbos, Greece

Kiran Prasad Department of Communication and Journalism, Sri Padmavati Mahila University, Tirupati, India

Constantinos Tsamadias Harokopio University, Athens, Greece

Paris A. Tsartas Department of Business Administration, University of the Aegean, Chios, Greece

George O. Tsobanoglou Centre of Urban and Regional Development Studies (CURDS), University of Newcastle, Newcastle, UK

Department of Sociology, University of the Aegean, Mitilene, Lesvos, Greece

Part I
Inside to Economic Integration: Limits and Prospects

Chapter 1
Inflation Convergence in Europe

Bettina Becker and Stephen G. Hall

1.1 Introduction

Convergence has been a popular theme in applied economics since the seminal papers of Barro (1991) and Barro and Sala-i-Martin (1992). The very notion of convergence quickly becomes problematic from an academic viewpoint however when we try and formalise a framework to think about these issues. In the light of the abundance of available convergence concepts, it would be useful to have a more universal framework that encompassed existing concepts as special cases. Moreover, much of the convergence literature has treated the issue as a zero-one outcome. We argue that it is more sensible and useful for policy decision makers and academic researchers to consider also ongoing convergence over time. Assessing the progress of ongoing convergence is one interesting and important means of evaluating whether the Eastern European New Member Countries (NMC) of the European Union (EU) are getting closer to being deemed "ready" to join the European Monetary Union (EMU), that is, fulfilling the Maastricht convergence criteria.

In this chapter, we build on our earlier work (Becker and Hall 2009) in considering some of the standard definitions of convergence and suggesting an alternative way to think about convergence based on a common factor framework which we implement using principal components analysis. We apply these ideas to a dataset of monthly inflation rates of the EMU countries, the NMC countries and three EU candidate countries (as of pre-2007) over the period 1996–2007. We consider

B. Becker (✉)
School of Business and Economics,
Loughborough University, Loughborough LE11 3TU, UK
e-mail: b.becker@lboro.ac.uk

S.G. Hall
Department of Economics, University of Leicester,
University Road, Leicester LE1 7RH, UK
e-mail: s.g.hall@le.ac.uk

E.G. Carayannis and G.M. Korres (eds.), *European Socio-Economic Integration*,
Innovation, Technology, and Knowledge Management 27,
DOI 10.1007/978-1-4614-5254-6_1, © Springer Science+Business Media New York 2013

groups between them and convergence of the NMC countries to the Euro Area aggregate and to a measure of inflation rates of the three best performing countries in the past 12 months, as a close proxy to the Maastricht convergence criterion. Among the questions we ask are as follows: Have there been any signs of convergence or divergence of the NMC inflation rates to each other or to the Euro Area? Are the NMC rates less homogeneous than the Euro Area, and are there subgroups between them? These are important questions to ask and answer in gauging the likely effects and sustainability of the European currency union, as (partial) convergence of inflation rates is one prerequisite of joining EMU. Nitsch (2004) suggests that inflation differentials have led to the dissolution of currency unions in the past.

This chapter is structured as follows. Section 2 considers the notion of convergence and shows how a common factor approach is a useful and in many ways more natural framework for defining convergence. Section 3 presents the empirical results of our application of this technique to a dataset of monthly harmonised inflation rates of the EMU (as of 2002), the NMC (as of pre-2007) and the three candidate countries. Gradual convergence patterns are examined for the 12 EMU member countries (Sect. 3.1), the ten NMC countries (Sect. 3.2), the NMC countries and EMU averages (Sect. 3.3), the 22 EMU and NMC countries (Sect. 3.4) and the 22 countries plus the three candidate countries (Sect. 3.5). Section 4 concludes.

1.2 Defining Convergence

While we have a clear idea regarding the importance of convergence as a prerequisite for economic changes such as the formation of a monetary union and we have a clear intuitive understanding of what convergence means, it is surprisingly difficult to find a satisfactory formal definition of convergence.[1] Hall et al. (1997) consider a number of formal definitions of convergence which illustrate the difficulty here. So consider the pointwise convergence of two series X_t and Y_t which we might define as occurring when

$$\lim_{t \to \infty}(X_t - \varphi Y_t) = \alpha \qquad (1.1)$$

where α is a non-stochastic constant which might often be required to be zero. This is a clear definition of convergence, but it is unrealistically strong as it requires the two series to exactly move together in the limit. A more reasonable definition would be to think of stochastic convergence or convergence in expectations.

$$\lim_{t \to \infty} E(X_t - \varphi Y_t) = \alpha \qquad (1.2)$$

---

[1]In the following, we will draw on our earlier work in Becker and Hall (2009).

This at first seems like a reasonable definition of convergence, but the problem here is that it implies convergence in many quite unreasonable cases. For example, if X and Y are both mean zero white noise processes, then this definition would suggest that the two series are converged even though they have no relationship. If X and Y are non-stationary, then sensible definitions may be offered through the notion of cointegration and the idea that convergence may limit the difference between the two series to a stationary difference either in the limit or over a given interval. However, while this is a useful operational notion of convergence, again it is limited by only being useful in the case of non-stationary series.

Here we propose a general measure of convergence which is based around the common factor representation of a group of series and which we believe more closely follows the basic conceptual idea which we have in mind when we talk about convergence. Consider a vector of 2 or more variables X which are determined by a set of factors F:

$$x_{it} = \lambda_i f_{it} \tag{1.3}$$

Then we may give the following definition of when X are converged.

Definition 1

The set of variables X are converged when the general factor representation in (1.3) may be restricted to the single common factor model given by

$$x_{it} = \lambda_i f_t + \varepsilon_{it} \tag{1.4}$$

and $\lambda_i \neq 0$ for all i, where ε_{it} are N specific factors.

The conventional assumption is that f_t and ε_{it} are uncorrelated across all i and t, and as Anderson (1963) pointed out, this is unlikely to be true of time series data, which is the primary interest here. Geweke (1977) however generalised this model to produce the dynamic factor model in the following way. The assumption is made that f_t and ε_{it} are strictly indeterministic and covariance stationary, which of course allows them to have a constant, time invariant correlation structure. Then by Wold's (1938) theorem, there exist two sets of white noise terms z and u_i such that

$$\lambda_i f_t = \sum_{s=0}^{\infty} a_{is} z_{t-s} = a_i^* z_t \tag{1.5}$$

and

$$\varepsilon_{it} = \sum_{s=0}^{\infty} b_{its} u_{it-s} = b_{it}^* u_{it} \tag{1.6}$$

hence,

$$x_{it} = a_i^* z_t + b_i^* u_{it} \tag{1.7}$$

where b is a diagonal matrix and the variances of z and u are normalised to be unity. This is then the dynamic single factor model. This model is a straightforward representation of one notion of what we mean by convergence. All the elements of X are moving in a similar way although they do each have an idiosyncratic element; as the elements of b^* go to zero the common feature completely dominates the behaviour of x and variables move perfectly together.

Of course not all series will satisfy the conditions for the decomposition in (1.7), and so Geweke (1977) proposes a formal test of this structure based on the restrictions to the covariance structure of X implied by (1.7). This test works both for individual intervals in the frequency domain (ω_1^j, ω_2^j], $j = 1, \ldots, p$ and a joint test for all the intervals. Of course in the context of convergence, the problem with this test is that like many other tests, it may not detect a process of developing convergence as it is designed to detect complete convergence over the entire sample being tested.

To consider this process of gradual convergence, we can return to the general factor model (1.3)

$$x_{it} = \lambda_i f_{it} \qquad (1.8)$$

and define the factors to be orthogonal to each other. If the factors are then ordered so that the first factor is calculated to have the maximum explanatory power, the second factor has the next highest power and so on (as in a principal components analysis), then the notion of ongoing convergence becomes rather straightforward. Pointwise convergence, as defined above, would imply that in the limit the first factor would be a complete explanation of X and so all the factors other than the first one would be zero. This would then collapse to the single factor model (1.7) where $b = 0$. Convergence in expectations would imply that the expected value of all the factors except the first one would be zero, and again in terms of (1.7), this would mean that the single factor model be accepted, but the b would not be restricted to zero. However, in a practical sense the usefulness of this approach becomes more obvious when we realise that there is a direct measure of the degree of convergence between the series in the form of the $\%R^2$ of the first factor. This shows the % of the total variation of X which is explained by the first factor. Pointwise convergence would imply that this is 1 and in general the closer this is to 1, the more complete is convergence between the set of series. This then allows us to deal with the problem of using convergence in expectations. Consider the case of n, mean zero IID distributed series; the expectation of the difference between these series on a pairwise basis would be zero, so they would all meet the condition for convergence in expectation, despite the fact that they are completely unrelated to each other. However, in the factor representation, the $\%R^2$ for the first factor would be $1/n$ as each factor would have equal explanatory power. The single factor model would be rejected, and this would indicate that there was no common underlying driving force linking the n series together. If the series began to move together, then the explanatory power on the first factor would rise, and so this becomes a natural metric for the extent to which convergence has occurred.

Definition 2

Convergence is taking place between a vector of 2 or more series over any given period 1 to T if the $\%R^2$ of the first principle component calculated over the period 1 to $T-t$ is less than the $\%R^2$ of the first principal component calculated over the period $T-t$ to T, $0 < t < T$.

This approach also works regardless of the stationarity properties of the data. So in the $I(1)$ case, if we have pairwise cointegration between the set of series so that between the n series there are $n-1$ cointegrating vectors, then in ECM form the model may be written as

$$\gamma(L)(1-L)X_t = \prod X_{t-1} + \upsilon + \varepsilon_t \tag{1.9}$$

where $\prod$ has rank $n-1$ and υ is the deterministic component. The moving average equivalent of this is

$$(1-L)X_t = C(L)(\varepsilon_t + \upsilon) \tag{1.10}$$

and the C matrix may be decomposed into

$$(1-L)X_t = C(1)(\varepsilon_t + \upsilon) + (1-L)C*(L)(\varepsilon_t + \upsilon) \tag{1.11}$$

where $C(1)$ has rank 1, and so there will be one common stochastic trend which is the dominant first factor in the factor representation. Asymptotically as the variance of this non-stationary trend will dominate any stationary terms, the $\%R^2$ will go to one and convergence in expectation is clear. Over a small sample, the size of the $\%R^2$ will be an indicator of how important the common stochastic trend is, relative to the noise in the series; again it becomes a direct measure of how much convergence has taken place. If any factor other than the first one shows signs of non-stationarity, then this would imply less than $n-1$ cointegrating vectors, and hence, full pairwise cointegration would not exist.

1.3   Empirical Application

In this section, we implement the common factor technique using principal components analysis and applying Definition 2 to identify gradual convergence processes over time. We apply this technique to a dataset of monthly harmonised consumer price inflation (HCPI) rates of the 12 EMU countries as of 2001,[2] the ten NMC of the European Union as of pre-2007[3] and three candidate countries of the EU as of

---

[2] These are Austria, Belgium, Finland, France, Germany, Greece, Ireland, Italy, Luxembourg, Netherlands, Portugal and Spain.

[3] These are Cyprus, Czech Republic, Estonia, Hungary, Latvia, Lithuania, Malta, Poland, Slovakia and Slovenia.

Table 1.1 Principal components analysis of inflation rates of the 12 EMU member countries ($\%R^2$ of first principal component)

Period	1997–2007	1997–2001	2002–2007	1997–2000	2001–2004	2005–2007
$\%R^2$	0.4758	0.6518	0.3778	0.6260	0.3785	0.4702

pre-2007, Bulgaria, Romania and Turkey.[4] The data begin in January 1997 for all countries except Bulgaria, for which the data are available from January 1998 only. Earlier HCPI data were not available from Eurostat. For each country sample under investigation, we conduct principal components analyses over a variety of time windows to examine gradual convergence or divergence through time. The windows are the total period (01/1997–12/2007), two consecutive sub-periods (01/1997–12/2001 and 1/2002–12/2007), three consecutive sub-periods (01/1997–12/2000, 01/2002–12/2004 and 01/2005–12/2007) and seven moving 5-year windows. Where Bulgaria is included in the sample, the earlier samples begin in 01/1998.

1.3.1   Gradual Convergence Patterns of EMU Inflation Rates

Table 1.1 shows the $\%R^2$ of the first principal component of the inflation rates of the 12 EMU countries. Over the sample period as a whole, inflation rates are not moving together very closely, as indicated by a low $\%R^2$ (0.48). Examination of the sub-periods reveals that in the period that includes the inception of EMU, inflation rates moved relatively more together than did post-EMU inflation rates. Most of the divergence is due to the time period 2001–2004 that includes most of years of the European recession.

Figure 1.1 shows the $\%R^2$ of the EMU12 inflation rates over the seven moving windows in graphical form. There seems to be a break between the first three and the last four windows, with inflation rates moving much closer together in the time periods that include the year of the inception of EMU, with a $\%R^2$ above or close to 0.6, while it is either below or only just above 0.4 over the later time windows. Between the beginning and the end of the sample period, inflation rates diverged substantially, as indicated by the fall of the $\%R^2$ from 0.65 over 1997–2001 to 0.35 over 2003–2007.

Figure 1.2 presents the individual country weights of the first principal component.[5] We see that over the period 1997–2007 as a whole (panel a), Finland, the Netherlands and in particular Greece moved least closely with the other countries, although there was little co-movement overall. Greece is the only country whose

---

[4]Slovenia joined EMU in January 2007 and Cyprus, Malta and Slovakia joined after the end of our sample period—Cyprus and Malta joined in January 2008, and Slovakia joined in January 2009. Bulgaria and Romania joined the EU in January 2007. We intended to include Croatia and Macedonia in our sample of candidate countries, but HCPI data for these two countries are not available from Eurostat.

[5]We are presenting a selection of sub-periods; full results are available upon request.

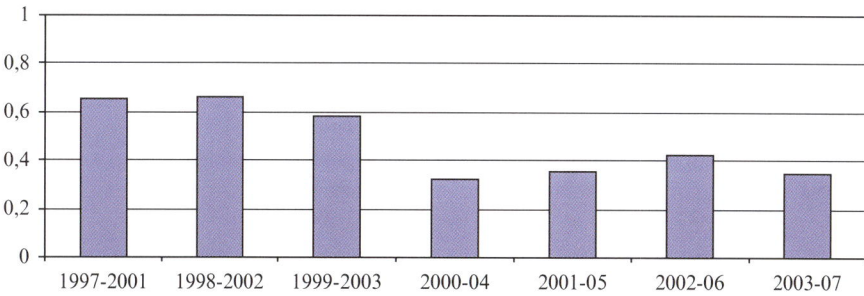

Fig. 1.1 Principal components analysis of inflation rates of the 12 EMU member countries ($\%R^2$ of first principal component, *5-year moving windows*)

inflation rate moved in the opposite direction than the other countries' rates on aver-age, as indicated by the opposite sign of its weight. Panel f reveals the disintegrating effect associated with the recession years and shows French inflation moving in the opposite direction than the others on average, if moving at all. The disintegration appears to subsequently have gained momentum (panels g and h), suggesting the emergence of two convergence clubs whose inflation rates moved into opposite directions. One of these groups includes most of the countries often called the "core" Euro Area countries, Austria, Belgium, France, Germany and Luxembourg, whereas the other includes the "periphery" countries. Over the final time window, 2003–2007 (panel i), all inflation rates moved in the same direction on average but at very different frequencies, with Spain's rate moving much more than the average. Overall, it is clear that inflation rates showed some signs of convergence around the incep-tion of EMU and in the early EMU years, but that little signs of convergence can be detected as we move on in time.

1.3.2   *Gradual Convergence Patterns of the New Member Countries' Inflation Rates*

Table 1.2, panel a, compared with Table 1.1, shows that for the investigation period as a whole, there is a somewhat surprising similarity between the extent to which the inflation rates of the EMU and those of the NMC, respectively, are converged to each other or not, as indicated by the $\%R^2$s of the first principal component over 1997–2007 (0.48 for each group). We can also observe that the $\%R^2$s moved in the same direction between the various time periods, that is, as the EMU inflation rates moved less closely together, so did the NMC inflation rates. The periods including the recession years are associated with less divergence for the NMC than for the EMU group.

Figure 1.3 (grey bars) presents the $\%R^2$ of the first principal component for the moving time windows. The results suggest that there has in general been relatively less change in the level of convergence or divergence over time than for the EMU countries, with the $\%R^2$s all moving between 0.4 and 0.6. There is also no apparent

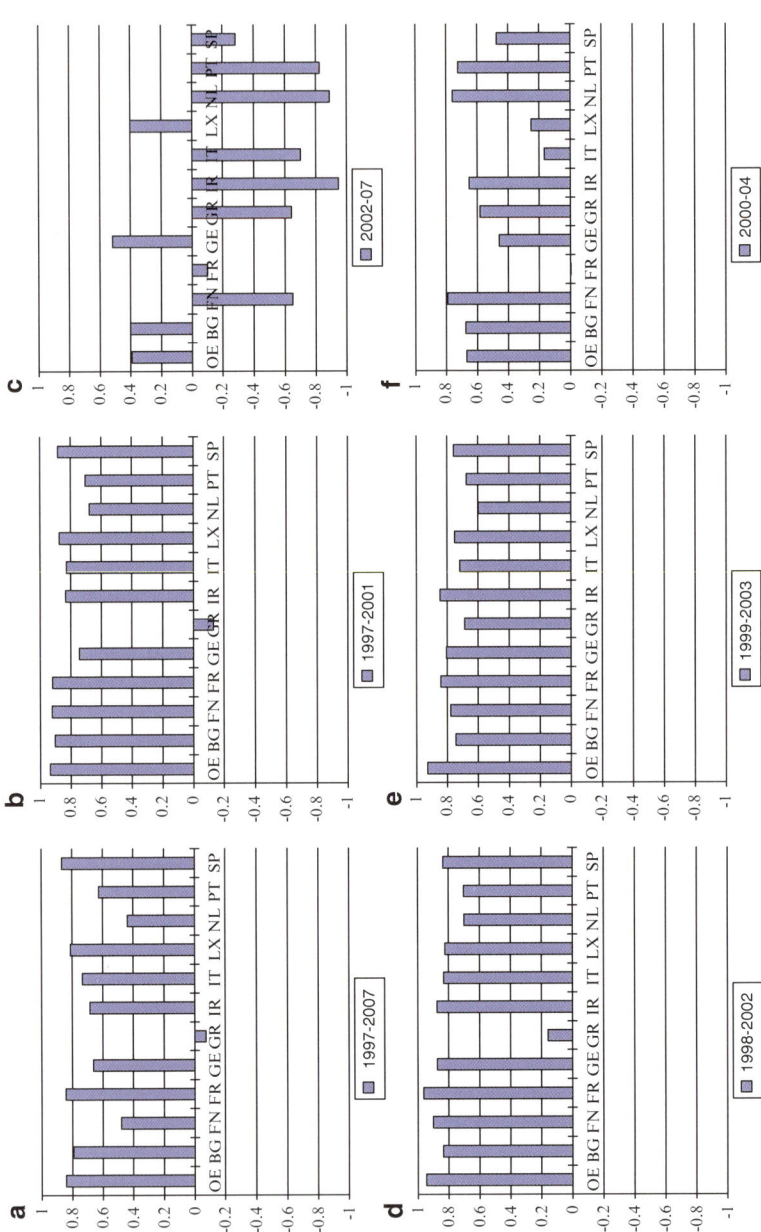

Fig. 1.2 Country-specific weights of first principal component, 12 EMU countries (*panel a*: total period, *panels b, c*: consecutive periods, *panels b, d–i*: moving windows). *Note*: The abbreviations used are OE (Austria), BG (Belgium), FN (Finland), FR (France), GE (Germany), GR (Greece), IR (Ireland), IT (Italy), LX (Luxembourg), NL (Netherlands), PT (Portugal), SP (Spain)

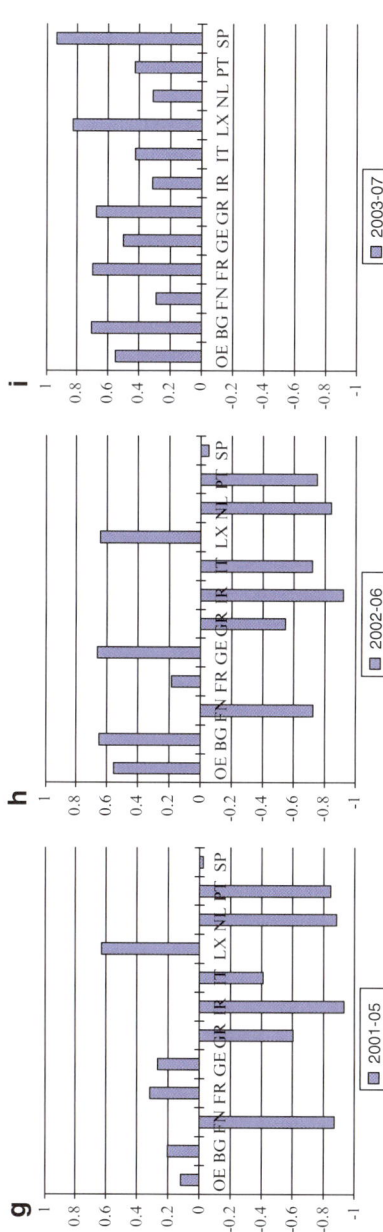

Fig 1.2 (continued)

Table 1.2 Principal components analysis of inflation rates of the ten New Member Countries ($\%R^2$ of first principal component) (*panels a* and *a'*: NMC inflation rates; *panels b* and *b'*: NMC inflation rates as a ratio to the average EMU inflation rate; *panel c'*: NMC inflation rates as a ratio to the average inflation rate of the three best performing EMU countries over the past 12 months (beginning of sample period: 1998 for panels a', b', c'))

	Period	1997–2007	1997–2001	2002–2007	1997–2000	2001–2004	2005–2007
a	$\%R^2$	0.4795	0.5905	0.4623	0.6318	0.4782	0.5717
b	$\%R^2$	0.6352	0.6728	0.4936	0.6522	0.4355	0.6063
	Period	1998–2007	1998–2001	2002–2007	1998–2000	2001–2004	2005–2007
a'	$\%R^2$	0.4163	0.5461	0.4623	0.6197	0.4782	0.5717
b'	$\%R^2$	0.6089	0.7270	0.4936	0.7241	0.4355	0.6063
c'	$\%R^2$	0.5639	0.6076	0.4443	0.5051	0.4898	0.5475

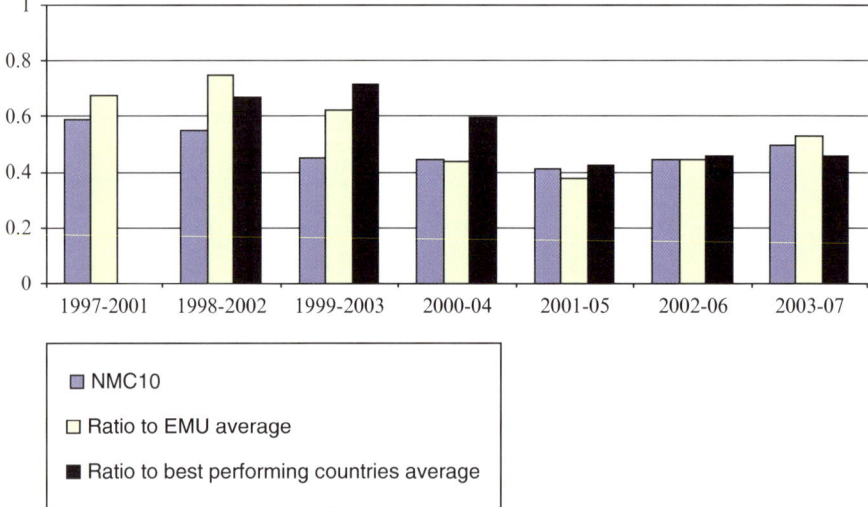

Fig. 1.3 Principal components analysis of inflation rates of the ten New Member Countries ($\%R^2$ of first principal component, *5-year moving windows*)

break over time. The NMC inflation rates diverged gradually until 2001–2005, after which they began to move more closely together with each other again. Between the first and the last 7-year windows, we can observe some small divergence ($\%R^2$ of 0.59 over 1997–2001 compared with 0.5 over 2003–2007), but this is much less pronounced than that for the EMU group. Comparison between Figs. 1.1 and 1.3 further indicates that the NMC inflation rates moved less in line with each other than did the EMU rates in the early years of EMU (1997–2001, 1998–2002, 1999–2003), but that the NMC countries moved much in sync with each other in the later years, and in particular over the last window of our sample (2003–2007).

Figure 1.4 presents the country weights of the first principal component for the NMC sample. Panel a indicates that over the period as a whole, the inflation rates of Cyprus, Latvia and Slovakia moved much less than the average, whereas the rates

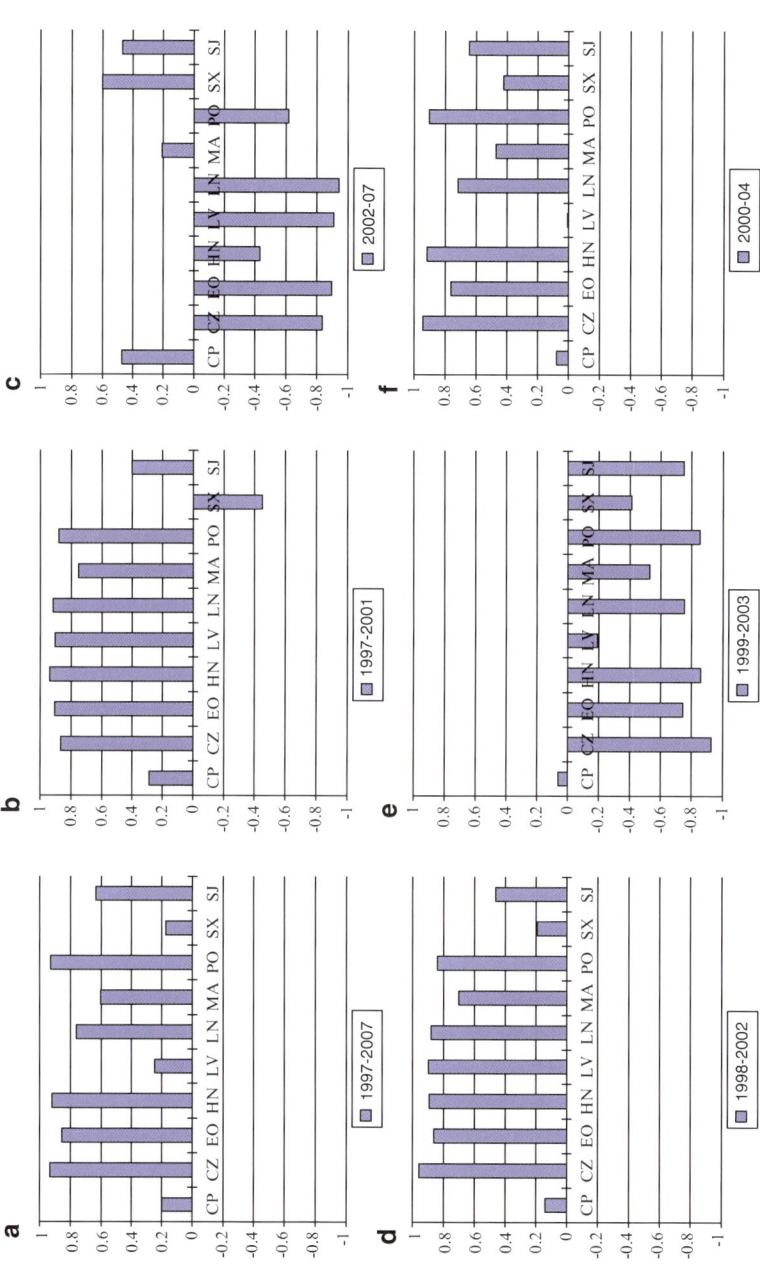

Fig. 1.4 Country-specific weights of first principal component, ten New Member Countries (*panel a*: total period, *panels b, c*: consecutive periods, *panels b, d–i*: moving windows). *Note*: The countries are denoted CP (Cyprus), CZ (Czech Republic), EO (Estonia), HN (Hungary), LV (Latvia), LN (Lithuania), MA (Malta), PO (Poland), SX (Slovakia), SJ (Slovenia)

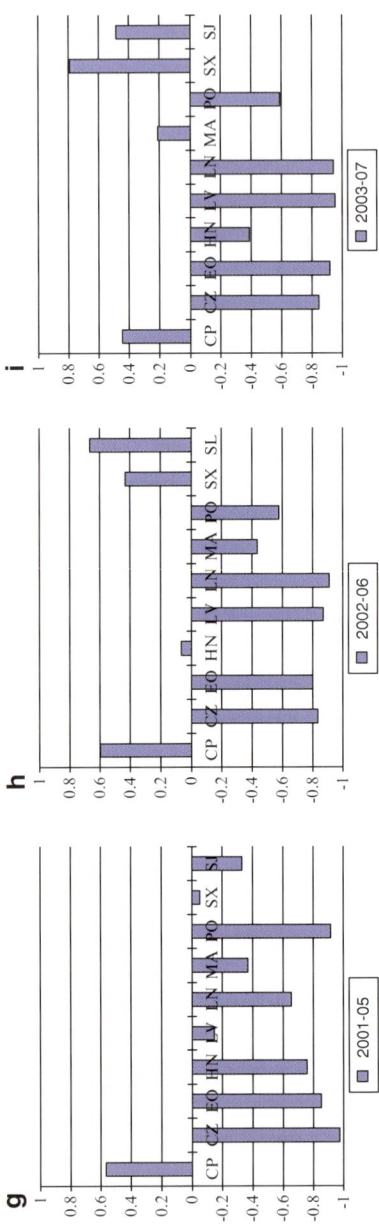

Fig 1.4 (continued)

of the Czech Republic, Hungary and Poland moved more. However, all rates tended to move in the same direction on average, as indicated by all weights having the same sign. The next two panels support the finding of divergence from Table 1.2 and suggest the formation of two general convergence clubs over time, whose inflation rates move into opposite directions. Interestingly, one of these consists of the four countries that joined EMU by 2009, Cyprus, Malta, Slovenia and Slovakia. The next panels confirm the evidence from Table 1.2 that there was not much change in the extent of convergence or divergence through 1999–2003 and 2002–2006, although the individual country weights change gradually and in particular towards the end of the period. Overall, comparison of the first and last time windows (1997–2001 and 2003–2007) suggests formation of two broad convergence clubs into new EMU members and non-members (as of the time of writing this chapter).

1.3.3   Gradual Convergence Patterns of the New Member Countries' Inflation Rates Towards EMU Rates

For the assessment of whether, from an inflation point of view, EU member countries are ready to join EMU, it does of course not matter how converged the countries are to each other, but how converged they are with EMU. To get a first idea of convergence of NMC inflation to EMU inflation, we examine potential co-movements between the inflation rates of the NMC countries as a group and the aggregate EMU or Euro Area inflation rate. We consider the ratio of each new member country's inflation rate to the average EMU rate. So if in this factor model the $\%R^2$ are relatively constant over consecutive time periods, this means the NMC inflation rates move closely together with the average EMU rate. As we have ten principal components in our model, complete convergence would imply a $\%R^2$ of 1/10 of each component, so if we find that the $\%R^2$ of the first principal component for the Euro rates exceeds 1/10 in the starting period, then a fall of the $\%R^2$ over time towards 1/10 would imply gradual convergence of the national inflation rates of the NMC to the EMU average rate.

Table 1.2, panel b, presents the $\%R^2$ of the first principal component of the NMC/EMU inflation ratios. The results suggest that as a group the NMC were relatively diverged from the EMU average over the investigation period as a whole ($\%R^2$ of 0.64). As the inflation rates of the NMC move less in line with each other between 1997–2001 and 2002–2007 (panel a), they move more in line with the EMU average (panel b). Figure 1.3 (white bars) shows that for the time periods that include the year of the inception of EMU, the NMC countries were much less converged to the EMU average than in the later periods. However, as the NMC rates converge to each other somewhat from 2001–2005 through to 2003–2007 (grey bars), they move less in line with the EMU average. Between the first and the last time windows, the NMC rates diverged slightly, while there was some convergence towards the EMU average. One reason for this may be that some NMC countries were on average more converged with EMU members than with other NMC countries.

However, what is relevant for EMU entry is of course not whether a country's inflation rate is well converged with the average of the EMU inflation rates. Rather, the inflation convergence criterion of the Maastricht treaty requires a country's inflation rate to be close to, that is, 1.5 percentage points around, the average rate of the three best performing EMU countries (BPC) over the past year for the three consecutive years prior to the country's EMU entry. This often means that an aspiring new EMU member will be required to exhibit a substantially lower inflation rate than existing EMU members, and hence, its inflation rate may need to be below rather than close to the EMU average. We generated a monthly series of the average inflation rate of the three BPC over the past 12 months to get some idea about convergence under the Maastricht criterion. Use of this series moved the beginning of the sample period forwards to 01/1998. We then conducted principal components analyses over the various time periods of the ratio of each NMC country's inflation rate to the BPC average rate.

Panel c′ in Table 1.2 presents the $\%R^2$s of the first principal components of the NMC to BPC inflation ratios. For comparison, panels a′ and b′ report the results of the previous two NMC analyses for the later start period of 1998. Over the whole period, 1998–2007, the inflation rates of the NMC countries as a group did not move much in line with the BPC average ($\%R^2$ of 0.56). However, they were marginally more in line with the BPC than with the average of all EMU. Inspecting the results through time, Fig. 1.3 (black bars) suggests some shift over time: In the early years of EMU, the NMC inflation rates moved rather independently from the BPC average, as indicated by the relatively high $\%R^2$s, while rates moved somewhat more closely in line with the BPC over the later periods. Between the first (1998–2002 in this case) and the last 5-year windows, as the NMC inflation rates diverged from each other slightly, they experienced some convergence towards the BPC average ($\%R^2$ of 0.67 in 1997–2001 compared with 0.46 in 2003–2007). One reason may be that the countries which joined EMU in 2007/2008 moved closely in line with the existing EMU members in the run-up to joining.

Figure 1.5 shows the country weights for the whole period (panel a) and the first and last 5-year moving windows (panels b, c). As explained in Sect. 2, in the present type of factor model, increasing convergence of the NMC inflation rates as a group to the BPC average rate would imply a more random distribution of the weights for the NMC countries over time. This is clearly the case when we compare panels b and c. Moreover, these results support the earlier finding of the formation of convergence clubs over time. The positive sign of the weights in panel c indicates that as the average inflation rate of the BPC moved up, so did, on average, the inflation rates of Cyprus, Malta, Slovenia and Slovakia, which all joined EMU by 2009, while the inflation rates of the remaining NMC countries moved down.

1.3.4 Gradual Convergence Patterns of the New Member Countries' Inflation Rates and the EMU Rates

Having looked at convergence or divergence patterns of the EMU countries and of the NMC countries as individual groups, and of the NMC countries as a group

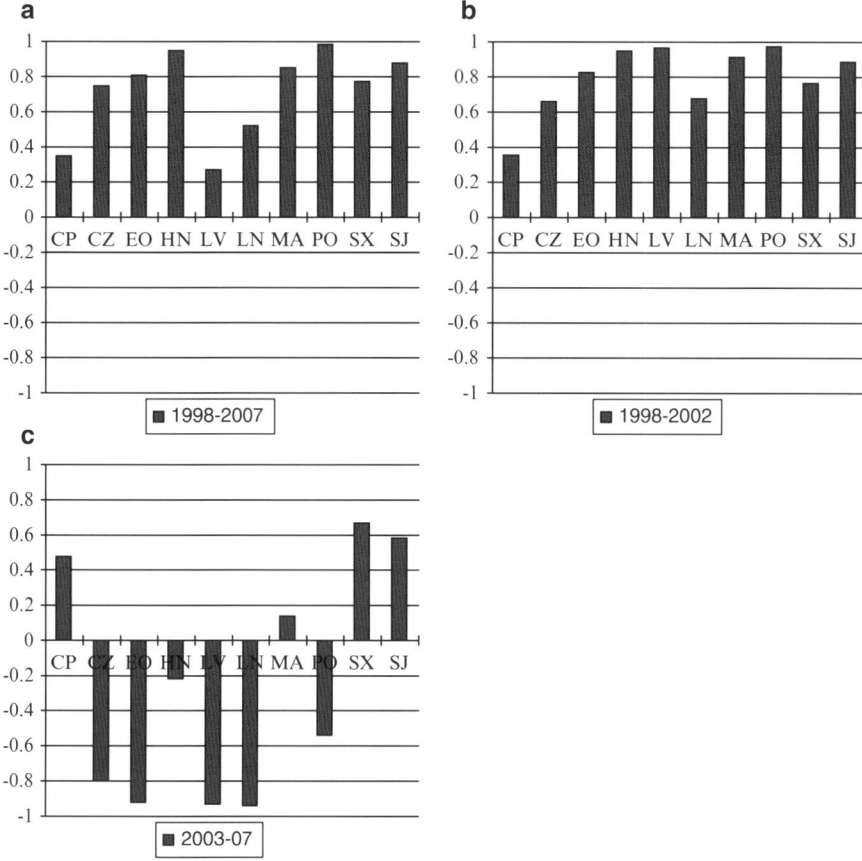

Fig. 1.5 Country-specific weights of first principal component, ten New Member Countries as a ratio to the average of the best performing countries over the past 12 months

Table 1.3 Principal components analysis of inflation rates of the 12 EMU member countries and the ten New Member Countries (%R^2 of first principal component)

Period	1997–2007	1997–2001	2002–2007	1997–2000	2001–2004	2005–2007
%R^2	0.3345	0.4438	0.3648	0.4223	0.3696	0.3808

towards EMU-related averages, it will now be interesting to examine all 22 countries as one group and see whether their inflation rates moved as two groups over time or whether there is evidence of convergence clubs between them. Table 1.3 shows the %R^2 of the first principal components for the total sample of the EMU and the NMC inflation rates. There is clear evidence of independent movements of inflation rates over all time periods considered, with the highest %R^2 being little above 0.4.

The results for the 5-year moving windows depicted in Fig. 1.6 confirm that there has been little change over time, even though some of the disintegration in the periods that include the recession carries over from the two individual samples to the

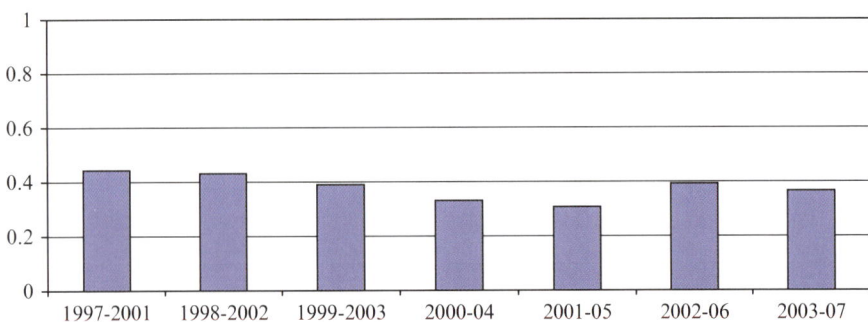

Fig. 1.6 Principal components analysis of inflation rates of the 12 EMU member countries and the ten New Member Countries (%R^2 of first principal component, *5-year moving windows*)

whole sample. There are signs of some small divergence between the first and the last 5-year moving windows.

Figure 1.7 depicts the country weights of the first principal component; the first 12 weights (bars) refer to the EMU countries; the last ten weights refer to the NMC countries. Inspection of the results reveals that the individual country patterns changed rather substantially over time. Examining first the results over the sample period as a whole (panel a, 1997–2007), there is a relatively clear split between the EMU12 and the NMC10 groups, with the exceptions of Greece and Cyprus, which by the sign of their weight move more in line with the respective other country group. This split is removed over time when we divide the whole period into two or three sub-periods (panels b, c and d–f). Examining the weights of the seven 5-year moving windows (panels b, g–l), we observe that the countries' inflation rates essentially move in the same direction on average over the period that begins with the EMU inception (panel h, 1999–2003), although the individual inflation rates clearly move at different frequencies. Comparing the first and the last periods (panel b and panel l) indicates that over time, the inflation rates disintegrate into groups that are unrelated to the initial split into the EMU and NMC groups. Cyprus, Malta, Slovenia and Slovakia move more closely in line with most countries of the "periphery" EMU countries than with most countries of the "core". Hence, there is some evidence for the formation of convergence clubs over time.

1.3.5 Gradual Convergence Patterns of the Inflation Rates of the New Member Countries, the EMU Countries and the Candidate Countries Bulgaria, Romania and Turkey

Finally, we add the three candidate countries Bulgaria, Romania and Turkey (BRT) to our country sample. Due to the lack of earlier data for Bulgaria, this moves the beginning of the sample period to 01/1998. The results for the %R^2 of the first principal components for the various time periods are presented in Table 1.4 and Fig. 1.8.

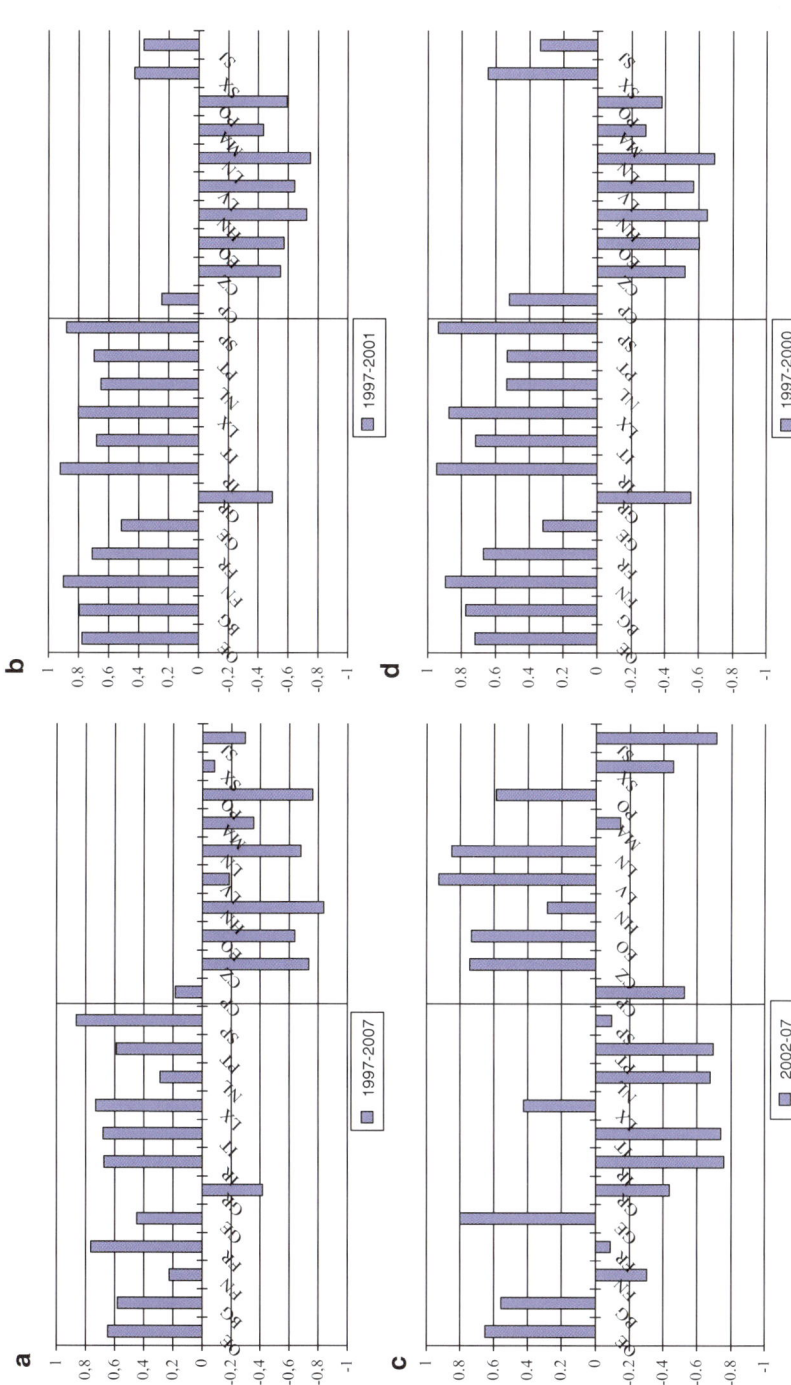

Fig. 1.7 Country-specific weights of first principal component, 12 EMU member countries plus ten New Member Countries (*panel a*: total period, *panels b–f*: consecutive periods, *panels b, g–l*: moving windows)

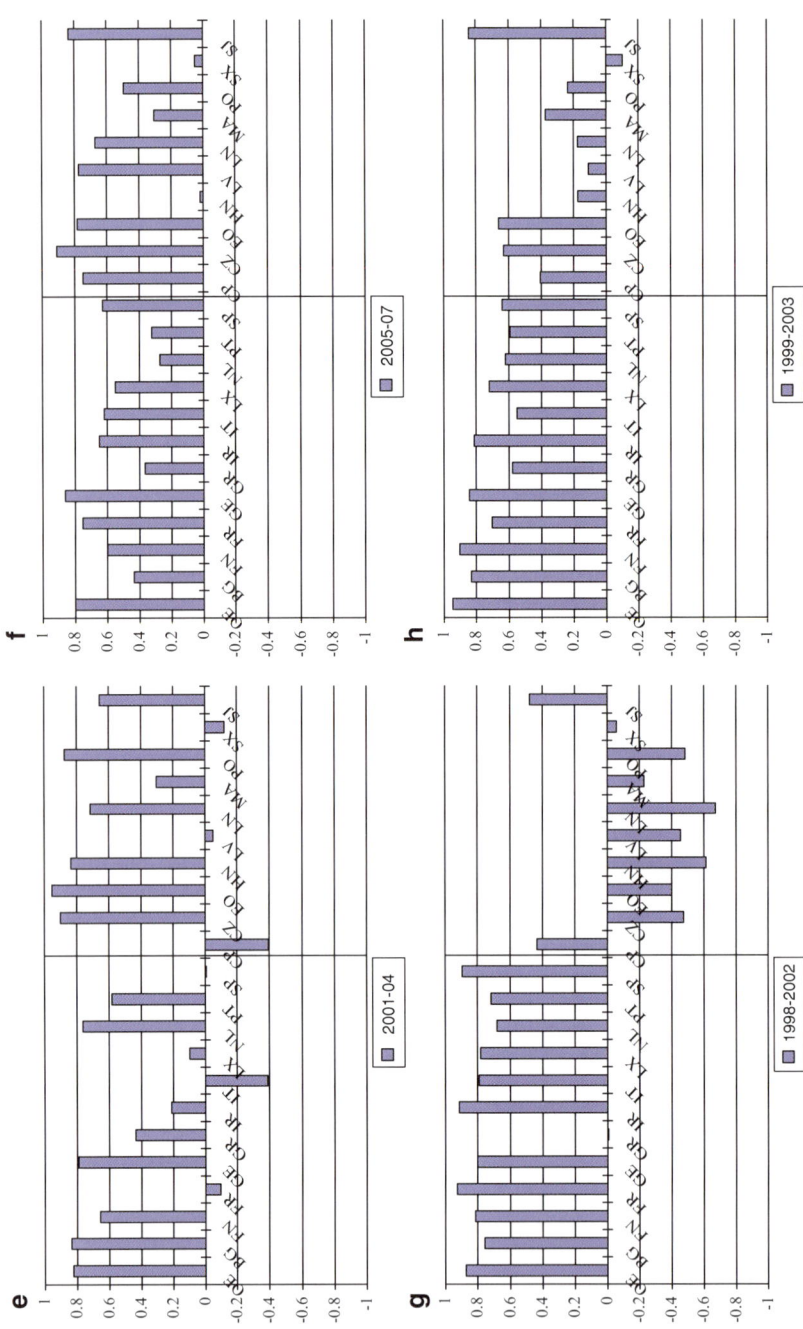

Fig 1.7 (continued)

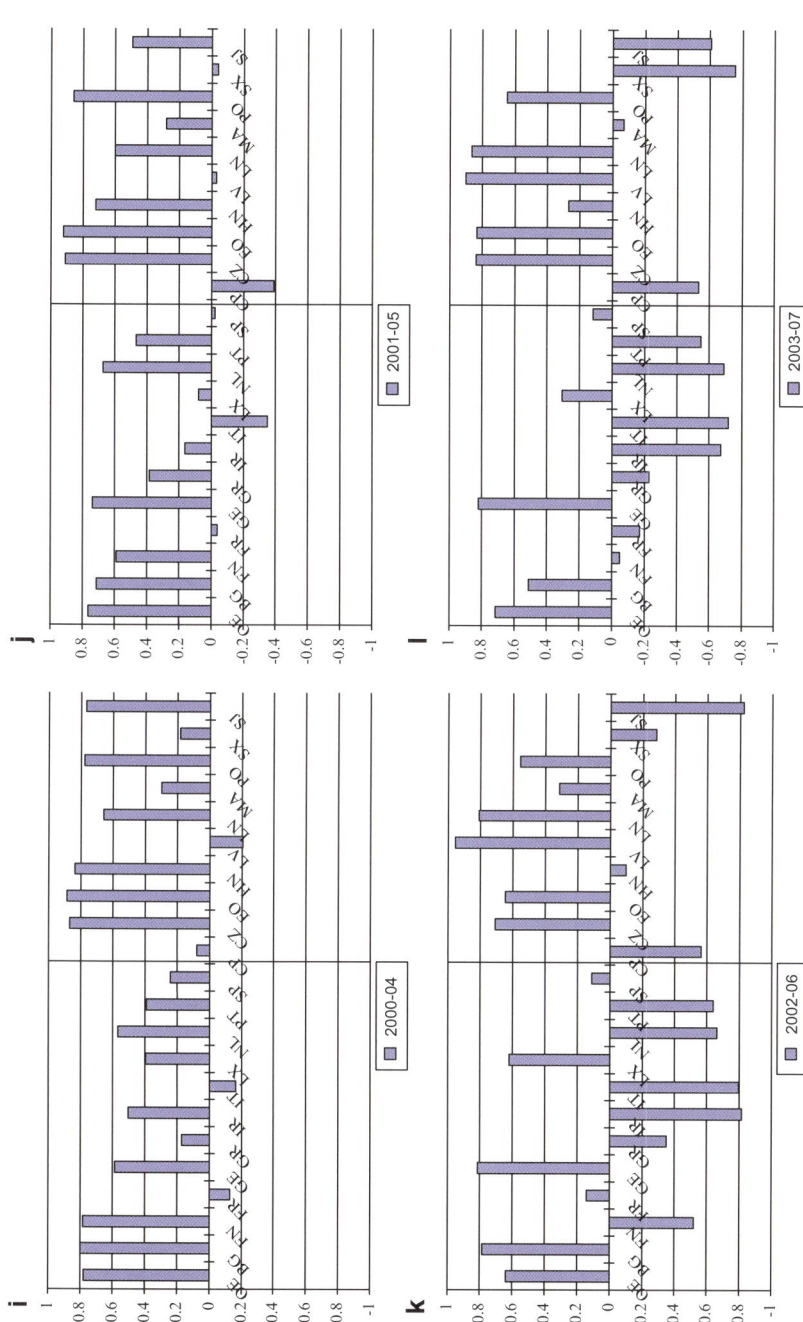

Fig 1.7 (continued)

Table 1.4 Principal components analysis of inflation rates of the 12 EMU member countries and the ten New Member Countries and three candidate countries (%R^2 of first principal component)

Period	1998–2007	1998–2001	2002–2007	1998–2000	2001–2004	2005–2007
%R^2	0.3085	0.4266	0.3815	0.4416	0.3918	0.3611

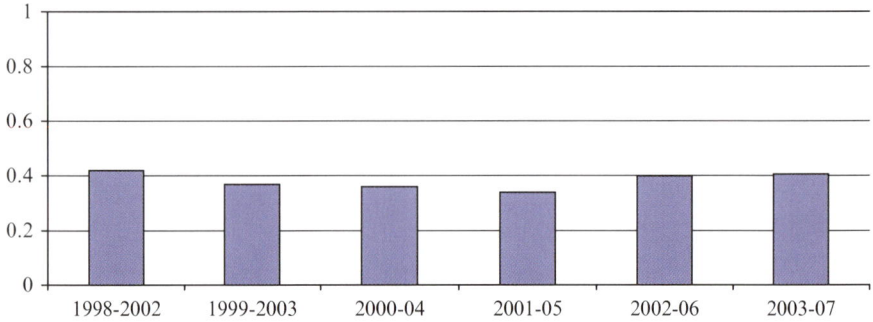

Fig. 1.8 Principal components analysis of inflation rates of the 12 EMU member countries and the ten New Member Countries and three candidate countries (%R^2 of first principal component, *5-year moving windows*)

Table 1.4 shows that the inflation rates of the 22 countries clearly move independently of each other as a group in all sample periods considered. The results also suggest marginal gradual divergence over time. Figure 1.8 indicates that between the first and the last 5-year moving windows, there has essentially been no change, with a %R^2 of around 0.4, indicating lack of co-movement.

Inspecting the country weights of the first principal component in Fig. 1.9, we can see that over the period as a whole, 1998–2007 (panel a), there are some signs of a split into two broad groups, EMU versus NMC plus BRT, as assessed by the sign of the weights. However, by this criterion, Finland, Greece and the Netherlands moved more closely in line with the second group on average, while Cyprus and Latvia moved more closely in line with the EMU group. Nonetheless neither group is homogeneous, as the differences in the size of the weights indicate that some inflation rates moved much more than the average while others moved much less. Panels b–g show the weights over the moving time windows. As the first window gives a lot of weight to the early EMU years, in line with our earlier results, the split into the two broad groups is much more evident here, and each subgroup is more homogeneous than over the period as a whole. In the period that begins with the year of the EMU inception (panel c), we observe, as before, that all inflation rates moved into the same direction, and interestingly the BRT rates are no exception here. Over time, however, there is disintegration which removes the split into the two broad groups evident at the beginning of the sample. With respect to the BRT countries, comparison of the first and the last moving windows suggests that Bulgaria has disintegrated from Romania and Turkey, with the latter two being more closely in line with Cyprus, Malta, Slovenia and Slovakia and most of the EMU "periphery" countries.

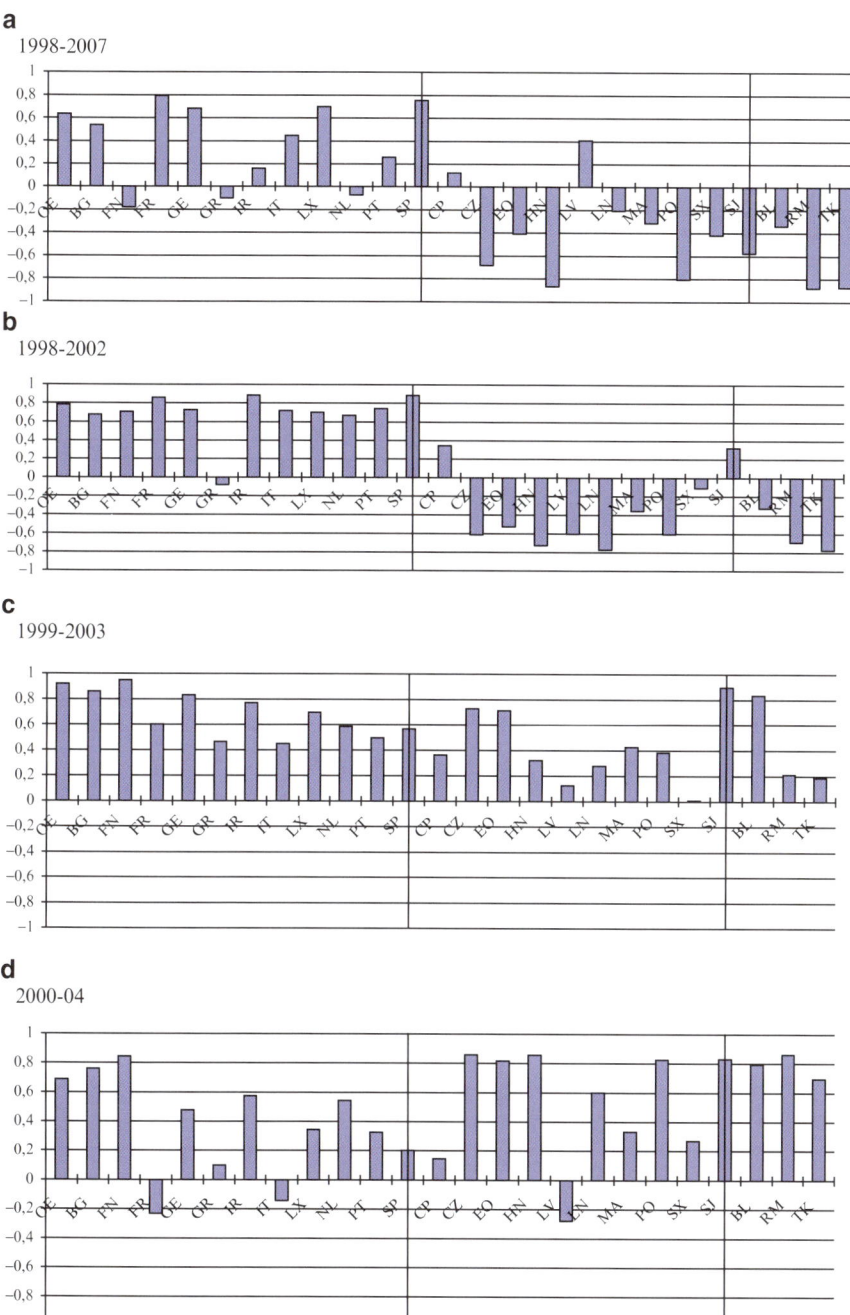

Fig. 1.9 Country-specific weights of first principal component, 12 EMU member countries and ten New Member Countries and three candidate countries Bulgaria (BL), Romania (RM) and Turkey (TK) (*panel a*: whole period, *panels b–g*: 5-year moving windows)

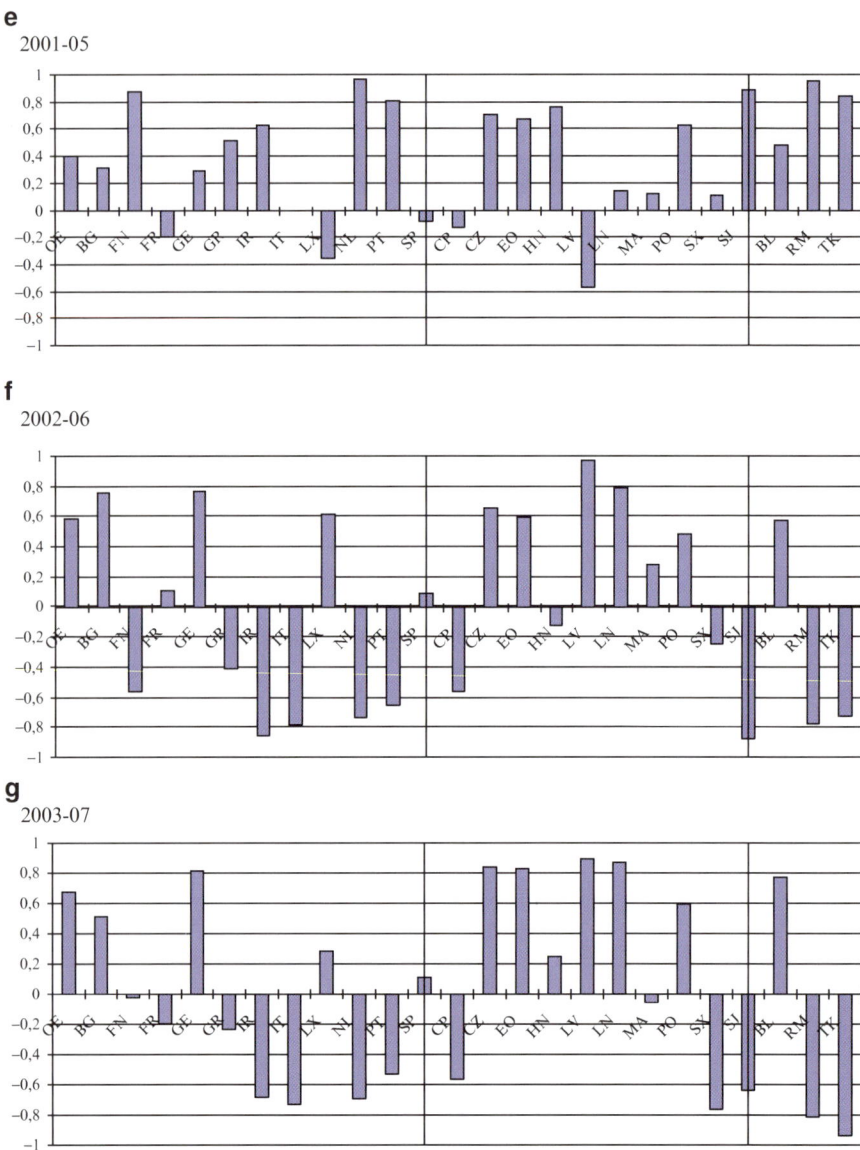

Fig 1.9 (continued)

1.4 Conclusion

In this chapter we have presented an alternative technique of approaching the convergence debate proposed in our earlier research and based on a common factor
framework which we implement using principal components analysis. We have
shown how this is in many ways a more natural way to consider the problem than

those conventionally used. We have applied these ideas to a dataset of monthly harmonised consumer price inflation rates of the EMU countries, the NMC countries and three EU candidate countries over the period 1996–2007. We have considered groups between them and convergence of the NMC countries to the Euro Area aggregate and to a measure of inflation rates of the three best performing countries (BPC) in the past 12 months, as a close proxy to the Maastricht convergence criterion.

The main results suggest that EMU inflation rates moved much closer together in the time periods that include the year of the inception of EMU, but little signs of convergence can be detected in the later periods. The NMC inflation rates moved less in line with each other than did the EMU rates in the early EMU years, but the NMC rates moved more in sync with each other than those of EMU in the later years of our sample period. Furthermore, in the earlier years, the NMC inflation rates moved rather independently from an average series of the three best performing countries over the past 12 months. Interestingly, our results indicate that the inflation rates of Cyprus, Malta, Slovenia and Slovakia, the three countries which joined EMU by 2009, moved in the same direction as the BPC rate, on average, while the inflation rates of the remaining NMC countries moved in the opposite direction. When examining the EMU and the NMC countries as one group, we find that while there was a split into the EMU versus the NMC group at the beginning of the sample period, there is evidence for convergence clubs across the two groups at the end of the period. Finally, adding three candidate countries to the sample of the EMU and the NMC countries does not substantially change the picture; however, the inflation rate of Bulgaria seems to have moved away from those of Romania and Turkey over time, with the latter two being more closely in line with Slovakia, Cyprus, Malta and Slovenia and most of the EMU "periphery" countries.

References

Anderson TW (1963) The use of factor analysis in the statistical analysis of multiple time series. Psychometrika 28:1–25

Barro R (1991) Economic growth in a cross section of countries. Quart J Econ 106:407–443

Barro R, Sala-i-Martin X (1992) Convergence. J Polit Econ 100:223–251

Becker B, Hall SG (2009) A new look at economic convergence in Europe: a common factor approach. Int J Finance Econ 14:85–97

Geweke J (1977) The dynamic factor analysis of economic time series models. Chapter 19. In: Aigner D, Goldberger A (eds) Latent variables in socioeconomic models. North-Holland, Amsterdam, pp 365–383

Hall SG, Robertson D, Wickens MR (1997) Measuring economic convergence. Int J Finance Econ 2:131–143

Nitsch V (2004) Have a break, have a … national currency: when do monetary unions fall apart? CESifo Working Paper No. 1113

Wold H (1938) A study in the analysis of stationary time series, 2nd edn. Amquist and Wicksell, Stockholm

Chapter 2
Economic and Monetary Integration in Europe: Evidence on Fiscal and Current Account Effects

Georgios Karras

2.1 Introduction

Both the economic and monetary aspects of European integration have always been understood to have benefits, as well as costs, for the countries involved. The advantages of freer trade, particularly within Europe, are generally acknowledged to generate benefits that vastly exceed any costs, so the project of European *economic integration* has almost always been viewed as greatly beneficial, as evidenced by the large number of countries which have wished to be considered as applicants over the years.

The project of *monetary integration*, however, has been a different matter. While a common currency is also known to generate both benefits and costs for the adopting countries, the issue of whether the benefits exceed the costs is more complex—and the answer less certain.[1] One way to pose the problem is in terms of whether the economies in question constitute an *optimum currency area*. The concept was introduced by Mundell (1961) who used factor (labor and capital) mobility as the most important criterion.[2]

More recently, the discussion has been based on the potential of a common currency to resolve or alleviate monetary policy's dynamic inconsistency problem,

---

[1] This ambiguity about the net benefits of monetary integration explains why some countries, already members of the EU, opted to stay out of the euro (Denmark, Sweden, and the UK).

[2] The concept attracted wide attention very quickly. McKinnon (1963) identified openness as a superior criterion, Kenen (1969) suggested product diversification as a crucial consideration, and several other contributors have proposed a number of different criteria. See Ishiyama (1975) for a survey of the early literature.

G. Karras (✉)
Department of Economics, University of Illinois, 601 S. Morgan Street,
Chicago, IL 60607-7121, USA
e-mail: gkarras@uic.edu

E.G. Carayannis and G.M. Korres (eds.), *European Socio-Economic Integration,*
Innovation, Technology, and Knowledge Management 27,
DOI 10.1007/978-1-4614-5254-6_2, © Springer Science+Business Media New York 2013

emphasized by Kydland and Prescott (1977), and Barro and Gordon (1983). Alesina and Grilli (1992), Alesina and Barro (2002), and Alesina and Stella (2010) are three characteristic examples of this very large literature. One of the central themes of this literature has been the identification of cost-benefit tradeoffs for economies that consider joining a monetary union. Thus, enhanced price stability has emerged as a prime benefit, especially for inflation-prone countries. On the other hand, increased cyclical volatility has been identified as a potentially sizable cost, a direct consequence of giving up the ability to conduct independent monetary policy under uncertainty.

Nevertheless, the euro's first decade proved highly successful.[3] It was only during the recent debt crisis that concerns started to mount and the very future of the common currency became in doubt.[4] Are these concerns justified? Can the euro be responsible for any of the factors that destabilize Europe today? More specifically, how do fiscal and current account balances (or, imbalances) respond after an economy has adopted the euro? How do these responses compare to those after an economy has joined the European Union?

These are the topics of this chapter. To address them, we first use a simple two-period optimizing model for a small open economy to derive a number of theoretical implications. We are mostly interested in testing two recently proposed explanations of how EU and/or euro membership may affect fiscal and current account imbalances. The first of these explanations argues that membership in the EU or the euro exacerbates (fiscal and trade) deficits because it reduces an economy's interest rate, lowering borrowing costs (see Krugman 2011; Roubini 2011; The Economist 2011). The second explanation claims that joining the EU or the euro creates increased expectations about future income levels, generating a positive wealth effect that causes increased borrowing. This chapter's simple theoretical model shows that both the interest-rate effect and the wealth effect are consistent with optimizing behavior.

Then, we look at the empirical evidence to test whether the actual responses of fiscal variables and the current account conform to these theoretical predictions. We average the responses of several countries, but also focus separately on the case of Greece, not only because of recent events, but also because the Greek case often deviates from the average in interesting ways. The results are mixed but can be summarized as follows.

Beginning with membership in the EU, it appears to be associated with an average medium-term restraining effect on fiscal policies and outcomes. This is only a temporary effect, however, and in the longer run, average government positions deteriorate again. The case of Greece here is different because EU membership produced no restraining effect, even in the medium term.

---

[3] Not so long ago, Chinn and Frankel (2008) were predicting that the euro would challenge the dollar's leading international reserve currency status by as early as 2015.

[4] See Rogoff (2011) and Roubini (2011) for recent examples.

With respect to the euro, the evidence suggests that on average there is fiscal consolidation before euro membership, which however gives way to a milder average fiscal expansion after the common currency is adopted. Greece is again different because both the pre-euro consolidation is weaker or nonexistent, and the post-euro expansion is more forceful.

The rest of this chapter is organized as follows. Section 2 outlines this chapter's basic theoretical framework. Section 3 introduces the data sources and the sets of economies to be used in the analysis. Section 4 presents the empirical evidence on the behavior of the variables of interest after EU membership and before and after euro membership, paying special attention to the case of Greece. Section 5 concludes.

2.2   Simple Theory

To keep things as simple as possible, the theoretical model builds on a two-period utility maximizing model for a small open economy with endogenously determined government expenditures.[5]

Using c for private consumption and g for government purchases, we assume that period utility is given by the logarithmic function

$$U_i = \ln c_i + \theta \ln g_i, \tag{2.1}$$

where θ is a parameter that depends on preferences and $i = 1, 2$. Intuitively, period 1 can be thought of as "the present," while period 2 as "the future." Denoting the subjective rate of time preference by ρ, the goal is to

$$\max_{\{c_1, g_1, c_2, g_2\}} \ln c_1 + \theta \ln g_1 + \frac{1}{1+\rho} (\ln c_2 + \theta \ln g_2), \tag{2.2}$$

subject to the present-value constraint

$$c_1 + g_1 + \frac{c_2 + g_2}{1+r} = y_1 + \frac{y_2}{1+r}, \tag{2.3}$$

where r is the market interest rate and y is income.

The first-order conditions can be solved for the optimal values of the consumption, government purchases, and current account (CA) for both periods. Focusing on the first period for the purposes of this chapter, these optimal values are

$$c_1 = \frac{1+\rho}{(1+\theta)(2+\rho)} \left[y_1 + \frac{y_2}{1+r} \right], \tag{2.4}$$

---

[5] Obstfeld and Rogoff (1996) consider a similar two-period model for a small open economy. The present model expands Obstfeld and Rogoff's by endogenizing government expenditures.

$$g_1 = \frac{\theta(1+\rho)}{(1+\theta)(2+\rho)}\left[y_1 + \frac{y_2}{1+r}\right],$$ (2.5)

and

$$CA_1 = y_1 - c_1 - g_1 = \frac{1}{2+\rho}\left[y_1 - \frac{1+\rho}{1+r}y_2\right].$$ (2.6)

Equations (2.4)–(2.6) can be used to illustrate and compare the wealth and interest-rate effects of an EU or euro membership, as discussed earlier.

The *wealth effect* refers to the expectation that membership in the EU or adoption of the euro will produce an increase in future income, here captured by y_2, over and above what was previously anticipated. Equation (2.4) implies that the optimal *current* consumption will then increase (as will, of course, the expected future consumption). The reason is that consumers here consume out of permanent (rather than out of current) income, so changes in future income growth influence consumption choices in the present.

Next, (2.5) says that current government expenditure will increase as well. The reason is simple: optimal provision of government services in this economy requires that government purchases equal a fraction θ of private consumption, so the increase in g_1 follows directly from the increase in c_1.

Finally, (2.6) implies that the current account will deteriorate—a result that follows immediately from the higher levels of period 1 absorption given the level of period 1 income.

The *interest-rate effect* refers to the reduction in interest rates that is often associated with membership in the euro or the EU. Lower levels of risk and exchange-rate premiums, whether fully justified or not, appear to be the main reason for this reduction. One of the most interesting aspects of (2.4)–(2.6) is that they demonstrate the similarities between the interest-rate effect and wealth effect. Indeed, a decrease in the interest rate the economy faces will result in higher current private consumption (2.4) and government purchases (2.5), and a deterioration of the current account (2.6). The economic intuition may be different, as these results are now driven by the reduction in the cost of borrowing that changes the intertemporal marginal rate of transformation. Note, however, that the results are qualitatively identical with those described in the last paragraph for the wealth effect.

2.3   The Data

All data are obtained from the IMF's World Economic Outlook (version of April 2011). We construct two data sets. Data Set I consists of the countries that joined the EU since 1980. Data Set II is comprised of the (relatively) small economies that have adopted the euro early on.[6]

---

[6] The larger economies of Germany and France are excluded because they do not fit the assumptions of the theoretical model as well as the smaller economies.

Data Set I includes Greece (member since 1981); Spain and Portugal (members since 1986); Austria, Finland, and Sweden (members since 1995); and Cyprus, Czech, Estonia, Hungary, Latvia, Lithuania, Malta, Poland, Slovakia, and Slovenia (members since 2004). There are 16 economies in Data Set I.

Data Set II includes Austria, Belgium, Finland, Ireland, Italy, Luxembourg, the Netherlands, Portugal, and Spain (using the euro since 1999), and Greece (using the euro since 2001). There are ten economies in Data Set II.

2.4 Empirical Results and Discussion

This section traces the behavior of several macroeconomic variables after joining the EU or the euro, averaged over the relevant sets of economies as outlined above. The list of variables includes three important fiscal measures: government spending, government deficit, and government debt. In addition, we also present the evolution of the same variables for Greece in order to compare their behavior with the average.

2.4.1 Evidence from Joining the European Union

Data Set I is used to compute averages of the 16 economies that have joined the European Union since 1980. For each of these economies, time period of 0 is set to equal the year before joining the EU, so that time period of 1 is the first year of EU membership, and, generally, time t corresponds to t years after joining the EU. We then compute simple (unweighted) averages of each of the series over the 16 economies.

We focus first on what happens to income per capita when an economy joins the EU. Figure 2.1 plots the evolution of real GDP per capita relative to Germany, averaged over the 16 economies. Real GDP per capita is measured in PPP terms, so it is comparable both over time and across countries. Figure 2.1 confirms the popular notion that EU membership facilitates income convergence. Income per capita on average increases from 64.5% of the German level the year before joining the EU to almost 72% of the German level by the fifth year of EU membership, though it slows to 70% by the seventh year. This appears to be consistent with a positive wealth effect.

Figure 2.1 also shows the relative GDP measure for Greece, and the difference with the average is striking. Not only does Greek GDP per capita fail to converge— it actually diverges: it falls from 86% of the German level the year before EU membership to 74% 7 years later.[7]

---

[7] It should be pointed out that Fig. 2.1 does not establish causality. The failure of the Greek GDP per capita to converge to the German level after EU membership does not imply that membership in the EU caused divergence. Greek and German income paths were determined by a variety of factors, including the economic policies of the two countries at the time. The graph is nevertheless significant because it will help explain the behavior of some of the other variables when expressed as percent of GDP.

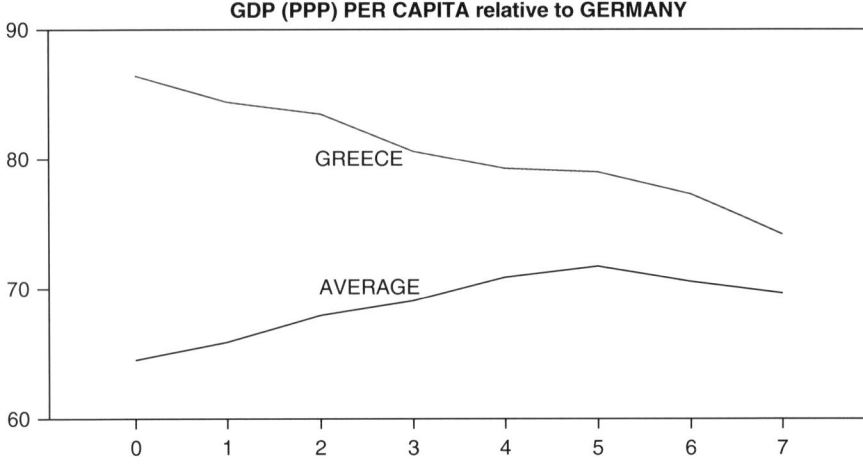

Fig. 2.1 GDP per capita (relative to Germany) after joining the EU

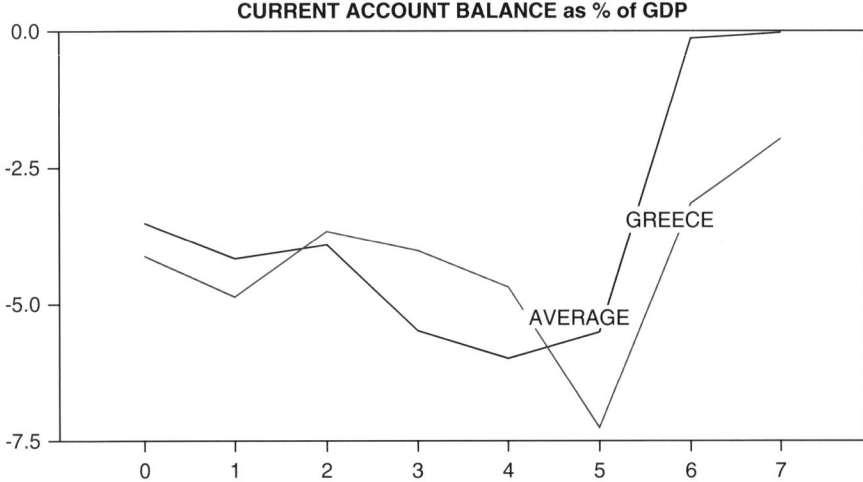

Fig. 2.2 Current account balance (as percent of GDP) after joining the EU

Next, Fig. 2.2 shows the response of the current account balance, as a percent of GDP, averaged over the 16 economies. The evolution of the current account is far from linear. The year before EU membership, the average current account is in deficit equal to 3.5% of GDP. Following membership in the EU, the current account balance deteriorates for a number of years, reaching an average minimum value of −6% of GDP 4 years later, but then improves markedly, achieving effectively zero

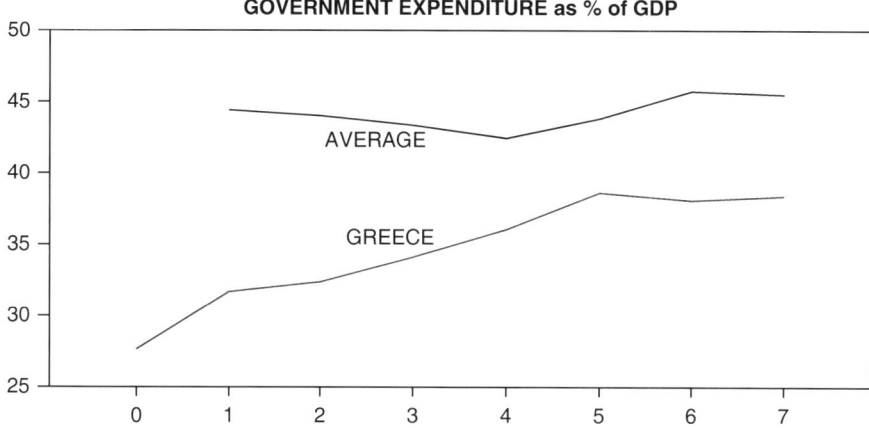

Fig. 2.3 Government expenditure (as percent of GDP) after joining the EU

balance by the seventh year of membership. This suggests that, however detrimental the effects of EU membership may be on the current account in the medium run, they have not been (on average) sustained in the long run.

Figure 2.2 also includes the current account for Greece. Unlike GDP per capita, the Greek current account responds in a way that is qualitatively similar to the average response: it first deteriorates, only to improve (and by more) later. Quantitatively, however, there are two important differences. First, the current account worsens by more than average in the medium term (from 4% of GDP to more than 7%); and, second, it shows a smaller improvement than average by the seventh year (to a deficit of 2% of GDP, compared to a virtually balanced account for the average).

Figures 2.3, 2.4, and 2.5 present three fiscal variables, the behavior of which is very interesting. Figure 2.3 shows that, upon entering the EU, average government expenditure as a fraction of GDP *falls* by two percentage points (from 44.5% of GDP to 42.5%) by the fourth year. It is subsequently increased, however, to almost 46% of GDP by the sixth or seventh year. On average, therefore, government size ends up higher, despite its short-run decrease.

Once again, the path of Greek government expenditure is very different: it steadily increases from 28% of GDP the year before EU membership to 38% 7 years later. Despite this more sustained increase, however, the government size in Greece remains lower than average throughout the period.

Figure 2.4 shows a path for the government budget deficit that is consistent with the path of government expenditure in Fig. 2.3. In particular, the average government deficit improves for 4 years after joining the EU, falling from 4.5% of GDP to about 1% of GDP. This is consistent with the decrease in government expenditure over the same period shown in Fig. 2.3. Subsequently, however, the budget deficit deteriorates, so that by the seventh year after membership, it is again higher than 4%

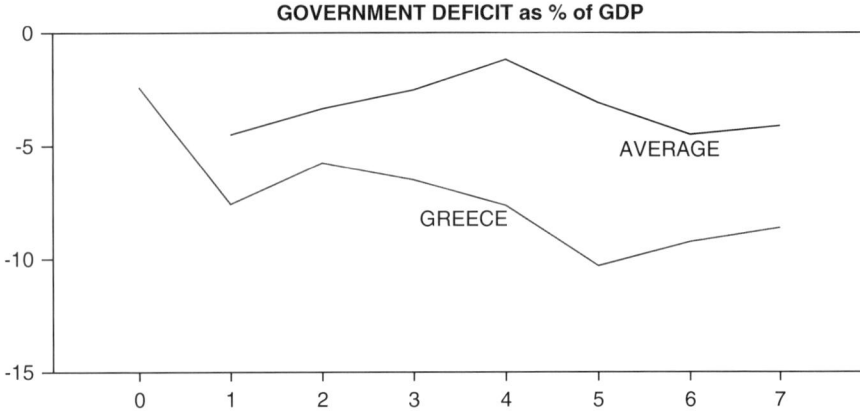

Fig. 2.4 Government balance (as percent of GDP) after joining the EU

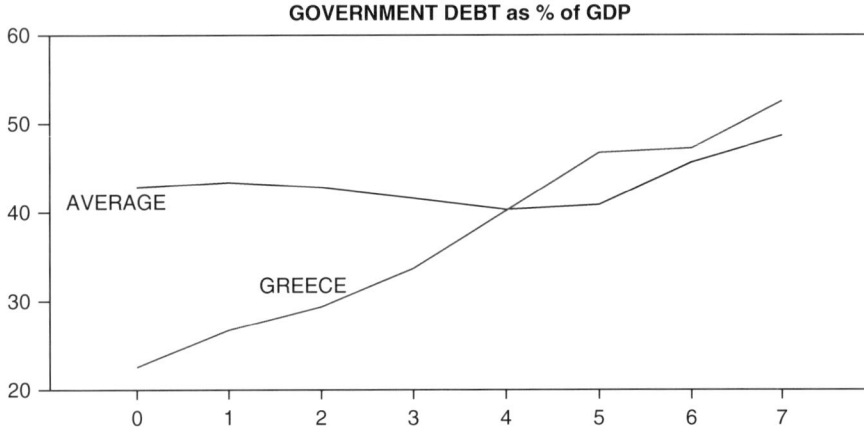

Fig. 2.5 Government debt (as percent of GDP) after joining the EU

of GDP. Once more, this is consistent with the expansion of government expenditure over this period noted in Fig. 2.3.

Greece shows a somewhat similar path, again with the exception that the deficit deterioration is larger and more permanent: the budget deficit widens from 2% of GDP the year before joining the EU to roughly 9% 7 years later.

Not surprisingly, Fig. 2.5 paints a picture for the government debt that is consistent with Figs. 2.3 and 2.4. Thus, average government debt improves modestly during the first 4 years of EU membership, declining from 43% of GDP to almost 40% of GDP. This is of course consistent with the earlier picture of reduced average fiscal deficits. Over the next few years, however, government debt accelerates, as suggested above by the deteriorating government budget balance. By the seventh year after EU membership, average government debt has risen to about 49% of GDP.

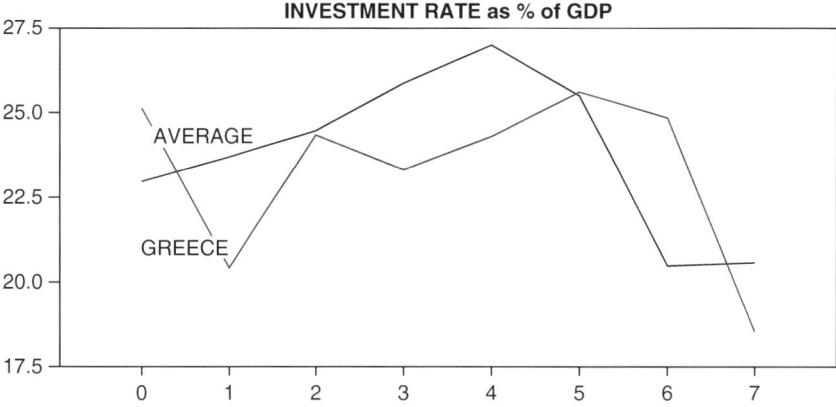

Fig. 2.6 Investment (as percent of GDP) after joining the EU

The picture is much more dramatic for Greece. Government debt increases from 22.5% of GDP the year before joining the EU to 52.5% 7 years later. This fiscal development is so acute that Greece government debt goes from about half of the average to higher than the average in just a few years.

For completeness, Fig. 2.6 reports the evolution of the investment rate after joining the EU. Average investment is 23% of GDP in the year before EU membership, but it increases rapidly to 27% of GDP by the fourth year after joining. However, it then falls even more sharply, so that by the sixth or seventh year it is 20.5% of GDP. This suggests that the investment momentum of membership is temporary. The evidence for Greece is very similar in this case.

2.4.2   *Evidence from Adopting the Euro*

We now use Data Set II to infer the evolution of the same set of macroeconomic variables for a sample of ten relatively small economies that have adopted the euro. Similar to the last section, for each of the economies, time period of 0 is set equal to the year before adopting the euro, so that time period of 1 is the first year of euro membership, and, generally, time t corresponds to t years after joining the euro. Once again, we compute simple (unweighted) averages of each series over the ten economies. Unlike the series for EU membership, data availability now allows us to compute averages for a few time periods *before* adopting the euro, so t can now take negative values as well.[8]

---

[8] The deciding factor is data availability from the IMF's World Economic Outlook (April 2011), where the earliest observation is for 1980. Data constraints prevent the use of negative values for t in our EU calculations and also prevent going back more than 4 years in the euro calculations.

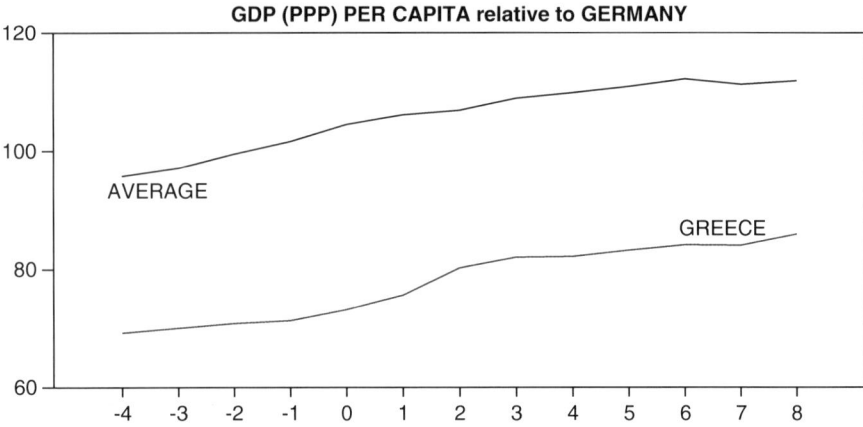

Fig. 2.7 GDP per capita (relative to Germany) before and after adopting the euro

First, we examine what happens to income per capita when an economy adopts the euro. Figure 2.7 shows the average real GDP per capita (in PPP terms) relative to Germany, averaged over the ten economies. Figure 2.7, just like Fig. 2.1 above, is consistent with the expectation that adopting the euro facilitates income convergence. Income per capita on average increases from 104.5% of the German level the year before joining the euro to about 112% of the German level by the sixth year of euro membership.

Note, however, that convergence is taking place even before the euro is adopted. Indeed, the rate of convergence is faster for the few years prior to joining the euro: average income per capita increases from 96% of the German level 4 years before joining the euro to 106% of the German level in the first year of euro membership.

Both of these findings also hold for the case of Greece. Greek GDP per capita increases from 71% of the German level the year before adopting the euro to 84% 8 years later. Just like the average, however, Greece was converging even before joining the common currency.

Figure 2.8 reports the current account balance, as a percent of GDP. Averaged over the ten economies, the evolution of the current account is almost linear. The year before euro membership, the average current account is in *surplus* of about 1% of GDP. Following membership in the euro, the average current account balance deteriorates steadily, until it reaches a *deficit* of more than 1% of GDP in the eighth year after the adoption of the common currency. This steady deterioration is consistent with the theoretical wealth and interest-rate effects of Sect. 2.

Note, however, that this worsening of the current account is already taking place before the adoption of the euro: the surplus shrinks from more than 2.5% of GDP 4 years before euro membership to <0.5% of GDP in the first year of the euro. Comparing this path with that of Fig. 2.2, it appears that the current account effects of adopting the euro have been more permanent than those of EU membership.

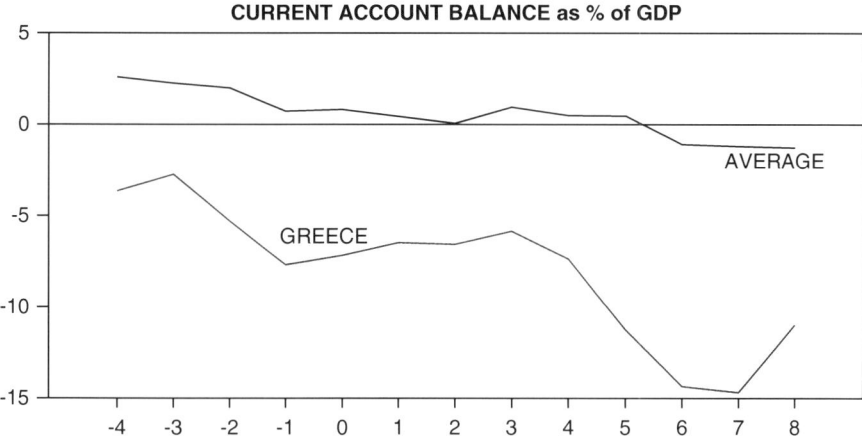

Fig. 2.8 Current account balance (as % of GDP) before and after adopting the euro

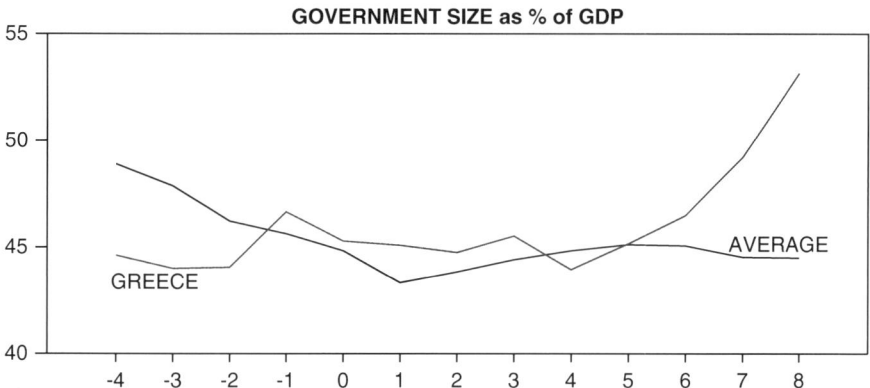

Fig. 2.9 Government expenditure (as % of GDP) before and after adopting the euro

The Greek path for the current account also shows a steady deterioration, but the difference in magnitudes is staggering. While it is true that the Greek current account is already in deficit (roughly 5% of GDP) prior to joining the euro, that deficit will widen to a massive 15% of GDP 7 years after adopting the common currency.

Figures 2.9, 2.10, and 2.11 plot the responses of the government variables, the behavior of which is again quite revealing. Figure 2.9 shows that, for several years prior to adopting the euro, average government expenditures as a fraction of GDP are steadily falling. To be precise, the average government size declines from 49% of GDP 4 years before entering the euro to <45% the year before membership: this is an average fiscal consolidation of more than 1% a year.

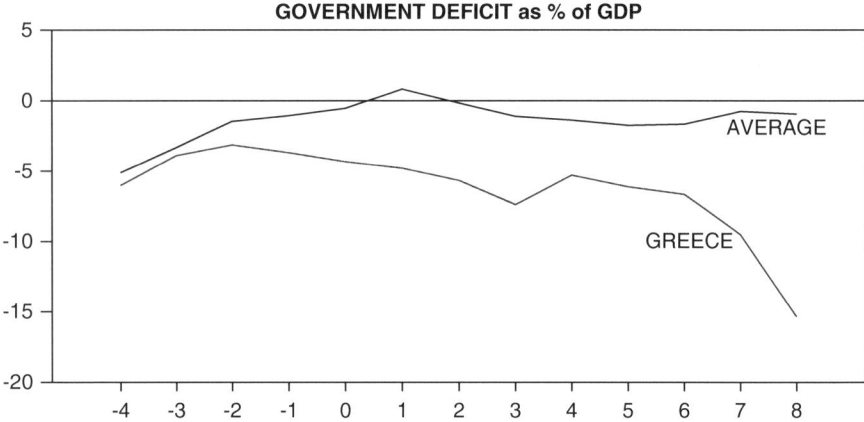

Fig. 2.10 Government balance (as % of GDP) before and after adopting the euro

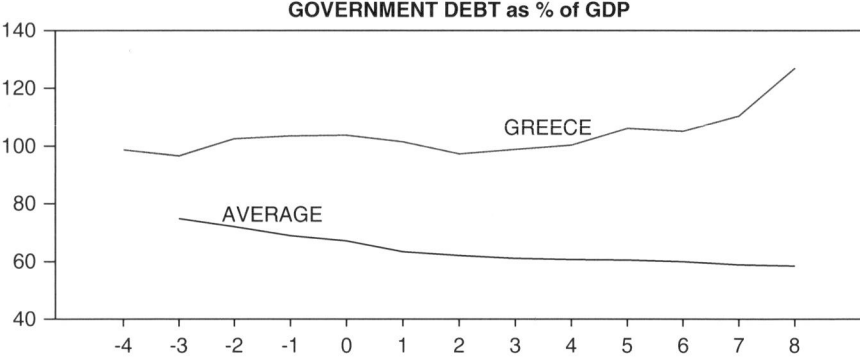

Fig. 2.11 Government debt (as % of GDP) before and after adopting the euro

This trend, however, is reversed following the adoption of the common currency: government spending expands from 43% in the first year to 45% of GDP by the sixth year after the euro. This is again consistent with the fiscal predictions of the two-period model, but note that the increase after the common currency is more gradual than the decrease prior to membership, so there appears to be a long-term reduction.

The picture for Greece is not very different. This, in fact, is one of the smoothest paths for the Greek variables. Thus, government spending fluctuates narrowly around 45% of GDP for several years before and after the euro. It is only 7 years or 8 years later that government size will jump up, actually exceeding 53% in 2009.

Figure 2.10 tracks the path of the government budget deficit. As expected, it is consistent with the evolution of government expenditure in Fig. 2.9. Note first that the average government balance improves markedly before the adoption of

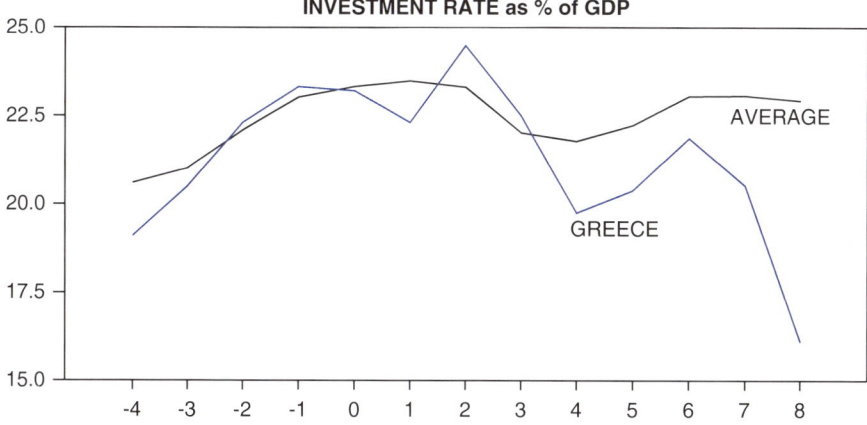

Fig. 2.12 Investment (as % of GDP) before and after adopting the euro

the euro: from a *deficit* that is larger than 5% of GDP 4 years before membership, to a *surplus* of almost 1% in the first year under the common currency. This trend, however, is once more reversed after the euro is adopted. Indeed, the budget fluctuates between an average deficit of 1 and 2% of GDP 5–8 years after adopting the euro.

The Greek picture is now much more dramatic. While the Greek budget deficit is not all that higher than average (6% of GDP) 3–4 years before the euro, it fails to improve in anticipation of the euro and steadily worsens thereafter, reaching almost 10% of GDP by 2008 and 15% in 2009.

Figure 2.11 plots the progress of government debt. Unlike the reversals of the fiscal variables that were apparent both for the government expenditure and deficit, the average debt to GDP ratio improves before euro membership and continues to improve after. In particular, average government debt falls from 75% of GDP 3 years before the adoption of the euro to 63% in the first year of euro membership and continues to fall to 58% by the eighth year under the common currency. It is clear that the beneficial effects of a rapidly expanding GDP (Fig. 2.7) offset the higher deficits under the euro (Fig. 2.10), stabilizing the average debt as a fraction of GDP. Note, however, that the debt falls much less rapidly after the introduction of the euro than before.

Once again, the Greek experience stands out. At around 100% of GDP, Greece's government debt has not only become larger than average even prior to adopting the euro, but it also fails to improve once the common currency is adopted. When the financial crisis hits, this will make it easier for the Greek government debt to rise to unsustainable levels.

Finally, Fig. 2.12 shows the behavior of the investment rate before and after adopting the euro. It is worth noting that average investment is noticeably increasing in the years before membership in the euro, from 20.5% of GDP 4 years before the euro to 23.5% of GDP by the first year of the common currency. It then fluctuates around this high value, dipping to a temporary low of 22% in the fourth year of membership.

Interestingly enough, the path of Greek investment is broadly similar. The Greek investment path diverges in earnest from the average path only after the effects of the financial crisis have become apparent.

2.5 Conclusions

What happens when a country joins the EU or adopts the euro? Do these decisions generate interest-rate effects and wealth effects that are significant enough to create large fiscal and/or current account imbalances?

This chapter uses data from a number of European countries to investigate the responses of fiscal variables and the current account after EU membership, and before and after adopting the common currency.

While the evidence is mixed, some broad trends are robust enough to summarize briefly.

Membership in the EU appears to be associated with an average medium-term restraining effect on fiscal policies and outcomes. This is only a temporary effect, however, and in the longer run, average government positions deteriorate again. The average response of the current account is almost the opposite, with a short-run deterioration followed by stronger long-term improvement. The case of Greece is different for the fiscal variables because EU membership produced no fiscal restraining effect, even in the medium term, but broadly similar for the current account.

The evidence also suggests that on average there is fiscal consolidation before euro membership, which however gives way to a milder average fiscal expansion after the common currency is adopted. The average current account balance worsens both before and after the euro is adopted. Greece is again different because the pre-euro fiscal consolidation is weaker or nonexistent, the post-euro fiscal expansion is more forceful, and the current account deterioration is more massive.

Overall, it appears that the effects of adopting the euro have not been the same with those of membership in the EU, as the responses of both the fiscal variables and the current account differ in meaningful ways. A promising avenue for future research would be an exploration of additional variables, such as saving and investment, employment and wages, and domestic credit and asset prices, which could shed additional light on the mechanisms involved.

References

Alesina A, Barro RJ (2002) Currency unions. Qual J Econ 117(2):409–436
Alesina A, Grilli V (1992) The European central bank: reshaping monetary politics in Europe. In: Canzoneri MB, Grilli V, Masson PR (eds) Establishing a central bank: issues in Europe and lessons from the US. Cambridge University Press, Cambridge

Alesina AF, Stella A (2010) The politics of monetary policy. NBER Working Paper No. 15856

Barro R, Gordon D (1983) Rules, discretion, and reputation in a model of monetary policy. J Monet Econ 12:101–122

Chinn MD, Frankel JA (2008) The euro may over the next 15 years surpass the dollar as leading international currency. NBER Working Paper No. 13909

Economist (2011) The euro crisis: a second wave. June 16, 2011

Friedman T (2011) Can Greeks become Germans? New York Times. July 20, 2011.

Ishiyama Y (1975) The theory of optimum currency areas: a survey. IMF Staff Pap 22:344–383

Kenen PB (1969) The theory of optimum currency areas: an eclectic view. In: Mundell RA, Swoboda AK (eds) Monetary problems of the international economy. The University of Chicago Press, Chicago, IL

Krugman P (2011) Can Europe be saved? New York Times. January 12, 2011.

Kydland FE, Prescott EC (1977) Rules rather than discretion: the inconsistency of optimal plans. J Polit Econ 85:473–490

McKinnon RI (1963) Optimum currency areas. Am Econ Rev 53:717–725

Mundell RA (1961) A theory of optimum currency areas. Am Econ Rev 51:657–665

Obstfeld M, Rogoff K (1996) Foundations of international macroeconomics. MIT Press, Cambridge

Rogoff K (2011) The global fallout of a Eurozone collapse. Financial Times. June 6, 2011.

Roubini N (2011, June 13) The Eurozone heads for break up. Financial Times. June 13, 2011.

Chapter 3
The Mathematical Capital and Its Economic Value

Constantinos Tsamadias

3.1 Introduction

At all the times, knowledge, research, technology, innovations and entrepreneurship have been the "engines" driving the whole process of economic and social evolution.

The economic growth on a global scale mainly depends upon the diffusion of knowledge concerning new techniques of production and management. Recognizing the growing significance of the knowledge-based economy, the OECD (1996) defines the latter as one "directly based on the production, distribution and use of knowledge and information," concluding that "knowledge and information tend to be abundant; what is scarce is the capacity to use them in meaningful ways." While all these are correct, it is also true that knowledge only reaches its full potential in creating economic value when it becomes embedded in organizational processes and routines.

Unlike physical goods that are consumed as they are used providing decreasing returns over time, knowledge, by contrast, provides increasing returns as it is used (Romer 1992). The more knowledge is used, the more valuable it becomes, creating thereby a self-reinforcing cycle. Stiglitz (1999) characteristically emphasizes that "it is the process of embodying knowledge in people (learning) and things (applications) that is costly in time and resources."

The "new economy of knowledge" is defined as possessing the following characteristics: highly intensive knowledge; rapid diffusion of information; extensive innovation networks; high levels of education, skill and training; as well as firms' linkages across complementary assets and competencies (Marceau et al. 1997). In this context, it is the efficient utilization of knowledge resources that offers a competitive advantage, and, in addition, there is need for a continuously increasing share of "intellectual workers" in labour force.

C. Tsamadias (✉)
Harokopio University, Athens, Greece
e-mail: ctsamad@hua.gr

E.G. Carayannis and G.M. Korres (eds.), *European Socio-Economic Integration*, Innovation, Technology, and Knowledge Management 27, DOI 10.1007/978-1-4614-5254-6_3, © Springer Science+Business Media New York 2013

During the last six decades, the contribution of technology, human capital, research, innovation and entrepreneurship on economic growth has been theoretically defended and empirically verified (Solow 1957; Abramovitz 1962; Schultz 1961, 1963; Becker 1964; Lucas 1988; Romer 1992). In addition, the impact of education on production, accumulation and diffusion of human capital, as well as on productivity, earnings, income distribution and social cohesion has also been theoretically and empirically validated and estimated (Schultz 1961, 1963; Becker 1964; Mincer 1974; Psacharopoulos 1994), but also critically debated (Bowen 1964; Arrow 1973; Spence 1973).

Throughout centuries, the role of mathematics in education, training and scientific research has been central. Mathematics operated as a catalyst for a very large number of communication processes among natural and/or social disciplines, engineering sciences and arts. After the Second World War, in a world driven by numbers, the scientific research has been increasingly using mathematical knowledge, while the new high technology has also embodied it. In fact, mathematics appears to pervade every study and technique in our modern world.

In turn, other sciences, having borrowed and employed the methods and "tools" of mathematics, pose new problems and generate new sources of inspiration for mathematics. Furthermore, technology has had a profound effect on mathematics. More specifically, the mathematical knowledge/technology constitute the core of the new knowledge economy—the so-called digital economy. Thus, it may be argued that the mathematical research, knowledge, education and technology are determining factors for the economic, social, cultural and political evolution of individuals, social groups and countries.

Yet, the development of mathematical research (in pure and applied mathematics), mathematical education and mathematical applications requires a share of the already insufficient private and social resources, which in turn raises direct questions with clear economic implications: How much mathematics does the economy and society need as consumption and investment[1]? How much mathematical research (in pure and applied mathematics) and mathematical technology is needed? How much and which mathematics is needed at the different levels and directions of education and training?

The purpose of this chapter is to introduce the concept of the individual and social mathematical capital and delineate its economic value, as well as detect a string of related issues open to discussion. Addressing these issues is a prerequisite for the optimization of planning concerning the procedures of production, accumulation and diffusion of mathematical capital and, by implication, for the more efficient contribution of mathematical capital to economic, social and cultural evolution.

The structure of this chapter is the following. Section 2 provides a brief answer to the question of "what is mathematics?" Section 3 introduces the concept of mathematical capital and its economic value. Section 4 presents a series of problems open to discussion. The last section offers some concluding comments.

---

[1] Consumption and investment are important concepts in economics. Whereas consumption refers to the purchase or use of goods and services which bring immediate but short-lived benefits, investment refers to the acquisition of assets which yield benefits over a long period of time.

3.2 What Is Mathematics ?

What is mathematics? How was it created? By whom has it been developed and practised? What is its role in the history of scientific thinking? What is its relationship with other disciplines? These are some of the old-standing questions that have been subject to intense discussion and to which, in the course of the evolving debate, new answers have been offered.

The word "mathematics" comes from the Greek "mathema" (sixth to third century BC), which means learning, study and science. Since the classical times, however, it came to have a narrower and more technical meaning as "mathematical study." Considering the richness of the definition of "mathematics" from the ancient to modern times, it is not prudent, for the purposes of this chapter, to attempt to give a single, precise and comprehensive definition. Nonetheless, it is sufficient to note that, contrary to a widespread opinion among non-scientists, mathematics is not a closed and perfect edifice. While it constitutes an autonomous and independent scientific field, mathematics also has the potentiality of mirroring and modelling all processes of thought and, perhaps, of sciences. In other words, mathematics represents an "extrovert" so to speak body of knowledge. In this context, it continuously collaborates with observational and laboratory sciences, yet, through its power to quantify and organize knowledge, it makes possible the application of such knowledge to problems extending over a vastly larger scope than that of the aforementioned sciences. One could even go so far as to say that mathematics was necessary for man's conquest of nature and for the development of the human race through the shaping of the modes of thinking.

Like other sciences, mathematics has been subject to great changes during the past 60 years. Not only has its scope vastly increased and not only has the emphasis on what were considered the central problems changed but also the tone and the aims of mathematics have to some extent been transmuted. There is no doubt that many great triumphs of physics, astronomy, biology, economics and other sciences arose, to a significant extent, from mathematics. Since the sixth century BC, mathematics has expanded and there has been a fruitful interaction with other sciences, to the benefit of both.

Broadly speaking, mathematics can be subdivided into the study of quantity, structure, space and change. It is the natural language of sciences and engineering, for example, and at the same time forms an essential tool for business, industry and generally for the "information revolution." In addition to these main classifications, there are also subgroupings focusing on the exploration of links between the core of mathematics and other fields, including logic, set theory, empirical mathematics of various sciences and, more recently, rigorous study of uncertainty.

In conclusion, mathematics is a field under continuous development and in constant search of new applications. Indeed, mathematics is deeply interconnected with modern life.

3.3   Mathematical Capital and Its Economic Value

In economic theory, "physical capital" or just "capital" refers to any manufactured asset that is applied to production, such as machinery and buildings. The "capital" is one of the three primary factors of production, with the other two being "natural resources" and "labour." All these three constitute the initial inputs in the production function.

Smith (1776) first pointed out that education helped to increase the productive capacity of workers, in the same way as the purchase of new machinery or other forms of physical capital. At the beginning of 1960s, the concept of human capital was introduced for the first time, and the human capital theory was shaped as an independent trend in the neoclassical economic theory (Schultz 1961, 1963; Becker 1964, etc.). Since then it constitutes new input in the production function.

Human capital refers to the stock of competences, knowledge, skills and personality attributes that are embodied in the ability to perform labour in order to produce economic value, and can be infinitely elastic, encompassing non-measurable variables, such as the personal character or relations with insiders. The concept of human capital was initially approached by Schultz (1961) and Denison (1962) and later on as "stock" by Lin (2003) or "flow" by Mankiw et al. (1992). The human capital theory suggests that education and training are the most important investments in human capital. All in all, mathematical capital appears to constitute the basic component of human capital.

Consequently, by analogy, "mathematical capital of an individual" may be construed as encompassing all inherent and acquired mathematical abilities, all acquired mathematical knowledge (logic, foundations and structure, critical thought, methodologies, techniques), skills, experiences and effectiveness in mathematical applications. By extension, "mathematical capital of a social group" may be interpreted as covering the sum of the overall mathematical capital of the social group's members and the mathematical tradition and culture of the group. The inherent mathematical ability/skill/talent is one of the seven attributes composing the "spectrum of human's intelligence" (Gardner 1993). The so-called "acquired abilities" are derived through the processes of education, research and experience.

The framework of hypotheses concerning the economic characteristics of mathematical capital and its function within the economy can be summarized as follows:

1. The research in pure and applied mathematics is the main mechanism of production accumulation and diffusion of the individual/social mathematical capital.
2. The education in mathematics is the main, institutional mechanism of diffusion, accumulation and production of the individual/social mathematical capital.
3. The rate of production and accumulation of the acquired part of the mathematical capital for each individual and social group depends, mainly, on the mathematical tradition; on the social, economic and cultural environment; and on the quality of research, education and training systems. The exploitation of mathematical capital occurs at different levels of effectiveness.
4. The research and education in mathematics can be considered as consumption but mainly as investment for both the individual and the society.[1] The consump-

tion and the investment element provide utility (now or later) and contribute to the discounted stream of utility enjoyed by the economic agent. The production and accumulation of the mathematical capital from every individual and/or society require investment in both time and economic resources. An individual or family decision unit selects an amount of investment in mathematical capital (or other self-investment) in order to maximize an objective function subject to some constraints. The objective function may be the lifetime income, appropriately discounted, or it may be a utility (i.e. a measure of well-being). The constraints include the limits imposed by a family's own financial resources, its capacity to borrow outside funds and the limits upon the time the individual (and, in earlier years, the parents as well) can devote to mathematical education or research. Costs include out-of-pocket payments plus earnings forgone. Benefits include the increase in expected lifetime earnings, as well as non-pecuniary returns, such as improved working conditions and job security. Optimal investment in mathematical capital occurs when the discounted value of the costs incurred equals the discounted value of the benefits expected. A society selects an amount of investment in mathematical capital in order to maximize an objective social welfare function subject to some constraints. Optimal social investment to mathematical capital occurs when the discounted social cost incurred equals the discounted value of the benefits expected.

5. Despite its long-term character, the investment in mathematical capital is accompanied by limited uncertainty (estimation methods: sensitivity analysis, risk analysis or new method) due to its continuing usefulness measured on both individual and social basis.

6. Expenditure on mathematical capital can be classified as either consumption or investment, although the borderline is not always precise.

7. The individual and social investment in mathematical capital is progressively reduced during an individual's life, tending to zero at the stage of retirement from work. Other things being equal, the earlier the investment, the longer will be the expected stream of benefits. Hence, maximization of lifetime utility implies that most formal mathematical education and training will occur during one's youth. The return on mathematical capital has a long-term character.

8. The mathematical capital reserves/stock borne by each individual cannot be transferred, cannot be bought and cannot be inherited in its entirety.

9. The quantity and quality of mathematical capital contribute to the improvement of individual productivity and to the total productivity of society. The mathematical capital increases productivity through the following basic channels: (a) it enhances the ability of an individual to perform standard tasks (factor efficiency) and learn to perform new tasks; (b) it improves the ability to receive and process new information; (c) it develops the ability to evaluate and adjust to changing circumstances (ability to deal with disequilibria); (d) it increases the ability to communicate and coordinate activities with one another; (e) it reduces the subjective uncertainty and unnecessary anxiety, on the one hand, whereas, on the other hand, it boosts the establishment of a more critical approach towards the status quo, fostering, in parallel, the probability of accepting new technologies and practises; and (f) it helps to

bring about new innovations in production processes and to develop new products.

10. The mathematical capital is a resource which increases rather than diminishes with use. It has little cost to generate and diffuse. Once mathematical knowledge is discovered and made public, there is essentially little marginal cost to adding more users.

11. The share of mathematical capital which is not used diminishes with the passage of time, or as the individual grows older, or with evolution and changes in sciences, technology and production. The mathematical capital which is not continuously replenished is to be quickly diminished.

12. The differences in quantity and quality of individual and social mathematical capital affect the inequities between individuals and societies and determine, to a significant extent, the hierarchies.

13. The benefits from mathematical research and education can be classified into private (accruing to the individual and the family) and social in both a direct-narrow (accruing to society at large) and indirect-wide (including externalities[2] and spillovers[3]) sense. The benefits could also be categorized into micro-level (monetary/private returns on investment in mathematical research and education and social returns in narrow sense) and macro-level (market and non-market, social benefits in wide sense, positive externalities and spillovers).

14. Mathematical capital embodied in new products and services has become a source of wealth creation.

15. The mathematical capital contributes to economic growth and development, and vice versa, that is, economic development contributes to mathematical capital development.

3.4   Open Problems for Evaluation and Planning

In order to achieve the optimal planning of policies and investments regarding the processes of production, accumulation and diffusion of mathematical capital, it is necessary to address the following problems:

1. The construction of methods and models to proxy for the quantity and quality of mathematical capital

2. The determination of private and social benefits (markets, non-markets, externalities, spillovers) derived from mathematical capital

3. The measurement of private and social cost of production, accumulation and diffusion of mathematical capital

---

[2] Externalities (positive) are those benefits to society that are above and beyond the private benefits realized by the individual "decision-maker," that is, the student or the family. These benefits are above and beyond private monetary and non-monetary consumption benefits, both of which are captured by the "decision-maker" and taken into account whenever the decision is made.

[3] Spillovers are a type of externality, since they are a benefit that is not captured by the decision-making unit within which occurs the mathematical educational process.

4. The estimation of the impact of mathematical capital on earnings of workers
5. The estimation of the return rates of private and social investments in mathematical capital (methods: cost–benefit analysis or new methods)
6. The economic and social evaluation of investment and policies in both mathematical research (pure and applied mathematics) and education (methods: cost-benefit analysis, cost-effectiveness analysis or new methods)
7. The assessment of public expenditures on mathematical capital (methods: cost-effectiveness analysis or new methods)
8. The estimation of mathematical capital contribution to economic growth/development/welfare, income distribution and social cohesion (methods: with models of new growth theory or new models)
9. Determining whether, in the interaction process between economic development and mathematical capital development, the latter comes first

3.5 Concluding Comments

This chapter highlighted the pivotal role of mathematical capital in the scientific research, education, applications and, more generally, new knowledge-based economy. The concept of individual and social mathematical capital was defined. The skeleton of the mathematical capital's economic characteristics was delineated, and its importance as an economic resource was stressed. The process of production, accumulation, transmission and diffusion of mathematical capital in economy and society was highlighted. Finally, a series of open problems was raised which deserve the attention of economists and mathematicians.

The economic and social evaluation of policies and investments concerning the production, accumulation and diffusion of mathematical capital leads to the efficient planning for the optimal use of scarce resources. It follows, therefore, from the discussion of this chapter that the mathematical capital has to be recognized and utilized accordingly by the scientific, economic, social and political elite as a strategically important resource.

References

Abramovitz M (1962) Economic growth in the United States. Am Econ Rev 52:762–782
Arrow K (1973) Higher education as a filter. J Public Econ 2:193–216
Becker G (1964) Human capital: a theoretical and empirical analysis, with special reference to education. National Bureau of Economic Research, New York, NY
Bowen W (1964) Economic aspects of education: three essays. Industrial Relations Section, Princeton University, Princeton, NJ
Denison EF (1962) The sources of economic growth in the US and the alternatives before us. Committee for Economic Development Supplementary Paper 13

Gardner H (1993) Frames of mind, the theory of multiple intelligences. Basic Books, New York, NY

Lin T (2003) Education, technical progress, and economic growth: the case of Taiwan. Econ Educ Rev 22:213–220

Lucas R (1988) On the mechanics of economic development. J Monet Econ 22:3–42

Mankiw G, Romer D, Weil D (1992) A contribution to the empirics of economic growth. Quart J Econ 107:407–437

Marceau J, Manley K, Sicklen D (1997) The high road or the low road? Alternatives for Australia's future. Australian Business Foundation, Sydney

Mincer J (1974) Schooling, experience and earnings. Columbia University Press, New York, NY

Organisation for Economic Co-operation and Development (OECD) (1996) The knowledge-based economy. OECD, Paris

Psacharopoulos G (1994) Returns to investment in education: a global update. World Dev 22:1325–1343

Romer P (1992) Two strategies for economic development: using ideas and producing ideas. In: Summers L, Shah S (eds) Proceedings of the World Bank Annual Conference on Development Economics. The World Bank, Washington, DC, p 63–91

Schultz T (1961) Investment in human capital. Am Econ Rev 51:1–17

Schultz T (1963) The economic value of education. Columbia University Press, New York, NY

Smith A (1776) The wealth of nations. W. Strahan and T. Cadell, London

Solow R (1957) Technical change and the aggregate production function. Rev Econ Stat 39:312–320

Spence M (1973) Job market signaling. Quart J Econ 87:355–374

Stiglitz J (1999) Public policy for a knowledge economy. Remarks at the Department for Trade and Industry and Center for Economic Policy Research, London, 27 January 1999

Chapter 4
Political Decision in a Game Theory Approach

George M. Korres and Aikaterini Kokkinou

4.1 Introduction

Neoclassical approach is based on the importance of the information problems in order to determine the inter-sequential behavior of agents and the necessity of considering the state as a major player in the strategic game. Using the hypothesis regarding the agents' rationality, we can examine the optimum way of using the information available at a certain moment in order to make decisions.

It is widely accepted that the analysis of actual regulatory decision should be considered within the context of the political structure and economic conditions, as, for instance, in the context of government–business relation. Consequently, there exists no single theory of regulation that could inform separately for both the establishment and the operationality of regulatory agencies. Decision theory is closely related with game theory and with the values, uncertainty, rationality, and optimal decision. In order to understand how in reality regulatory decisions were to be made, we must first understand where agencies are situated.

A political decision-making model attempts to analyze all the forces that may impact a change that is made. This is described as "recognizing the role of stakeholders in affecting and shaping matters of significance to the organization" (Fulop and Linstead 1999:316). In addition, the political decision-making model is

G.M. Korres (✉)
Centre of Urban and Regional Development Studies (CURDS),
University of Newcastle, Newcastle, UK

Department of Geography, University of Aegean,
Mytilene, Greece
e-mail: George.Korres@ncl.ac.uk; gkorres@hol.gr; gkorres@geo.aegean.gr

A. Kokkinou
Department of Economics, University of Glasgow,
Adam Smith Building, G12 8QQ Glasgow, Scotland, UK
e-mail: a.kokkinou.1@research.glasgow.ac.uk

E.G. Carayannis and G.M. Korres (eds.), *European Socio-Economic Integration*,
Innovation, Technology, and Knowledge Management 27,
DOI 10.1007/978-1-4614-5254-6_4, © Springer Science+Business Media New York 2013

described as being based on "reconciling the interests of different stakeholders" while recognizing the organization as "a system adapting and learning to cope with a variety of internal and external constraints" (Fulop and Linstead 1999:316). These models can be applied, for instance, in this situation where the company needs to increase production and is deciding how to achieve this.

The decision theory can also be used in order to explain the study of public choice. In the procedure of public choice, one of the main subjects is the origin of government and more particularly the fundamental problem of collectively choosing and the constitutional rules. Furthermore in the "behavioral decision theory" that contributed to a reevaluation of what rational decision-making requires, it is possible to relax the assumptions of perfect information, rationality, and so forth in various ways and produce a series of different prescriptions or predictions about behavior (Black 1958; Lehmann 1950). Decision theory and public choice is also closely related with the so-called Arrow's "impossibility theorem" (Arrow 1963), based on "voting paradox" suggesting that voters have no reason to expect a decision on a public choice under myopia, which can lead to the kind of consistency attributed to individual choice. In particular, the paradox that more choices may lead to a poorer decision or a failure to make a decision at all is observed in many cases. The decision theory and public choice is also related to the rational choice theory, also known as choice theory or rational action theory, that is a framework for understanding and often modeling social and economic behavior. The game theory can be used to explain the decision theory and studies the behavior in conflict situations, where each of the "opposite" parties involved has analytical authority and the capability to make decisions in order to achieve its objective. It marks the meaning of the rationality hypothesis when the individual satisfaction is altered by the decisions of other agents and describes solutions for different situations of conflict. According to the game theory, each player is an independent decision unit consciously aiming to a particular purpose. Moreover, these players are given the rationality feature. This is the reason why the game theory studies the making of rational decisions by individuals in interactive situations where the results of their action depend directly on the actions of others. According to the rational choice theory, we are assuming that all individuals choose the best solution and action according to stable preference functions and also to all possible constraints which they face. The basic idea of rational choice theory is that the behavior of individuals and societies reflects the choices to maximize their benefits and minimize their costs. In other words, they should act by comparing the costs and benefits of different courses of action (Schwartz 2004). The idea of rational choice, where people compare the costs and benefits of certain actions, is easy to see in economic theory, as, for example, in the case that individuals compare prices and costs and also in the case that they will choose the object that provides the greatest benefits at the lowest cost. In the decision theory, the following main questions may rise for public choice:

• How the government can hire competent and trustworthy individuals to whom decision procedure can be delegated?

- How to set up an effective system and identify the optimum-best decision assuming an ideal decision maker who is fully informed and also is able to compute with perfect accuracy and full rationality?

This chapter proposes a study using the game-theoretical approach for the political decision problem. It also attempts to analyze and examine the constraints, the rules, and the effects and moreover to develop a model for the political decision problems.

4.2   Decision Theory and Public Choice Policy: A Literature Review

The game theory issue is historically linked to 1944 when the mathematician John von Neumann and the economist Oskar Morgenstern published the famous work: *Theory of Games and Economic Behavior*. However, we can classify the following main stages of evolution in the game theory related to the decision theory (Sîrghi Nicoleta 2009):

- Bertrand (1833) studied the operation of oligopolistic markets where companies whose returns are constant produce the same product establishing the selling price. The result stated by Bertrand is known as the *Bertrand paradox*. For instance, if in case of equilibrium situation each company chooses the price that would maximize its profit taking into account the prices given by the other companies, then the equilibrium price is equal to the marginal cost.
- Cournot (1838) studied the operation of oligopolistic markets where each company acts knowing that its production volume affects the market price. Cournot described equilibrium as this situation where each company chooses the output which would maximize the profit but taking into account the production declared by other companies, showing that such a balance leads to a price above the marginal productivity.
- Stackelberg (1934) showed that certain companies may have a leading role and are able to impose the price to the other companies. The leading company knows best the market situation and has the means necessary in order to control the opponents.
- In World War II, "strategic games" were developed according to the military tactic games and those of "zero-sum." According to this, the game theory is a research method of strategic interaction situations where each part of economic agents is aware of the interdependence between them and they make their decisions according to others' behavior.
- Morgenstern and von Neumann (1944) determined cooperative games theory focused on coalitions which can occur between rational individuals in order to maximize their earnings, an approach which lasted until the 1970s.
- Since the 1970s, the rational forecasts school focuses on rational forecasts which include forecasts for the future. The rational forecasts school creates the hypothesis according to which the economic agents make the forecasts using the best way any

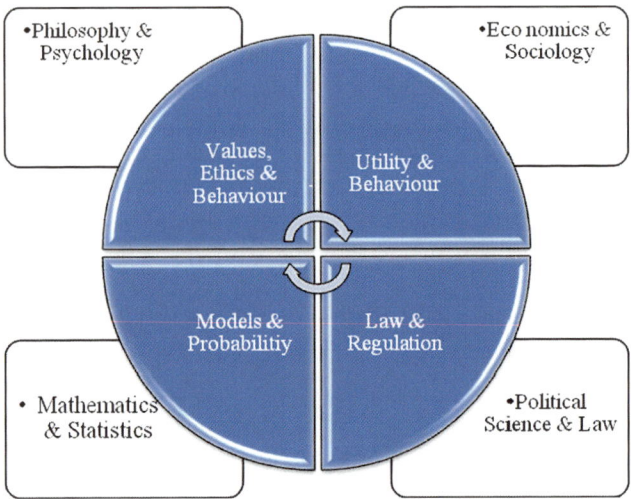

Fig. 4.1 The framework of decision-making

information they have (Arrow 1989). According to this school, the economic agents' control of economic mechanisms is taken into account. In these circumstances, economic agents will use in an optimal way all relevant information likely to influence the forecast value. After having passed the maturation period, marked by Nash (1951), game theory became in the late 1980s a powerful instrument for analyzing strategic interaction situations, presented in the work of Friedman (1990).

The most important determinant factors in a decision-making process are philosophy and psychology, such as ethics and values; economics and sociology, such as utility and behavior; mathematics and statistics, such as probability and models; and finally the political and anthropology fields, such as law, regulation, and behavior (Amartya 1987, 2008). Figure 4.1 illustrates the framework and factors that affect a decision-making process.

4.3 Modeling Government Intervention and Political Decision Using a Game Theory Approach

Following the public choice and the decision theory, one of the most fundamental subjects is the government intervention and the political decision process. In the decision process and theory of public choice, the government and policy interventions aim to reduce the distortions, risk, and uncertainty (Bicchieri 2003). In the political decision process, the government and policy interventions usually refer to the institutional arrangements that regulate the pattern of interactions. The study of regulation and government intervention is quite important for the political decision process and also has affected the evolution of political economy. The governance structure is also the focal point of policy intervention and affects also the political decision process (Dixit 1996). Furthermore, another important factor in the government and political decision theory is bureaucracy. In a process of a political decision model, the main constraints and characteristics are:

- The risk and uncertainty of decision process
- Short-term horizon
- Constraints in the budgeting
- Compromise decision-making strategy
- No bounded rationality
- Ambiguous objectives
- Incremental or marginal choices
- Potential best outcome (optimal solution) and acceptable outcomes

Bureaucratic decision-making does not only imply decision-making in a bureaucratic setting but also extends to include any organizations that have bureaucratic characteristics and notably highly hierarchical structure and are constrained, to a large extent, by political influence. In order to be able to solve the problems of bureaucracy and to reduce the distortions, risk, and uncertainty, we can use the efficient management tools in the decision problems (Williamson 1999). In summary, the main determining factors for political decision process are:

- Complex decisions
- Conflict and disagreement over problems and solutions
- Coalition building
- Management, information, and technology

Figure 4.2 illustrates the modeling of government and public policy decision for both business and public policy. One of the main points of the foundation of the model is management or alternatively stakeholder approach that derives from staging an issue set as focal point and then accommodates the various choices that policy decision maker has to make as the issue set goes through the various decision-making processes (Mc Gowan 1995). The political decision and government intervention affect and formulate the public policy, the public choice, and, moreover, the business policy. The outcome from public and business policy involves a new legislation and regulation framework and also implies new strategies for industries and firms, respectively. The management of new legislations and regulations reduces the existence of any distortions, risk, and uncertainty of the market and consequently is easier for the market, firms, and industries to develop their own long-term strategies (Dixit 1996). Among the main determinant factors for the best outcome (the optimal solution) in a political decision problem is the management of any available information and technology so to eliminate the constraints and, consequently, the uncertainty, risk, and ambiguity that coexisted in a political decision process. Figure 4.3 shows the main factors affecting a political decision-making process.

Let us assume a political model where consensus is introduced. Furthermore, we can assume that parties try to reach consensus in forming a political decision. Structuring this model, an important criterion for government intervention is the

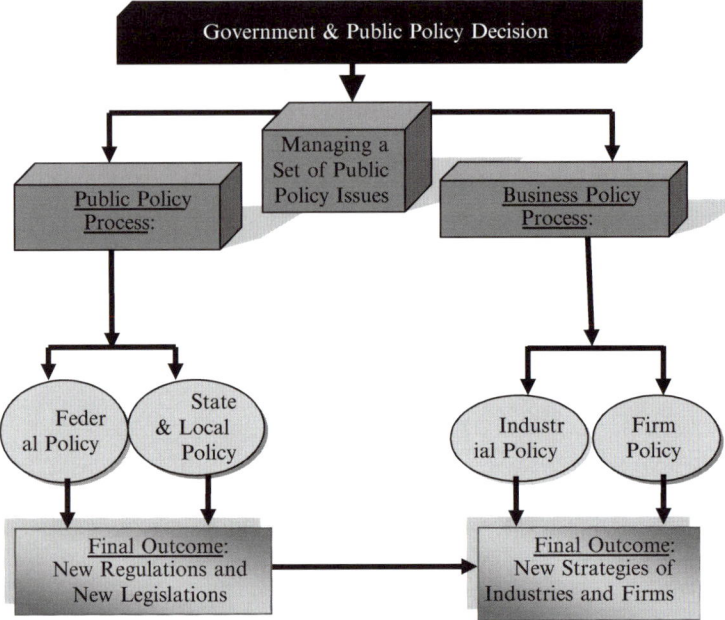

Fig. 4.2 Modeling government and public policy decision: business–public policy (*Source*: Adjusted from Mc Gowan (1995))

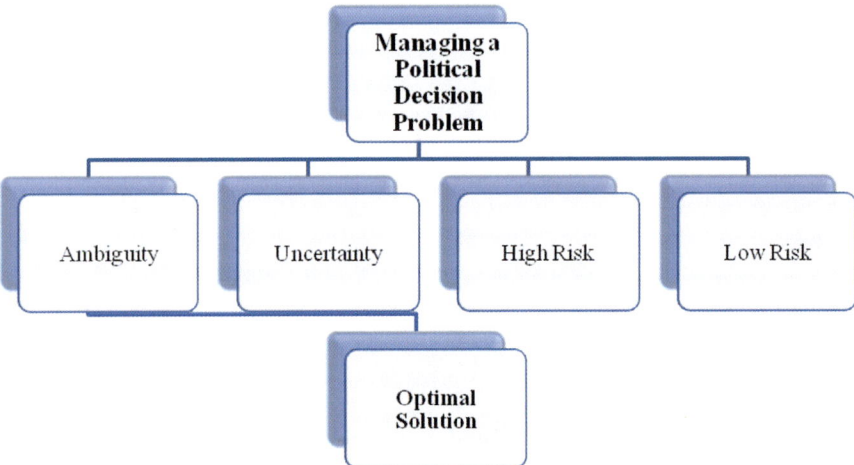

Fig. 4.3 Factors affecting a political decision process

coalition and evaluation. Let us denote N ($N = 1, \ldots, n$) the set of all different parties (i.e., in a parliament) and MC the set of all majority coalitions, respectively. Let us also assume that a majority coalition needs to form a solid governmental strategy; however, this does not mean that it is necessary to have the majority of different parties. Furthermore assuming that the set of MC (majority coalitions) containing party ($i \in N$) are acceptable to party i. Furthermore, let us also assume that p denotes the set of all possible policies that are acceptable to party i ($i \in N$). Therefore, a governmental policy can be defined as a set of majority coalition and policy, $g = (MC, p)$. A feasible government is that government with both the set of majority coalition and policy is acceptable to each party that belongs to the majority coalition. The decision theory evaluates the importance of criterion of majority coalition and that of policy (assuming that the evaluation of the importance of these criteria should be relatively close to each other) in order to reach an optimum decision (best solution). The final output from the evaluation of governmental decisions should be positive and preferably close to 1 (total final output, $\sum F = 1$). According to this, government intervention and the political decision aim to result toward the more advanced solution (Riker 1962).

Furthermore, using game theory approach, let us assume that we are not sure for the final outcome from government intervention and the probability from a political decision to be inefficient may be anything from 0 to 1. Therefore, this is an example of decision-making under ignorance. The government intervention and the political decision process affect the public choice and consequently the socioeconomic growth. Management is related with the possible level of success and security and furthermore with the existence of any distortions and the elimination of risk and uncertainty (Friedman 1990).

Let us first see what we can do with only a preference relation, as, for instance, with no exact information (Noll 1989). The preferences can be classified as follows:

- Government intervention with an efficient political decision can imply high socioeconomic effects; low public budget *is better than*
- Government intervention with an efficient political decision can imply high socioeconomic effects; high public budget *is better than*
- Government intervention with an inefficient political decision can imply poor socioeconomic effects; low public budget *is better than*
- Government intervention with an inefficient political decision can imply poor socioeconomic effects; high public budget *is better than*

We should note that among the decision criteria proposed for decisions under ignorance is the "maximin rule" that means for each alternative, we can

	Scenario A (effects and externalities)	Scenario B (effects and externalities)
Strategic Plan A (policy and government intervention)	• Efficient policy and high socioeconomic effects • High budget	• Inefficient policy and poor socioeconomic effects • High budget
Strategic Plan B (policy and government intervention)	• Efficient policy and high socioeconomic effects • Low budget	• Inefficient policy and poor socioeconomic effects • Low budget

define and prefer another alternative "security level" as the worst possible outcome with that alternative. Alternatively, in other words the "maximin rule" recommends us to choose the alternative that has the maximal security level or, alternatively, "*maxi*mize" the "*min*imal" outcome. The "maximin" principle was first proposed by von Neumann as a strategy against an intelligent opponent and furthermore (Dixit 1996) extended the use of game theory. In our case, the security level of "high budget of a political decision" is "an efficient policy resulting with high socioeconomic effects," and the security level of "low budget" is "an inefficient policy following with poor socioeconomic effects." Thus, the "maximin rule" recommends us to adopt a high-budget decision policy.

The "maximin rule" does not distinguish between alternatives with the same security level. Alternatively, a variant of this approach is the "*lexicographic maximin*," or, in other words, "*leximin* rule." This approach can distinguish between such alternatives by comparison of their second-worst outcomes. Moreover, if we are assuming that two alternatives have the same security level, then the one with the highest second-worst outcome is chosen. Finally, if both the worst and the second-worst outcomes are on the same level, then the third-worst outcomes are compared (Amartya 1987, 2008).

The "maximin" and "leximin" approaches are often said to represent extreme prudence or pessimism. It is in general quite difficult to justify the "maximax" principle as rational principle of decision (Friedman 1990). The other extreme is represented by the "*maximax* rule" that can choose the alternative which is the best possible result (the "hope level"), that is, the best outcome. Following this approach for our case study, the "hope level" can choose between two alternatives, that of "high budget of a political decision" that may imply "an efficient policy implying high socioeconomic effects," and that of "low budget of a political decision" with "an efficient policy with high socioeconomic effects." In summary, a "maximaxer" approach will be in our case study a "low budget of a political decision."

There is an obvious need for a decision criterion for which we need perfect information that does not force us into the extreme pessimism of the "maximin" or "leximin rule" or into the extreme optimism of the "maximax rule." Let us assume that we have such information for the government intervention and political decision, with the following values:

A middle way between "maximin pessimism" and "maximax optimism" is the "optimism–pessimism index." It is often called the "Hurwicz a-index," proposed by

	Scenario A (high effects)	Scenario B (poor effects)
Strategic Plan A (policy and government intervention with a high budget)	15	15
Strategic Plan B (policy and government intervention with a low budget)	18	0

Hurwicz (1945). According to this decision criterion, the decision maker is required to choose an index (*a*) between 0 and 1, which reflects the degree of optimism or pessimism level. For each alternative *A*, let *min*(*A*) be its security level, for instance, the lowest utility to which it can give rise, and let *max*(*A*) be the hope level, for instance, the highest utility level that it can give rise to. The "*a*-index" of *A* is calculated according to the following formula:

«*Optimism-pessimismindex*»(«*Hurwicz* a *index*») = $a \times min(A) + (1-a) \times max(A)$

Obviously, if this index (*a*)=1, then this procedure reduces to the "maximin criterion," and if this index (*a*)=0, then it reduces to the "maximax criterion."

Furthermore, utility information also allows for another decision criterion, namely, the "*minimax regret* criterion" or in other words "minimax risk," "minimax loss," and simply "minimax" (Friedman 1990). Suppose, in our example, that we may prefer the government intervention with a low budget and it may imply a poor performance with an inefficient level of socioeconomic effects and then you may feel regret. Your degree of regret correlates with the difference between your present utility level (0) and the utility level of having an efficient level of performance with high socioeconomic effects (for instance, 15).

Similarly, in the alternative case, you may prefer the government intervention with a low budget, and it can imply an efficient and high performance with positive and high socioeconomic effects. Therefore, your degree of regret may similarly be correlated with the difference between your present utility level (15) and the utility

	Scenario A (high effects)	Scenario B (poor effects)
Strategic Plan A (policy and government intervention with a high budget)	3	0
Strategic Plan B (policy and government intervention with a low budget)	0	15

level of having an efficient performance with high socioeconomic effects with a low budget (for instance, 18).

A "regret matrix" may be derived from the above utility matrix. To produce a "regret matrix," assign to each outcome the difference between the utility of the maximal outcome in its column and the utility of the outcome itself.

The "minimax regret criterion" advices you to choose the option with the lowest "maximal regret" (to *mini*mize "*maxi*mal *regret*"), for instance, in this case to prefer the decision with a high budget. Both the "maximin criterion" and the "minimax regret criterion" are rules for the cautious who do not want to take risks. However, we should note that these two criteria do not always make the same recommendation.

4.4 Conclusions

Alternative forms of governance mechanism and contractual arrangements play the major role in the literature of the new decision theory. With the advancement in the analytical tools, such as game-theoretical modeling, many political scientists are now able to have a more balanced treatment toward regulation by concentrating on the intricate interactions of politics and economics through institutions. The recent development in game-theoretical model has enabled analysts to consider many features such as unforeseen contingencies and incomplete information. Among the main questions of this chapter are:

- How to hire a competent and trustworthy decision?
- How to set up an effective system of oversight and sanctions for such decisions?

As a modern working instrument in economics, the game theory can be used to analyze the inequality of changes conducted between economic agents; changes are inevitably subject to transaction costs. Thus, the game theory makes available to the economic agents a set of possible strategies (game scenarios) to simulate different market situations and especially to create and adopt the decisions that lead to the best result possible.

In socioeconomics, especially in public choice model, the regulatory process was explicitly treated as a system of market-like exchange, self-interested rational actor seeking to exchange inducements such as favorable votes and regulation (Becker 1985). It is shown that firms often seek relief from the pressures of a competitive market via the process of rent-seeking in the regulatory processes (Buchanan 2003, Tullock 1991). What could have lost in competitive market can be recovered from political market, and thus, there is always a market for regulation.

The game theory allows the consequences assessment of the coordination limits and of informational problems inherent for the various transactions related to the government intervention and political decision that affect socioeconomic development and growth. In conclusion, the policy makers can use the game theory to provide strategic interaction simulation situations starting with simplified patterns of game and ending with the most complex ones. From this perspective it is important to build these patterns as close as possible to the social reality. Summarizing for a political decision process, the implications from management, information, and technology are important:

- Improved effectiveness
- Increased efficiency
- Evaluating information
- Enhanced collaboration and networking
- Organizational learning
- Succeed an optimal solution

Starting with the rationality hypothesis, taking into account the information available to the economic agents and the constraints required by the rules of the game, the instruments offered by the game theory in economics are, at present, one very generous and useful. In this instrument, interaction patterns of rational agents are included in the social field.

References

Amartya S (1987, 2008) Rational behavior. New Palgrave: Dictionary Econ 3:68–76

Arrow KJ (1963) Social choice and individual values, 1951, 2nd edn. Yale University Press, New Haven, CT

Arrow K.J (1989) Economic theory and the hypothesis of rationality, in *The New Palgrave: Utility and Probability,* p. 25-39.

Becker GS (1985) Public policies, pressure groups, and dead-weight costs. J Public Econ 28(3):329–347

Bertrand J (1883) Review of "Theorie mathematique de la richesse sociale" and "Recherche sur les principes mathematiques de la theorie des richesses", Journal de Savants 48, 499-508.

Bicchieri C (2003) Rationality and game theory in: The handbook of rationality. The Oxford reference library of philosophy. Oxford University Press, Oxford.

Black D (1958) The theory of committees and elections. Kluwer Academic Publishers, Boston, MA

Buchanan JM (2003) Public choice: the origins and development of a research program. Center for Study of Public Choice at George Mason University, Fairfax, VA

Cournot A (1838) Researches into the Mathematical Principles of the Theory of Wealth. Macmillan Co.: New York, Transl. by Nathaniel T. Bacon (1897).

Dixit AK (1996) The making of economic policy: a transaction-cost politics perspective. MIT Press, Cambridge, MA

Friedman JW (1990) Game theory with applications to economics. Oxford University Press, Oxford

Fulop L, Linstead S (1999) Management: a critical text. Macmillan, Basingstoke

Hurwicz L (1945) The theory of economic behavior. Am Econ Rev 35(5):909–925

Lehmann EL (1950) Some principles of the theory of testing hypotheses. Ann Math Stat 21(1):1–26

Mc Gowan RA (1995) Business politics and cigarettes: multiple levels, multiple agenda. Greenwood Press, Westport, CT

Morgenstern O, von Neumann J (1944) Theory of games and economic behavior. Princeton University Press, Princeton, NJ

Nash J (1951) Non-cooperative games. Ann Math 54(2):286–295

Noll RG (1989) Economic perspectives on the politics of regulation. In: Schmalensee R, Willig R (eds) Handbook of industrial organization. North-Holland, Amsterdam, pp 1253–1287

Riker WH (1962) The theory of political coalitions. Yale University Press, New Haven, CT

Schwartz B (2004) The paradox of choice. HarperCollins Publishers, New York, NY

Sirghi N (2009) The New Microeconomics and the Oligopoly Strategic Behaviour, Annals of University of Bucharest, Economic and Administrative Series, Nr. 3 (2009) 201-213.

Von Stackelberg H (1934) *Marktform und Gleichgewicht (Market Structure and Equilibrium),* Vienna.

Tullock G (1991) Creative maverick of public choice, vol 1. Kluwer Academic Publishers, Dordrecht, pp 41–148

Williamson OE (1999) Public and private bureaucracies: a transaction cost economic perspective. J Law Econ Organ 15:306–342

Chapter 5
Small States and the Nontraditional Effects of Economic Integration

Rose Marie Azzopardi

5.1 Introduction

Economic integration is a process which has, in recent decades, gained increased attention, particularly following the development of the European Union and the expansion of the regional integration agreements (RTA) lodged with the World Trade Organization, especially after 1995.

Traditional economic theory indicates that the effects of economic integration are likely to be relatively stronger for small economies than for larger ones. The main reason is that small states cannot affect trading conditions, and thus, the power of imposing tariffs and other barriers to trade is negligible in influencing trade in international fora. The negative effects of tariffs are the loss in national welfare, with a redistribution of income from consumers (who are asked to pay higher prices) to local inefficient producers (who get protected) and governments (who use tariffs as a revenue-generating mechanism). For these reasons, economic integration for small countries is expected to offer more benefits than costs. The evaluation of the overall economic effect, however, depends on various factors.

Economic effects can be classified as static and dynamic ones. Static effects follow Viner's (1950) analysis, distinguishing between trade creation and trade diversion. The dynamic effects build on increased specialization, which then translate into economies of scale, the attraction of foreign direct investment and impetus to local investment creation. This leads to relocation of industries that choose the most competitive of the countries in the regional agreement and thus drives towards an efficient resource allocation. This has effects on technical change and technological diffusion, instilling an increase in the growth potential of the countries involved,

R.M. Azzopardi (✉)
University of Malta, Room 301 Humanities B (FEMA),
San Gwann, Malta
e-mail: rose.m.azzopardi@um.edu.mt

E.G. Carayannis and G.M. Korres (eds.), *European Socio-Economic Integration*,   63
Innovation, Technology, and Knowledge Management 27,
DOI 10.1007/978-1-4614-5254-6_5, © Springer Science+Business Media New York 2013

especially those which reform to meet the challenges of competitive pressures from a larger, unified and freer market. Such effects depend on the level of development of the country involved and the type of integration engaged in, with the impacts being stronger for deep rather than shallow integration projects (Evans et al. 2006).

However, it has become more complicated to analyse the full impact of agreements which do not classify as shallow, nor are really deep ones, but are a cross or a blend of both. In fact,

> … over the past three decades trade agreements have gone beyond border measures, such as tariffs, and have integrated a number of domestic policies and regulations, including intellectual property rights, product standards, competition and investment policies. (WTO 2011, p. 109)

This research has studied the integrative process of two small states, Malta and Cyprus, into the European Union. Results from the analysis indicate that static effects were meagre, whilst dynamic effects depend significantly on the commitment of the countries to reform and the restructuring programmes undertaken by the economies. Furthermore, the 7 years since EU accession does not provide for a long enough timescale in which to analyse the full impact of dynamic effects, since data is limited (covering at best 5 years) and because the recent international crisis may have thwarted business decisions in terms of expansion of operations, new investments and foreign direct investment, which are the basic conditions for longer term and wider impact of dynamic effects.

Therefore, the research turned to investigate what other benefits were accruing according to the prime proponents on the two islands, of this deep integrative course of action. The research question asked and explored in what manner the stakeholders were expecting to profit from the integration agreement and what type of gains were expected from the process. Interviews and focus groups with the main stakeholders on the islands were conducted 1 year and 6 years after accession. Results indicate that in the case of these two small islands, there were other nontraditional effects which encouraged almost all the main leaders in the two states to push for EU membership and sustain the significant process which entailed changes to the status quo. These effects include lock-in mechanism, credibility, "big brother" and opportunity, which reflect some of the aspects referred to by Fernandez and Portes (1998), discussed further on.

The remainder of this chapter is divided into four sections and a conclusion. The first section gives the theoretical framework regarding the effects of economic integration and their measurement. The second section deals with the literature on economic integration and small states. The third section provides the methodology used for the analysis. The fourth section presents the results of the research conducted in Malta and Cyprus. The final section concludes.

5.2 The Theoretical Framework

The literature on economic integration traditionally distinguishes between static and dynamic effects. The former represent changes in the allocative efficiency of member states, taking their productive capacity as given. By contrast, dynamic effects measure the impact of integration on the productive capacity of member states (Sapir 1992, p. 1498).

Theory suggests that the removal of tariffs could be beneficial for all those involved in the trading environment. Therefore, any form of trading agreement which lowered tariffs was believed to be positive. However, Viner (1950) suggested that such agreements may not always offer the best option and in fact referred to them as "second best policy," with global free trade remaining the best policy option.

Viner described the welfare effects of a customs union with his suggestion that benefits can be greater than costs only if trade creation is more than trade diversion. Trade creation is when trade is created with the new members of the agreement without detracting from the trade already engaged in with countries outside the agreement. Trade diversion is when trade previously conducted with countries outside the regional bloc becomes more expensive because of the common external tariff and gets diverted and conducted with countries inside the bloc, even if the latter are not as efficient, but prove to be cheaper only because they are protected behind tariffs. Estimating these two effects becomes important in the analysis of whether it is beneficial for one country to engage in a closer economic relationship with another country or a group of countries. These effects are however considered as static in that they tend to occur in the initial stages of the agreement and lead to a more efficient allocation of existing resources.

In later decades, other researchers suggested that other important aspects may have a more profound effect on the outcome of an RTA. Wonnacott and Wonnacott (1981) indicated that static effects were not enough for valuable empirical analysis and other issues had to be taken into consideration. Hamilton and Whalley (1985) suggested that the size of the regional bloc, the tariff structures of the participating countries and the existing trade pattern among the countries within the agreement with each other and with countries outside were to be considered as critical conditions for the evaluation of the agreement. Nonetheless, even if static effects estimates are at best "ambiguous" (Schiff and Wang 2003), analysis has often focused on such impacts.

Trade creation is expected to have a stronger impact if certain conditions prevail. These include high pre-regional trade agreement trade barriers (as this would lead to more trade among the agreement members without diverting trade from other countries outside the agreement); economies that are competitive rather than complementary (as this would encourage more specialization and competitive pressures rather than accommodating attitudes); geographical closeness (as this decreases transportation costs which can influence trade flows); a large number of countries forming part of the agreement (as this provides for a bigger, wider and more competitive market) and sources that are available at the lower end of the cost structure (since this would act as an attraction and provide to minimize trade diversion) (Tweeten 1992). A group of academics at the University of Sussex have used these six rules of thumb to develop what has come to be termed the Sussex Framework as a means of primary analysis of RTAs (for a full explanation of the methodology, see Evans et al. 2006 and CARIS 2007).

Another effect also taken into consideration when evaluating the effects of an RTA is the terms of trade one. However, empirical analysis indicates that the impact is not very important. Johnson (1960) suggests that positive terms of trade effects occur when initial tariff levels are high, partner's export supply curve is elastic, initial cost structures of foreign partners are small and the foreign demand for the country's export is inelastic. Petith (1977), Kreinin and Plummer (1992) and Gasiorek et al. (1992) conducted research on the terms of trade of the EU and the results differed. Winters and Chang (2000) and Chang and Winters (2002) similarly find that the results show that the terms of trade effects are small. Some researchers even suggest that a group of small countries, joining together in a RTA, tend to suffer a loss as a group since they are all price-takers on the international trading arena. Kowalczyk (2000, p. 492) maintains that "the small country's first best trade policy … is to seek membership of all free-trade areas" as this widens its market base.

Dynamic effects are likely to continue to have their impact on the relevant economies in later years since this influences the productive capacity of the country, by encouraging more investment, expansion of activities and new business ventures, leading to the attraction of factors of production where returns are higher. These effects relate to increased competition which intensifies market forces in a larger internal market, favouring specialization and thus economies of scale, stimulating investment, joint ventures and mergers across countries, leading to an overall more efficient use of RTA resources in an enlarged market, expanding the capabilities of the resources, whilst attracting others from outside the regional bloc. Regional integration researchers maintain that such impacts are more significant than the static effects of trade creation. Baldwin (1989) suggests that the gains can be "significant." Their estimation however, may be more difficult to ascertain and there can be variation in the results obtained depending on the methodology being used to make such calculations. For example, estimates for the EU internal market, looking at economies of scale and competition effects, reached 3% (quoted in Dyker 2001, p. 1001). However, Brada and Mendez (1988) estimated two effects in six RTAs, and their result showed that over 20 years the cumulative effect was lower than 1%.

Dynamic effects are stronger in deep integration projects, such as a common market or an economic union, and since few international projects have actually gone this far, the analysis has rested mainly on the impacts evidenced within the European Union and the single market of the bloc. De Rosa (1998, p. 48) maintains that this creates a vacuum in the analysis and there are "still unresolved questions about appropriate theoretical models and quantitative methods for determining the impacts of regional integration under imperfect competition." However, several ex ante quantitative studies have been conducted, mainly using general equilibrium models [see, e.g. Haaland and Norman 1992; Gasiorek et al. 1992; Harrison et al. (1996)].

Deeper integration leads to more labour and capital movements within the single market, since markets open up for both goods and services. For these reasons, skill and expertise movement and foreign direct investment are directly linked to deep integration and thus to the dynamic effects resulting from a more integrated market space. The emphasis on tariffs in static effects analysis turns to more complicated barriers to trade such as those affecting investment (Lawrence 1996). Therefore, whilst in shallow integration projects such as a free-trade area the focus is on border barriers, deeper integration calls for the elimination of across the border barriers, leading thus to more policy harmonization in the process. Rutherford and Tarr (1998, p. 5) sustain that it is the simplification and harmonized regulatory framework, allowing for easier factor mobility, which "realize the large gains." These deeper integration projects work within a framework where tariffs have already been lowered or even in some cases eliminated (Pomfret 2006a and 2006b), and therefore, the Vinerian analysis is no longer applicable. For this reason, across the border impediments, in the many forms of nontariff barriers (NTBs) to trade, gain increased importance and become more pronounced (Anderson and Van Wincoop 2004). NTBs are often less transparent and apparent than tariff structures and thus more difficult to ascertain and deal with. Some may appear justifiable from a national standpoint but create difficulties on the regional plane and hinder the smooth operation of market forces in a wider single market.

In spite of these conditions relating to both static and dynamic effects and more specifically to their measurement, RTAs have continued to proliferate over the years especially since the birth of the WTO, possibly as a consequence of the apparent success of the European Union and the attraction this has been to countries outside the agreement, both those who have joined in recent years and those who are lined up for the future. Apart from Luxembourg as a co-founder, other small states have however only recently become interested in becoming members. These include Malta and Cyprus and very recently Iceland and Montenegro. Other smaller states such as Andorra, Liechtenstein, Monaco, and San Marino have special arrangements and have not shown any inclination to go for full membership. The issue of small states and RTAs is considered in the following section.

Apart from the pure economic effects of RTAs, other impacts which affect the sociopolitical arena have been suggested by several researchers. De Melo and Pangariya (1993) indicate that regional integration has to be analysed by looking at other issues which focus beyond trade-related aspects. These aspects include gains which may influence the decision to join a regional bloc, thus impinging on economic decision-making, but in themselves need not result from an economic assessment of the possible benefits to be gained from regional integration. Fernandez and Portes (1998) suggest these gains to be "credibility, signalling, coordination, insurance and bargaining power."

RTAs involve reforms and changes in the economy: politicians tend to focus on the short term and can fall victim to pressures from an electorate which makes demands based on vested interests. The accumulation of such small favours will, in the long term, distort the economy whilst continuing to operate under the impression that various forms of special treatment and protectionism will persist. The RTA can thus act as a commitment mechanism for governments not to comply with such requests, because the RTA regulations need to be enforced and monitored by an entity outside the country. The government thus can "blame" someone else for its inability to comply with their demands. The commitment mechanism provides government with the *credibility* needed to enforce changes and binds not only present governments but future ones too. This creates a credible environment for investment scenarios since governments are believed to be able to carry out necessary macroeconomic policy reforms (Pass et al. 2000). Burfisher et al. (2000, 2003) also see an RTA as a force for national policy changes.

Signalling is also important, as this means sending a message to indicate a commitment to reform. This message is sent to all across the board, such as the electorate, business entities, and foreign investors. For example, joining an RTA entails a more liberal approach to economic management, and this signals that the country wants to work to become more competitive. The fact that the agreement also binds future governments means that the commitment is long-term. The signals include the condition that there is no room for the accommodation of vested interests. RTAs are also a means of *coordination*, especially of the benefits to be gained from reciprocal liberalization since all the members need to make the same pledges. An advanced RTA may also have a centralized budget which provides for temporary movements of financial aid in order to minimize the effects of the opening up of market sectors. Coordination of economic policies thus helps to provide for a level playing field with commitments from all members.

The RTA also acts as an *insurance* policy, whether this is in terms of cross-border problems, regional goods or merely as a wider market. The RTA has a better possibility of dealing with regional issues than a country can on the national level. Perroni and Whalley (1994) even indicate that RTAs can act as "safe havens" for small countries so that they gain a wider market. This is possibly more realistic when small countries engage in an RTA with larger countries, then if the RTA is among small countries only. Within an RTA, *bargaining power* can increase in two ways. For a small country, its power is minimal, but this increases in relative terms in the case of joint decisions taken internally within an economic bloc (e.g. by putting forth suggestions which on its own it can never realize). Externally the power of the bloc as one entity is bigger than the sum of the single member states participating in the RTA. In this manner, the political power of the small country is amplified in relative terms.

According to Schiff and Winters (1998b), some countries appear to use the RTA as a form of diplomatic strategy since it improves the conditions for security, especially for small states. Other countries see it more from a political perspective and view the RTA as a means of securing peace, strengthening democracy and political institutions and providing for greater security (Schiff and Winters 1998a, 2003). Baldwin (2005) says that political economy considerations also come into play since market forces and economic interdependence continue to encourage deeper integration which needs increased political commitment and the relinquishing of aspects of national sovereignty. Alesina and Spolaore (2003, p. 27) even maintain that "the cost of being politically small is decreasing with economic integration" and size becomes in essence less important in a regional bloc.

Estimates of RTA effects have generally centred round trade flows. Both ex ante and ex post studies look at changes in trade values. However, few have looked at the behaviour of actors in the process and how these can influence the outcome. In the final analysis, it is the accumulated economic behaviour of individuals and entities which influences the level of increased economic activity across borders and thus the success or failure of the endeavour.

The following section looks specifically at the experiences of small states within economic integration projects and the likely consequences for these small economic microcosms.

5.3 Economic Integration and Small States

The benefit of country size on economic performance should decrease with the increase of international economic integration and removal of trade barriers (Alesina and Spolaore 1997, p. 1042).

Small states depend more heavily on trade as they lack natural resources and thus need to sustain more open economies. Evidence suggests that small countries which relied on their openness and trade relations appear to have fared better than closed economies. In essence, trade was a significant part of their development strategies. In general, small states tend to be more open than larger countries and thus are more affected in a slowdown in the global economy as their integration is relatively more intense. Graph 5.1 shows the trade to GDP ratio of six EU countries (the smallest three and the biggest three) which shows that generally speaking, the smaller the country, the more it relies on trade. Whilst this is true for Malta and Luxembourg, it is not the case for Cyprus, which shows a lower level of trade openness than

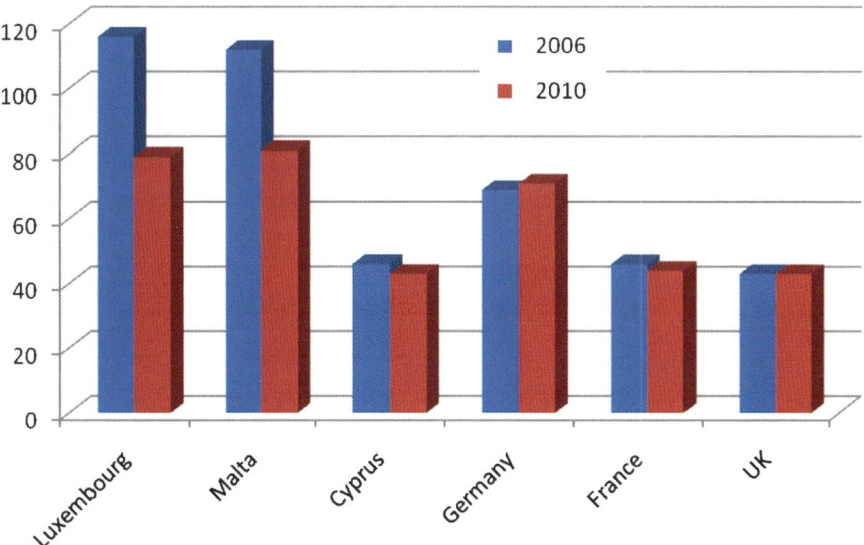

Graph 5.1 Trade to GDP ratio for selected European Economies, 2006 and 2010. *Source*: Based on Eurostat data (2011)

Germany. The difference between 2006 and 2010 also brings out the effect of the international crisis in the intervening years and the impact this had on trade flows, especially for Malta and Luxembourg, where the reduction in trade was relatively higher than in the bigger states. Within such a framework, it is reasonable to assume that any removal of barriers to trade is likely to have more of an effect on small open economies, and consequently, economic integration projects have a relatively stronger impact on small-sized countries. This is because the main force behind an RTA is to facilitate and augment trade among the member states by removing impediments to trade.

In the economic literature, the only distinction made between large and small states is in fact in relation to trade and the effect of a tariff. The main issue surrounding size in economic literature is linked to trade, in the case of the imposition of a tariff by a small country (which has a negligible effect on world trade and also leads to a lowering of welfare for consumers in such economies), and leads to the assumption that the total removal of tariffs, especially possible within a RTA, is the best option available to small countries.

However, there are two schools of thought on the issue of small states in general: one which sustains that small states have innate disadvantages which limit their economic achievements (Kuznets 1960; Demas 1965; Dommen 1980; Selwyn 1980; Jalan 1982; Dommen and Hein 1985; Briguglio 1995, 1998; Streeten 1993; Commonwealth and World Bank 2000; Davenport 2001); and the other which, whilst recognizing certain intrinsic factors, does not see the small size as an inhibitor for economic growth and development (Milner and Westaway 1993; Easterly and Kraay 1999; Armstrong and Read 1995, 1998, 2000, 2002a, b, 2004).

The first group maintains that the innate characteristics of the small economies hinder full exploitation of, for example, economies of scale because of the limited internal market. Furthermore, small states may face issues of indivisibilities, which tend to increase costs per unit, particularly transportation costs, leading to less competitive exported products and services. Due to lack of internal resources, there is a higher dependence on imports and subsequently exports to pay for these imports, making the country more exposed to exogenous shocks. Small states can also be regarded as riskier to invest in, which makes attracting investment and financing opportunities more problematic.

The second group puts forth examples of successful small states, which in some cases even have higher income per head than their larger neighbours (e.g. Armstrong and Read 1998). This group presents success stories such as Singapore or Hong Kong to sustain their arguments. Empirical evidence even shows that only four countries with population over one million actually feature in the top ten richest countries in the world (in GDP per capita), Alesina (2002) signifying that "clearly size and prosperity do not go hand in hand." By 2010, only two countries with population under one million (Luxembourg and Brunei) actually feature in the IMF's ranking, with six others under the ten million threshold, and only two over this limit.

Some researchers speak of certain advantages which play in favour of small-sized economies, and these include flexibility, the very openness of the economy and thus the ability of the small country to integrate and participate in the world economy, elements such as the cohesiveness of the small society and the marketing strategies of small countries as relaxing idyllic places to visit, thus the ability to continue to be attractive tourism destinations (Blazic-Metzner and Hughes 1982; Streeten 1993; Armstrong and Read 1995; Baldacchino 2000).

Empirical evidence indicates that there are several instances where small states have engaged in economic integration agreements. Some agreements have been more successful than others. It is safe to say that the global impact has not been significant, but such agreements have had an effect on the economies of the small states involved. These agreements have not only been among small states themselves but involve small countries and larger and more developed states as well. In general, such agreements tend to be of a shallow type of integrative agreement although aspirations for a deeper form exist. Examples include CARICOM (Caribbean Community), PICTA (Pacific Island Countries Travel Agreement) and IOC (Indian Ocean Agreement), which are all agreements among small island states. Some small states have reached trade agreements (in some cases, on a preferential basis although still within the regulations of the WTO) with bigger and more developed countries such as SPARTECA (South Pacific Regional Trade and Economic Cooperation Agreement), CBI (Caribbean Basin Initiative) and COMESA (Common Market for Eastern and Southern Africa).

With the increased proliferation of trading agreements, it could prove disadvantageous for countries to remain outside RTAs seeking mainly to encourage trade amongst themselves and in some cases being accused of overprotective policies. Moreover, the smaller the country remaining outside, the more harmful the situation can become. Krugman (1991, p. 21) refers to this as the "innocent bystander problem," where the largest costs of increased formation of big economic blocs "would likely be borne not by countries in the blocs but by those left out in the cold" (p. 22).

> Inward-looking free trade areas, whilst doing little damage to themselves or to each other, can easily inflict much more harm on economically smaller players that for one reason or another are not part of any of the big blocs (Krugman 1991, p. 23).

The innocent bystander concept was further developed by Kose and Reizman (1999). They conclude that for a small state, free trade remains the best option. In the case of free-trade areas, small countries should opt to remain outside the agreement as the bystander cost is relatively low. With deeper forms of integration such as customs unions and common markets, staying out of the agreement puts more pressure on the small fragile economy. Therefore, it becomes more beneficial for the small country to become a member of the economic integration agreement. However, the authors do not define what a small state is and also make some implausible assumptions. For example, they assume that the reliance of a small country on international trade is less than larger countries. Empirical evidence contradicts this. Since small countries depend more on trade, the removal of barriers to trade is more significant for these little economic players.

5.4 Methodology

The analysis for static and dynamic effects was carried out using the Sussex Framework and various indices, based mainly on published statistical data. The fact that both Cyprus and Malta had signed an Association Agreement with the EC in 1970 meant that they could export industrial goods duty-free. Some sensitive sectors such as agriculture and textiles were excluded from the agreement. The results from static effects proved to be negligible with some elements of trade diversion in the case of the agricultural sector. To analyse dynamic effects, an evaluation was conducted in terms of intra-industry trade, foreign direct investment flows, trade in services, capital and labour movements, trade facilitation and competition policy. The results indicate that whilst some positive steps have been registered, more developments in these areas require reforms and structural changes and thus depend on the commitment of governments and economic actors on both islands. This analysis is however, not the scope of this chapter, which focuses on other nontraditional effects, apart from static and dynamic ones.

No referendum was held in Cyprus; therefore, it is difficult to adequately gauge the sentiment on the island regarding EU membership, unless this is through surveys which may not always reflect reality, as a referendum does. Malta did hold a referendum and proved to be the most sceptical from all nine prospective candidates who gave the people a voice through a referendum. Those in favour accounted for 53.65%, needing a general election, conducted the following month, to push the process forward (Cini 2003). However, from official reports and the general intuition among several academics on both islands, EU membership was seen to be a very positive step in the development strategy of the two states. The research thus sought to discover if there were other beneficial outcomes which were not linked to pure economic calculations.

Analysis of economic integration project has generally been through quantitative techniques. Qualitative research in economics is considered to be rather unorthodox (Poire 2006). Whilst quantitative techniques were used for static and dynamic effects, qualitative analysis was undertaken to understand economic behaviour under the circumstances of the economic integration development, derived from the expectations of the economic agents in the process. The complexity of issues involved, including the small-size perspective, political powerlessness, social cohesion dimension and economic flexibility, could better be evaluated using a qualitative approach. The main tools utilized were in-depth interviews and focus groups, conducted with different stakeholders which brought to the fore a rich blend of socio-economic and political factors. Economic behaviour is best understood within the cultural, historical, political, legal and social milieux within which it is influenced and ultimately acts.

Thirty-one semi-structured, in-depth, one-on-one interviews were conducted with the main stakeholders on the two islands, 15 in Cyprus and 16 in Malta. These stakeholders included government officials, representatives of both employers' associations and unions, small business agents, private consultants and academics. These interviews were complemented with two focus groups, one on each island. The focus group in Cyprus consisted of seven members, whilst that in Malta had eight participants. These interviews and focus groups were conducted 1 year after accession, June 2005 in Cyprus and May/July 2005 in Malta. Six years after accession, in the summer of 2010, four more focus groups were conducted in order to compare the results of the two time frames and to evaluate if a change in attitudes had resulted in the intervening years. There were minor differences in the examples provided, which do not, however, influence or change the original result.

The focus on stakeholders was based on the assertion that their behaviour and decisions influence the way society behaves. "Economists have long understood that interest groups can affect international trade policy, and by extension RIAs" (Schiff and Winters 1998a, p. 187).

Primary data was thus generated, which was then coded, sorted, categorized and analysed using HyperResearch™ Version 2.0, a software package. HyperResearch™ is a computer-assisted qualitative data analysis software (CAQDAS), which provides for the coding and retrieving of data, to allow the researcher to build theories based on the coded material. HyperResearch™ is extensively used in the social sciences, since it gives the researcher the possibility to evaluate and classify trends and patterns. According to Richards and Richards (1991), in order for a programme to be capable of building theories, it should be possible for it to look for overlapping codes, to find their counter-evidence and to classify codes in sequential order. All these three features are possible with HyperResearch™.

Coding is analysis. To review a set of field notes, transcribed or synthesized, and to dissect them meaningfully, whilst keeping the relations between the parts intact, is the stuff of analysis (Miles and Huberman 1994, p. 56).

The coding conducted for the interviews and focus groups involved two processes: descriptive (or factual) coding (codes emerge directly from the transcripts and describe a state of fact as perceived by the interviewee) and interpretative coding (codes interpret the attitudes or meaning of the words used by the interviewees). The former type of codes describes actions, definitions, processes, properties, settings and events. The latter brings out viewpoints and causal conditions.

The analyst's reports do not summarize and organize what interview participants have said, as much as they "deconstruct" participants' talk to show the reader both the *hows* and the *whats* of the narrative drama conveyed, which increasingly mirrors an interview society (emphasis in original) (Silverman 2000, p. 127).

It is within this context that the results of the research emerged, taking into account that they mirror the attitudes of the stakeholders of these two small economies, against the background of their particular contextual circumstances. However, since they reflect issues related with small size, the results may be relevant to other small countries facing regional integration decisions.

5.5 Analysis and Results

The analysis brought forth several nontraditional factors which were influential and thus impinged on the decision for both islands to join the EU. The main stakeholders and economic agents, as the prime movers in this process, saw this decision as another step in the development strategy of the countries. The governments pre-sented EU membership mainly as an economic project; however, the acceptance of the stakeholders of it was not solely on economic terms but also in a sociopolitical vein. The EU was seen as an insurance policy for the future, which would increase the bargaining power of the small players, augment the credibility of the islands' commitment for reform and thus signal to the global trading environment that it was ready to make the necessary changes in order to integrate more in world affairs, even if only small countries. The data revealed that references were made to the EU providing the small states with a stronger voice, offering an element of burden-sharing, security issues, as an insurance policy, a coordination force for reforms and regional goods, and a mechanism to lock in transformations. In various forms, these impact on economic decisions and can facilitate decision-making and coordination between economic agents. The importance of these impacts is more pronounced for small states since this may influence investment opportunities, international supply chains, access to bigger markets for the mobility of goods, services, labour and capital and also lend credibility in terms of standards and product quality.

These various effects have been grouped into four main factors, with the EU act-ing as "a lock-in mechanism; increasing the level of credibility; 'big brother'; and offering opportunities" (Azzopardi 2007). These four factors, provided with exam-ples, are shown in Fig. 5.1.

The stakeholders on both islands were and still are firmly convinced that the EU would be acting as a *lock-in mechanism* for structural reforms, changes demanded by EU regulations which would make the economies more efficient and stream-lined, thus becoming more competitive in an enlarged market. The economic envi-ronment would need to become more liberalized. Reform was not expected purely on the policy level, to become in line with EU requirements, but also in terms of institutional set-ups, in order to be compliant with the needs of the regional bloc. These bodies include agencies for the administration of EU funds, commissions for competition policy, consumer protection authorities, regulators in various market sectors and environmental safeguards. Prior to EU membership, policies and orga-nizations had existed; however, accession entailed more harmonization with EU directives. This gives more direction and certainty, and thus, the EU acts as a force for the necessary modifications to the economy.

Politicians are time-constrained performers, in that whilst acknowledging that changes are needed for a country to remain competitive, reforms bring casualties, and these can translate into a loss of votes. Thus, politicians can fall prey to electoral considerations and do not undertake the much needed adjustments required by a modern economy in a fast-changing global economic environment. Therefore, poli-ticians make promises, but political exigencies can retard the actualization of these pledges, because the main aim of any politician is re-election.

Within an economic integration project, there is an "external discipline" or force which is requesting more restraint, sustainability and thus pushing for reforms. "Others" are considered to be answerable for any alterations that need to be engaged in, and the responsibility to push forward any unpleasant changes (Alesina and Spolaore 2003). Within this context, the EU is seen as the external discipline for the

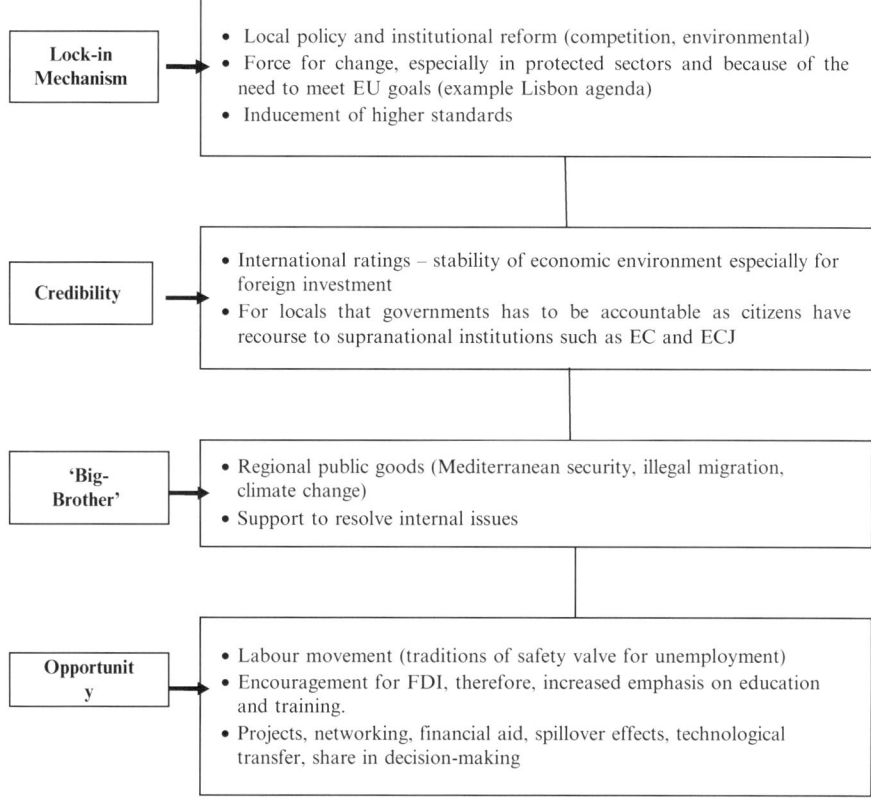

Fig. 5.1 Non-traditional effects of economic integration. *Source*: Azzopardi 2007

stakeholders on both islands, in order to transform their economies. In sensitive and traditionally protected industries, this could lead to redundancies or even closing up of companies. Such events are easier to sell to the people if the blame for such occurrences is put on outsiders.

Moreover, when there are regional goals to meet, such as deficit levels, inflation targets or employment participation rates, such goals impose more pressure to be met than national ones do. On the regional level, comparisons and rankings are made with other members in the bloc, and this can instigate local endeavours and sacrifices in order not to feature low in these rankings. Sacrifices are perhaps more readily made within this context. Expectations were also high in terms of standards for products, from which consumers benefit since EU standards are considered to be of a higher level, but also producers gain since national products can witness an improvement in their image.

All these characteristics of the lock-in mechanism are directly linked to the issue of *credibility*, which can improve both on the national and international levels.

On the local level, governments need to become more accountable because nationals have further recourse on the regional level. These supranational institutions include the European Commission and the European Parliament (via their European Members of Parliament) but more significantly the European Court of Justice. Governments thus have more responsibility to shoulder because if national citizens take their government to the European court, there is more exposure of administrative mistakes or wrongdoings, and thus stronger pressure on governments to regulate and comply with EU regulations, rather than be exposed of their incompetence outside national borders. Such a possibility can act as a deterrent, like a "name and shame" strategy often used to curb abuses and non-compliance. The regional dimension of such a strategy has greater credence and acts as a force for governments to regulate their roles and actions within the bloc. For example, if competition and other business policies are credible, then investors have positive expectations of stability, and the feel-good factor can be built upon. In this manner, economic integration increases the reliability and standing of governments. It also acts as a force for change, acting as a guarantee for consumers, businesspersons and even future governments.

The credibility increases also on the international scene. The first sign comes from the credit rating agencies, such as Standard and Poor's, Fitch Ratings and Moody's Investor's Service (these three control more than half of the market although other agencies exist). Their ratings are seen as a reliable source of credit worthiness of a country and are used by investors, bond markets, finance corporations, government regulators, and politicians. When countries accede to a strong regional integration project, these ratings are expected to see an improvement.

Moody's reports on Malta registered an improvement in the ratings when EU accession became a certainty for the island. In 1997, Malta had a negative outlook, mainly because of fiscal problems and external accounts issues registered by the country. This negative rating remained in place because of the need for structural and institutional reforms which were expected of the country in the integration process. It was only in 2003, after the EU referendum and subsequent general election results, which finally guaranteed the EU accession process, and Malta's future as an EU member state, that Moody's changed the rating from negative to stable. Two years after accession that is in 2006, the situation further improved from stable to positive, based on expectations of further restructuring and the island's endeavours to adopt the euro at the earliest time possible. Euro adoption came about in 2008 and upgraded Malta's ratings from A2 to A1.

Similarly Cyprus's rating had been lowered to negative from stable in 2000. With EU accession on the agenda, the rating was initially restored to stable and then became positive in 2006. After euro adoption in 2008 its rating was upgraded to Aa3 from A1.

Moody's views the adoption of the euro by Cyprus and Malta as a significant credit positive because it all but eliminates the risk of a currency crisis, thereby insulating their economies from external financial shocks (Reuters 2008).

EU membership pushed forward reforms, which created a more secure business and economic environment and this fed back into the ratings issued by international

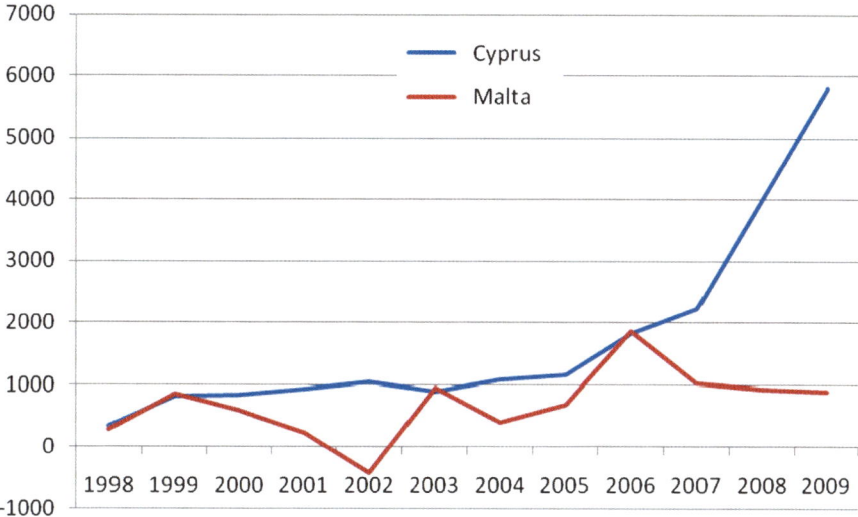

Graph 5.2   Foreign direct investment in Cyprus and Malta, 1998–2009. *Source*: UNCTAD 2011

credit rating agencies, which in turn brought in more investment into the countries, especially in the 2 years before euro adoption in the case of Malta, and an escalating amount in the case of Cyprus since EU membership. Cyprus appeared more credible for investment purposes as reforms had been ongoing for EU membership for quite some time, even before full accession. This is shown in Graph 5.2.

The third factor relates to the EU being regarded as a "*big brother*" by the two small islands. Two main reasons underlie this: regional goods and internal issues. The regional goods characteristic, that is, when a group of countries can make more of a coordinated effort to solve problems on the regional level, or to tend to regional goods, has been proposed as a convincing reason for regional integration projects, especially those among small states (Schiff 2002). In a situation where a small state engages in a regional bloc which comprises of much bigger countries, the impact is even more powerful, since the power of the bloc is massive compared to the puny influence of a small country.

Several examples of regional goods can be quoted in the case of the two Mediterranean islands. One is the security issue of the region, including the Middle East (especially for Cyprus) and the Northern coast of Africa (particularly for Malta). Coupled with a potential thriving EuroMed process, which would engage most countries touching the Mediterranean coast, this could lead to increased trade and investment flows, bringing a renewed economic interest in the area and considerable positive externalities, particularly for the two small players in the neighbourhood. A second issue is illegal migration in the region, deriving not solely from Africa but also from Asia and making their way towards the European continent via the Mediterranean Sea.

According to EUROSTAT's official data, the Republic of Cyprus ranks first among European states in regard to the number of illegal immigrants. The flow of illegal immigrants is widely attributed to the geographical position of Cyprus, which is at the crossroads of Middle East and North Africa (Stylianou 2010).

Both islands witness a significant amount of migrants, particularly in summer, and this is creating problems because of the limited resources of the islands. After the revolutions and riots on the African continent, the surge of migration increased during 2011. Stylianou (2010) maintains that "illegal immigration is not solely a Cypriot problem" and Cyprus should "seek the necessary help from the European Union." According to estimates issued by the Hamburg Institute of International Economics, Cyprus and Malta have the highest relative percentage of irregular foreigners as a percentage of their population, both registering 1.89%, with Bulgaria and Romania having the lowest amount at 0.05% of their population (Kovacheva and Vogel 2009).

The EU's response to the issue of illegal migration was the setting up of Frontex in 2005. This agency was established "to ensure that the EU's external borders remain permeable and efficient for bona fide travellers whilst being an effective barrier to cross-border crime" (Frontex 2011). Malta was chosen by the EU to host the European Asylum Support Office, which has the role of tackling the administrative side of the illegal migration problem. This was viewed by the Maltese authorities as a sign that Malta had first-hand knowledge and experience on the issue and was in a position to deal with the matter more effectively. Another example of regional goods is in terms of climate change and possible rising sea levels. As islands, such an event would affect their coastlines more seriously than larger mainland states. Such a global problem needs an international perspective, and small states have meagre possibilities of influencing decisions dealing with climate change. A regional bloc has more clout.

The small states see the EU as having a mediating role to resolve internal issues. In the case of Cyprus, the matter is political and surrounds the divide between the northern and southern parts of the island. In Malta's case, the question was more economic, such as funds for restructuring, social projects to increase employment or environmental upgrading. The conviction among the stakeholders was that the EU would be the "big brother," looking out for them, because it was protective and strong enough to deal and resolve both internal and external eventualities.

The fourth factor deals with *opportunity*. Traditional effects such as the encouragement of competition and investment, the provision of a larger market, certain spillover effects, the diffusion of technology and other positive externalities are assumed to take place in economic integration. However, results show that there are other opportunities which the local citizens and businessmen see as possible with EU membership. These include, mainly the opportunities available for work, study and business activities.

Both Cyprus and Malta have seen their people migrate in order to seek particularly work opportunities abroad, and families of Cypriot or Maltese origins can be found in traditionally migrant countries such as Australia, Canada and USA. The facility for Cypriots and Maltese to find these opportunities closer to home on the

European continent presents the EU as the "twenty-first century land of opportunity." This fact was further accentuated since the other ten new member states from Central and Eastern European countries had to wait 7 years before being provided with the opportunity of labour mobility. The EU thus provides the prospect of increasing the standard of living for those who are willing to seek higher returns on their education or capital. For two small states which have limited resources and a lower level of opportunities, the EU is the new haven, which offers more openings and options.

The EU also offers the chance for spillover effects in other sectors of the economy, for example, FDI may create needs for higher level type of education, skills and expertise. This may push for increased labour market participation rates, technological exposure and jobs in new areas. The regulatory framework of the market creates stability in the economic environment, pushing forward for more growth prospects. Such changes need not even emanate directly from EU accession; however, they are viewed by local stakeholders as indirectly related to it. Even if influenced by global rather than regional events, such opportunities are seen to be attributable to and possible because of EU membership.

EU membership has led Malta to tackle its macroeconomic fundamentals, restructure its economy, strengthen internal competition through liberalization, increase efficiency through privatization, protect its citizens by tightening environmental regulation and management and open new avenues to its exporters of goods and services, both within the EU and beyond, thus giving incentive to diversification (Pace 2006, p. 47).

The incentives which economic integration presents are considered to be made available by various authors, who believe that political economy forces increase the integrative process and open up prospects and affect economic decisions undertaken by governments, businesses and consumers. "The integration itself will change the political economy forces in each nation in a way that will make deeper integration easier" (Baldwin 2005, p. 22).

The EU is regarded as a sort of panacea which offers solutions to problems faced by the two islands. It is the prime mover in locking in reforms which increase the credibility of the islands' economic environment, thus making them more attractive for investment, more competitive and stable. It is the land of opportunities for education, investment, business and employment, and it is the big brother, ensuring a secure atmosphere and acting as a protective shield against possible difficulties, which the small states feel ill-equipped to find solutions to on their own.

These nontraditional effects emanating from a deep economic integration project resulted from research conducted with the main stakeholders in Cyprus and Malta. As small states, within the volatile Mediterranean basin, they are surrounded by certain contextual circumstances, which may not always be thought to be applicable to other small states. However, if one were to analyse the arguments put forth by a significant cadre of small states' researchers, it is evident that small countries in general have attributes which influence their economic decisions, and this also includes regional trade agreements. Therefore, the results obtained from this research may be relevant to other small states elsewhere.

5.6 Conclusion

Traditional economic theory has always sustained that small states are likely to gain the most from joining economic integration projects, basically because of their powerlessness in international trading fora and thus their inability to have any real effect when imposing trade restrictions.

This chapter has evaluated the process of Malta and Cyprus towards EU membership. Their long-term relationship with the European Community dating back to a 1970 Association Agreement signified that only small changes were expected to result from static effects of full membership. Dynamic effects depend primarily on internal reforms and commitments which national actors need to undertake, and the time frame is generally of a longer perspective than that available for this research. Data after 2004 membership is only available at best 5 years after accession, which cannot do full justice to the possible impact of adhesion within the deep integration project of the EU.

The focus of the research was on other nontraditional effects which influenced the expectations and aspirations of the prime movers of the accession process. These individuals heralded from government entities, business environments, labour unions, academia and consultancy groups. They were chosen, as their leadership and behaviours impact on the action of smaller economic agents in the economy.

Four main political economy considerations came to light from the evaluation. These included the EU acting as a lock-in mechanism, as a big brother, offering a myriad of opportunities and providing or increasing the credibility of the new member states. Due to the small size of the two member states involved, the effect of these factors are expected to be significantly stronger than they would be for bigger countries.

This research has thus shown that even if the initial economic impact of a regional trading agreement is not directly seen to be fundamental, there are more important issues which are taken into consideration by small economies in their quest to gain a better grasp of their role in the international trade environment. The RTA augments the spectrum of possibilities for small states, and their membership of strong economic blocs increases their potential.

References

Alesina A (2002) The size of countries: does it matter? NBER
Alesina A, Spolaore E (1997) On the number and size of nations. Q J Econ 112(l4):1027–1056
Alesina A, Spolaore E (2003) The size of nations. Massachusetts Institute of Technology, Cambridge, MA
Anderson J, Van Wincoop E (2004) Trade costs. J Econ Lit 42(3):691–751
Armstrong H, Read R (1995) Western European micro-states and EU autonomous regions: the advantages of size and sovereignty. World Dev 23(7):1229–1245
Armstrong HW, Read R (1998) Trade and growth in small states: the impact of global trade liberalization. World Econ 21(4):563–585

Armstrong HW, Read R (2000) Comparing the economic performance of dependent territories and sovereign states. Econ Dev Cult Change 2:285–306

Armstrong HW, Read R (2002a) The importance of being unimportant: the political economy of trade and growth in small states. In: Murshed SM (ed) Issues in positive political economy. Routledge, London

Armstrong HW, Read R (2002b) The phantom of liberty? Economic growth and the vulnerability of small states. J Int Dev 14(3):435–458

Azzopardi RM (2007) Economic integration and small states: case studies of Cyprus and Malta. Unpublished doctoral thesis, University of Sussex

Baldacchino G (2000) The challenge of hypothermia: a six-proposition manifesto for small island territories. Round Table 353:65–79

Baldwin R (1989) Measurable dynamic gains from trade. National Bureau of Economic Research. Working Paper No. 3147

Baldwin RE (2005) Sequencing and depth of regional economic integration: lessons for the Americas from Europe. World Econ 31(1):5–30

Blazic-Metzner B, Hughes H (1982) Growth experience in small economies. In: Jalan B (ed) Problems and policies in small countries. Croom Helm, London

Brada JC, Mendez JA (1988) An estimate of the dynamic effects of economic integration. Rev Econ Stat 70(1):163–167

Briguglio L (1995) Small island developing states and their economic vulnerabilities. World Dev 23(9):1615–1632

Briguglio L (1998) Small country size and returns to scale in manufacturing. World Dev 26(3): 507–515

Burfisher ME, Robinson S, Thierfelder K (2000) Small countries and the case for regionalism vs. multilateralism. International Food Policy Research Institute. Trade and Macroeconomics Division Discussion paper no. 54

Burfisher ME, Robinson S, Thierfelder K (2003) Regionalism: old and new, theory and practice. Paper presented at the International conference "Agricultural Policy Reform and the WTO: Where are we heading?" Capri, Italy

CARIS (Centre for the Analysis of Regional Integration at Sussex) (2007) Assessing preferential trading agreements using the Sussex Framework. Briefing Paper No. 1. http://www.sussex.ac.uk/Units/caris/wps/Carisbp01.pdf (received via Email from CARIS)

Chang W, Winters LA (2002) How regional blocs affect excluded countries: the price effects of MERCOSUR. Discussion paper no. 2179. Centre for Economic Policy Research, London

Cini M (2003) Malta votes twice for Europe: the accession referendum and the general election, March/April 2003. South Eur Soc Polit 8(3):132–146

Commonwealth Secretariat/World Bank Joint Task Force on Small States (2000) Small states: meeting challenges in the global economy. Commonwealth Secretariat/The World Bank, London/Washington, DC

Davenport M (2001) A study of alternative special and differential arrangements for small economies. Commonwealth Secretariat. A study prepared for the Economic Affairs Division

De Melo J, Pangariya A (eds) (1993) New dimensions in regional integration. Cambridge University Press, New York, NY

De Rosa DA (1998) Regional integration arrangements: static economic theory, quantitative findings, and policy guidelines. Background paper for the World Bank Policy Research Report "Regionalism and Development"

Demas WG (1965) The economics of developments in small countries: with special reference to the Caribbean. McGill University Press, Montreal

Dommen EC (1980) Some distinguishing characteristics of Island states. World Dev 8(12):931–943

Dommen EC, Hein PL (eds) (1985) States, microstates and islands. Croom Helm, London

Dyker DA (2001) The dynamic impact on the central-eastern European economies of accession to the European Union: social capability and technology absorption. Eur Asia Stud 53(7): 1001–1021

Easterly W, Kraay A (1999) Small states, small problems? Income, growth and volatility in small states. World Dev 28(11):2013–2027

Eurostat (2011) http://epp.eurostat.ec.europa.eu/portal/page?_pageid=1090,30070682,1090_3307 6576&_dad=portal&_schema=PORTAL

Evans D, Gasiorek M, Ghoneim A, Hayes-Prempeh M, Holmes P, Iacovone L, Jackson K, Iwanow T, Robinson S, Rollo J (2006) Assessing regional trade agreements with developing countries: shallow and deep integration, trade, productivity and economic performance. UK, DFID Project Number 04 5881

Fernandez R, Portes J (1998) Returns to regionalism: an analysis of non-traditional gains from regional trade agreements. World Bank Econ Rev 12(2):197–220

Frontex (2011) Frontex: libertas, justitia. http://www.frontex.europa.eu/origin_and_tasks/origin/

Gasiorek M, Smith A, Venables T (1992) "1992", trade and welfare: a general equilibrium model. CEPR Discussion Paper no. 672. Centre for Economic Policy Research, London. http://www.cepr.org/pubs/dps/DP672.asp. Accessed 13 May 2005

Haaland J, Norman V (1992) Global production effects of European integration. In: Winters LA (ed) Trade flows and trade policy after "1992". Cambridge University Press, Cambridge

Hamilton B, Whalley J (1985) Geographically discriminatory trade arrangements. Rev Econ Stat 67(3):446–455

Harrison GW, Rutherford TF, Tarr DG (1996) Increased competition and completion of the market in the European Union. J Econ Int 11(3):332–365

Jalan B (ed) (1982) Problems and policies in small economies. Croom Helm, Beckenham

Johnson HG (1960) The economic theory of customs union. Pakistan Econ J 10(1):14–32

Kose MA, Reizman R (1999) Understanding the welfare implications of preferential trade agreements. Rev Int Econ 8(4):619–633

Kovacheva V, Vogel D (2009) The size of the irregular foreign resident population in the European Union in 2002, 2005 and 2008: aggregated estimates. Hamburg Institute of International Economics (HWWI), Database on Irregular Migration, Working paper No.4

Kowalczyk C (2000) Welfare and integration. Int Econ Rev 41(2):483–494

Kreinen ME, Plummer MG (1992) Effects of economic integration in individual countries on ASEAN and the Asian NIEs. World Dev 20(9):1345–1366

Krugman P (1991) Geography and trade. MIT Press, Cambridge

Kuznets S (1960) Economic growth of small nations. In: Robinson EAG (ed) The economic consequences of the size of nations. Macmillan, London

Lawrence RL (1996) Regionalism, multilateralism, and deeper integration. The Brookings Institute, Washington, DC

Miles MS, Huberman AM (1994) Qualitative data analysis: an expanded sourcebook. Sage Publications, Thousand Oaks, CA

Milner C, Westaway T (1993) Country size and medium-term growth process: some cross-country evidence. World Dev 21(2):203–211

Pace R (2006) Malta and EU membership: overcoming "Vulnerabilities" and strengthening "Resilience". J Eur Integr 28(1):33–49

Pass C, Lowes B, Davies L (2000) Collins dictionary of economics. HarpersCollins Publishers, Glasgow

Perroni C, Whalley J (1994) The new regionalism: trade liberalization or insurance? Can J Econ 33(1):1–17

Petith HC (1977) European integration and the terms of trade. Econ J 87:262–272

Poire MJ (2006) Qualitative research: does it fit in economics? Eur Manage Rev 3:17–23

Pomfret R (2006a) Regional trade agreements. In: Fratianni M, Rugman A (eds) Regional economic integration. Elsevier, Amsterdam

Pomfret R (2006b) Is regionalism an increasing feature of the world economy. Paper presented at a IIIS Seminar at the Trinity College Dublin, 23 May 2006

Read R (2004) The implications of increasing globalization and regionalism for the economic growth of small Island states. World Dev 32(2):365–378

Reuters (2008) Cyprus and Malta ratings raised by Moody's. http://www.reuters.com/article/2008/01/03/economy-moodys-cyprusmalta-idUSWNA253620080103. Accessed 3 Jan 2008

Richards L, Richards T (1991) The transformation of qualitative method: computational paradigms and research processes. In: Fielding NG, Lee RM (eds) Using computers in qualitative research. Sage, London

Rutherford TF, Tarr DG (1998) Trade liberalization and endogenous growth in a small open economy: a quantitative assessment. Paper presented in Milan Italy at a conference on Technology Diffusion and Developing Countries, Apr 1997

Sapir A (1992) Regional integration in Europe. Econ J 102:1491–1506

Schiff M (2002) Regional integration and development in small states. World Bank, Development Research Group. Institute for the Study of Labor. World Bank Policy Research Working Paper No. 2797

Schiff M, Wang Y (2003) Regional integration and technology diffusion: the case of the North America Free Trade Agreement. World Bank Policy Research Working Paper 3132

Schiff M, Winters LA (1998a) Dynamics and politics in regional integration arrangements: an introduction. World Bank Econ Rev 12(2):177–195

Schiff M, Winters LA (1998b) Regional integration as diplomacy. World Bank Econ Rev 12(2):271–295

Schiff M, Winters LA (2003) Regional integration and development. Oxford University Press, New York, NY

Selwyn P (1980) Smallness and islandness. World Dev 8(12):945–951

Silverman D (2000) Doing qualitative research: a practical handbook. Sage Publications, London

Streeten P (1993) The special problems of small countries. World Dev 21(2):197–202

Stylianou N (2010) Illegal migration: a first glance at the case of Cyprus. Research Institute for European and American Studies. http://www.rieas.gr/research-areas/editorial/1352-illegal-migration-a-first-glance-at-the-case-of-cyprus-.htm. Accessed 9 Nov 2010

Tweeten L (1992) Agricultural trade: principles and policies. Westview Press, Boulder, CO

UNCTAD (2011) http://www.unctad.org/Templates/Page.asp?intItemID=1584&lang=1

Viner J (1950) The customs union issue. Carnegie Endowment for International Peace, New York, NY

Winters LA, Chang W (2000) Regional integration and import prices: an empirical investigation. J Int Econ 51:363–377

Wonnacott P, Wonnacott R (1981) Is unilateral tariff reduction preferable to a customs union. The curious case of the missing foreign tariffs. Am Econ Rev 71:704–714

World Trade Organization (WTO) (2011) World Trade Report 2011: the WTO and preferential trade agreements: from co-existence and coherence. WHO, Geneva

Chapter 6
The Greek Crisis & CO.D.TRA (Code of Digital Transactions): Mobile Payments and the Global Info-Cash (GIC)

George K. Gantzias

6.1 Introduction: Info-Communication Globalization and Culture

Info-communication globalization is a dynamic process concerning transformation through digitalization of transactions in social, political and cultural systems (also see, Urry 2003; Gantzias 2001; Webster 2002; Nash 2008; Gantzias 2012). This type of digital globalization exerts strong pressure on the traditional banking and monetary systems. Mobile payments and the digital form of money, i.e., the Global Info-Cash (GIC) are likely to be a way for Greece to emerge from crisis by the 2015. The digitalization of payment transactions for sums exceeding 1,500 Euros together with the forthcoming new electronic taxis system after Greek elections are serious indications that the Code of Digital Transactions (CO.D.TRA), as an idea for mobile payments in Greece is an alternative way for battling tax evasion (also see, Gantzias 2012; Mavros 2011; The Daily Mirror 2011; Dicker 2007; Gantzias 2010; Tapscott 1996).

Traditional banking and monetary systems have recently been seriously challenged by the domination of the digital technology, mobile payments and the global monetary crisis. Global companies such as Google together with central banks are likely to play a key role in switching on the digital form of money by 2015, both globally and locally. Global companies and central banks are going to negotiate how to share mobile payments revenue in info-communication globalization. Google

G.K. Gantzias (✉)
Department of Cultural Technology and Communication,
University of the Aegean, Lesvos 81100, Greece
e-mail: ggantzias@aegean.gr; ggantzias@yahoo.gr

E.G. Carayannis and G.M. Korres (eds.), *European Socio-Economic Integration*,   85
Innovation, Technology, and Knowledge Management 27,
DOI 10.1007/978-1-4614-5254-6_6, © Springer Science+Business Media New York 2013

and a group of partners including Sprint Nextel, Citibank, and MasterCard plan to jump-start the mobile payments market in the USA with a system based on a free "Google Wallet" app and a technology called "Near Field Communications" (NFC) (Taylor and Palmer 2011).

Within this, new cultural patterns have been creating an info-communication culture which is challenging the traditional cultural, political, social and economic systems. According to the academic research "Info-Communication Globalization, Participatory Freedom and the Global Info-Cash (GIC)," *info-communication culture is subject to both globally and locally cultural patterns which are* (Gantzias Forthcoming):

- Consumerism (signified by brands)—refers to culture of consumerism which is directly related to the formation of global capitalist markets. Most countries now live under capitalism—sharing of market values and consumer culture.
- Networked individualism—refers to a set of values and beliefs that gives priority to the satisfaction of individual needs and desires.
- Cosmopolitanism (be it ideological, political, or religious)—refers to small but influential minority people—there is consciousness of the shared destiny of the planet we inhabit, be in terms of the environment, human rights, moral principles, global economics interdependency or geopolitical security.
- Multiculturalism—refers to existence of a multicultural global cultural characteristics by hybridization and remix of cultures from difference origins—as the diffusion of hip hop music in adapted version throughout the world or remixed video that populate YouTube.
- Communalism—is a set of norms, values and beliefs that place the common goods over the individual satisfaction of its members on the basis of public interest principles.

New cultural patterns, broadband networks and info-communication multifunctional devices (i.e., mobile phones, tablets PCs, etc.) together with the emerging mobile payments methods have been the causal dynamics for creating "Code of Digital Transactions" (CO.D.TRA) and the Global Info-Cash (GIC) in the emerging info-communication landscape. Within this, context, European countries, and in particular Greece, should consider the recent technological challenges for digital reformation of their traditional political, cultural, social, and economic systems as soon as possible (also see, Gantzias 1998; Negroponte 1995; Gantzias 2001; GeBloch and Fontela 2003; Webster 2005; Brown 2010; Gantzias 2010, Manolopoulos 2011).

This chapter examines and analyzes the role of mobile payment, the info-communication industry, the *"Code of Digital Transactions" (CO.D.TRA)* and the *Global Info-Cash (GIC)* in the recent cultural and economic crisis. It outlines mobile payment methods and the role of digital transactions in info-communication globalization. Finally, it introduces actions programs switching on the digital form of money as an alternative way of physical payment in free market economy after the Greek elections of 2012 (also see, McKnight et al. (2001); Palmer 2011; Gantzias 2012; Mavros 2011).

6.2 Info-Communication Industry: Digital Technology and the "Code of Digital Transactions"

Information and Communication Technologies (ICT) have radically reformed the way we conduct business in info-communication globalization. The domination of digital technology has been transforming local, national and international economies throughout the world. Instant capital transaction across geographic nodes that would have taken days and months to cross with physical means, almost "cancels" the concept of time as an obstacle or expense in the accounting books of transnational companies (also see, Castells 1996–1998; Seaberg et al. 1997; Terranova 2004; Selwyn and Laszlo 1997; Gantzias 1998).

The dynamics of digital technology and the free market philosophy have irrevocably challenged the analogue networks, products, services and content of the cultural industries. The domination of broadband networks and the rise of social media networks have affected our everyday life, by changing the way people do everything, from shopping to concert attending. According to Castells (2009) "...networks do not have fixed boundaries; there are open-ended and multi-edge...their expansion or contraction depends on the compatibility or completion between the interests and values programmed in each network and the interest and values programmed into networks they come into contact with their expansionary movement" (p. 25). The Internet, wired society, and social media networks are very important issues in info-communication globalization. Within this context, social media networks are made up by individuals and organizations engaged in a variety of info-communication industry's platforms on a voluntary, autonomous basis, without the interference of state or business enterprises. The condition of social and economic networks is widely seen as essential to the condition of society in cultural crisis. It is within the sphere of social networks and the digital transactions that individuals and groups can act as agent, capable, insofar as the resources and the constraints upon them allow, of creating and sustaining their own cultures and values in free market economy (also see, Gantzias 2000; Littlechild 2000; Terranova 2004; Herman 2005; Lievrouw and Livingstone 2002; Pilbeam 2010).

The third generation mobile phones, broadband connections, wireless applications, social media networks, cyberspace, electronic commerce and the digital form of money—i.e., the Global Info-Cash, the contactless visa cards, etc.—are subject to five digital platforms in the emerging new info-communication industry. Creative industries, mobile payments and the recent economic crisis have recently set up a global digital environment to create the info-communication multi-functional devices (i.e., iPhone, iPad, tablet PC, etc.), which empowers people to produce, distribute to and receive broadband information from anything that has IP (Internet Protocol) address (also see, Gantzias and Kammaras 2000; Gantzias 2001; Webster et al. 2003; Palmer 2011; Gantzias 2012).

Within this context, new technologies expand opportunities and increase the social, political, cultural and economic rewards by creating new info-communication products and services. Nowadays, info-communication networks are creating compatible digital platforms to develop global networks and mobile payments in order to bring together multicultural business startups, research institutions, social media and digital markets in our everyday life. Just as electricity, telephony, railroad and automobile, each providing a major stimulus to cultural, political and economic growth and significant restructuring of economies and societies during the twentieth century, so the domination of digital technology and the social mass media are likely to create a new "paradigm shift." This new "paradigm shift" is the digital transformation from the semi-detached paradigm of creative industries to the unitary paradigm which called "Info-Communication Model" (also see, Gantzias 1998; Gantzias 2000; Gantzias 2001).

According to the unitary paradigm, info-commutation industry may be the unitary global platform to link together different locations within and between a company's office, a town, a region and indeed the entire info-communication economic activities in the free market economy. According to Frank Webster (2002) "as the electricity grid runs through an entire country to be accessed at will by individuals with the appropriate connections." So we may imagine now the info-communication industry being likely to operate at national, regional, and global level to provide compatibility between info-communication networks, info-communication devices, info-communication content, info-communication services and info-communication security to each home, bank, university, governmental department and office (also see, Gantzias 1998; Gantzias 2001; Gantzias 2012; Webster 2005; Gantzias 2012).

Figure 6.1 shows how the key drivers (technology, markets and regulation) will be digitally transformed into the info-communication technologies, info-communication markets and info-communication regulations in order to support the emerging new info-communication landscape. According to the Info-Communication Model, there are five compatible digital platforms, which are activating both globally and locally the info-communication industry. These five digital platforms are (also see, Gantzias 2001; Gantzias Forthcoming):

- Info-Communication Devices (ICD)—digital access system.
- Info-Communication Networks (ICN)—digital distributing system.
- Info-Communication Content (ICC)—digital content system.
- Info-Communication Services (ICSer)—digital services system.
- Info-Communication Security (ICSec)—digital security system.

In the Info-Communication Landscape the Info-Communication Security platform is the main factor for activating mobile payments and the "Code of Digital Transaction" (CO.D.TRA). In the recent financial crisis, digital transactions have been changing the traditional monetary system because broadband, wireless information and content can be sent to anything that has IP (Internet Protocol) address. We have already got IP-enabled PCs, digital television with set top boxes, Personal Digital Assistants (PDAs) with wireless protocols (e.g. wireless protocol 802.11b) and mobile phones as "digital wallets."

Latest technological developments in broadband networks, multimedia services and content and IP based products have irrevocably challenged traditional

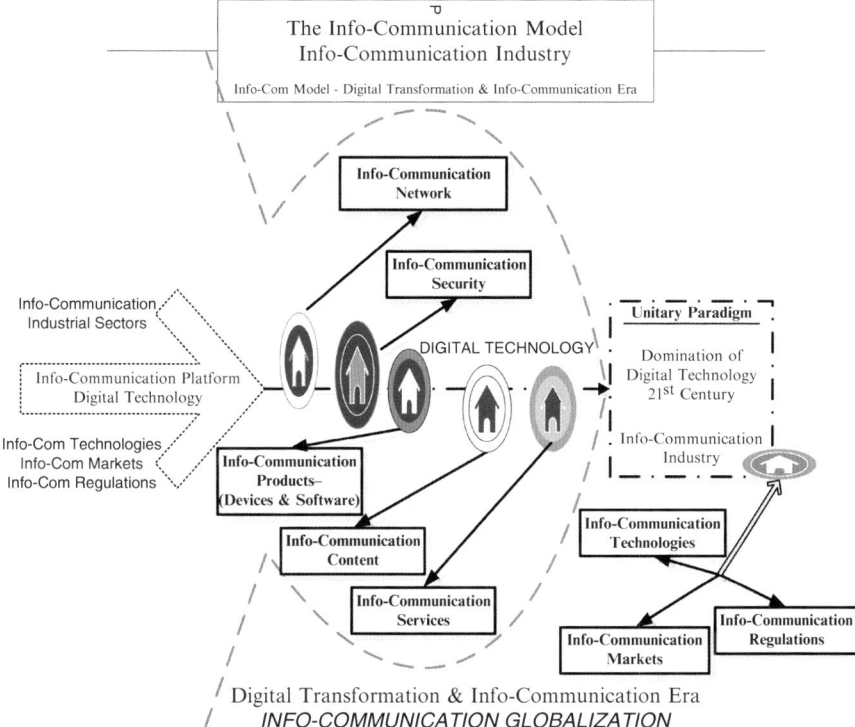

Fig. 6.1 The unitary paradigm: the info-communication model

communication systems, i.e., wireless communication encompasses voice, data, video and graphics by Internet connectivity. New Info-Communication multi-functional devices such as iPhone, iPad, smart phones, tablets, etc.—bring cars, vending machines, kiosks, toys, and household equipment, all with IP address. The advancement in wireless communication and the mobile phone as "digital wallets" together with the emerging of the info-communication industry are very important factors for all the countries to consider developing a policy to switch off the physical form of money and switch on the digital form of money (i.e., the Global Info-Cash) (also see, Tapscott 1996; Bell 2003; Webster et al. 2003; Gantzias 2010; BBC 2011; Mavros 2011).

A number of countries—including Turkey, Sweden, Estonia, the Philippines, South Korea and Japan—have started to discuss how to end the use of cash all together. One of the most prominent campaigns has been in Sweden, where the anti-cash lobby group has high-profile support from Abba's Björn Ulvaeus, co-writer of pop hits including "Money, Money, Money." One reason experts believe we could be coming to a tipping point is that smartphones have made it easy not just to make but also to receive electronic payments. Emerging Info-Com multi-functional devices and services that can turn any phone into virtual cash till—just as accessible to small traders, such as window cleaners and babysitters, who have hitherto have to operate on a cash basis, as for bigger enterprises (Taylor and Palmer 2011).

The Greek government has recently introduced a tax legislation which is encourages to develop a new culture of digital transactions in the Greek free market economy, i.e., to allow payments using cash (physical form of money) for sums not exceeding 1,500 Euros. According to the research, "Info-Communication Globalization, Participatory Freedom and the Global Info-Cash (GIC)" (Gantzias Forthcoming):

It is more expensive for governments to produce, manage, store, control and regulate the transactions using the money as physical form than using the money as a digital form in the recent crisis. In info-communication globalization, the physical form of money is like a "corpse with a perfume"…and the digital form currency (the Global Info-Cash (GIC) with its digital subdivision, such as the Info-CashGR, the Info-Cash EU, the Info-CashUS, etc.) is a practical solution for all governments around the world who want to:

- Cut spending
- Collect taxes
- Improve services and products
- Reduce their debt
- Be transparent and accountable in their policy making
- Introduce local focused and global ranged regulatory bodies.

Moreover, the above research project introduces "the Global Info-Cash (GIC) as an alternative digital form of money in monetary crisis." It also introduces "'Code of Digital Transactions' (CO.D.TRA) as dynamic multi-cultural economic system for developing a multicultural payment, i.e. multicultural payments on the Internet by transmitting unique, authenticated tokens (unique encrypted numbers) for various digital and physical transactions both locally and globally. This type of dynamic system (i.e. CO.D.TRA) seeks to emulate the functionality of a system of regular physical form of money in monetary free market economy. In particular, the most important functions of the CO.D.TRA. are the following: (a) to authenticate the citizen thought the use of reliable encryptions system, (b) to store and transfer value both globally and locally, (c) to secure the payment process, (d) to create specific digital rights transactions which are subject to public interest principles" (Gantzias Forthcoming).

6.3 Mobile Phone as "Digital Wallets": Mobile Payments

The digital form of money is not inherently good or evil. Technological options have to be translated into social, political and economic realities. Within this context, the need to understand the role of digital money in free market economy is a very important issue, at the time when mobile phones as "digital wallets" have become a reality. The info-communication industry and the digital form of money deserve a new attention in recent cultural and economic crisis, because digital technology and the economic crisis are pushing forward by breaking obsolete boundaries in traditional cultural market sectors and by setting up a new system of digital transactions, digital content and digital markets. No individual, organization, business, or government can ignore the important role of speed in cyberspace and refuse to accept the role of the digital transactions in information and knowledge society (see also Crawford and Marks 1998; Terranova 2004; Webster 2005; Castels 2009; Gantzias 2010).

The emergence of the new info-communication industry together with the social media and the info-communication cultural patterns are challenging the physical form of money by placing a lot of pressure to free market system. According to "Info-Communication Globalization, Participatory Freedom and the Global Info-Cash (GIC)" research project "the difference between the physical form of money and the digital in economic crisis is enormous because a hand-to-hand transaction could be opaque, and thus deprive the state of valuable resources for payment of salaries and pensions, spending on health and education and investments in development projects. Conversely, digital transaction is unavoidably recorded and thus taxed. Therefore, the digital form of money are likely to reform the way in which we communicate, make transactions and conduct business in info-communication globalization"(Gantzias Forthcoming).

Citizens/users/customers have recently used their mobile (smart) phones (i.e., info-com multi functional devices) as digital wallets in order to pay their cups of tea or coffee. According to the Daily Mirror newspaper, there are more than 12 million contactless credits and debit cards in circulation. David Chan, chief executive of Barclaycard Consumer Europe, said:

> "This is the first time that customers can use their mobile to pay for goods and services in shops across the UK rather than using cards or cash. They'll be able to do this, safe in the knowledge that this is a secure technology brought to them by the biggest names in payments and mobile technology" (The Daily Mirror 2011).

Electronic payments are here! From Sweden to Afghanistan digital transactions have become routine. In an age of more than 7 billion people in the world and 182 different official currencies in 192 states of the United Nations, the penetration of mobile phones and the Internet has shaped the Info-Communication landscape of digital transactions. According to most academic studies, 50% of the world have already communicated via different types of mobile phones and over two billion people have Internet access (Gantzias 2012).

Mobile phones have already been the "digital wallets" in some countries of our planet. A striking example is Afghanistan, where in 2001 the penetration of mobile phones reached from 0 to 30% of the population. As a result, in more than 95% of Afghans not having bank accounts conduct their daily financial transactions digitally via mobile phones. For instance, more than 2,000 police officers in Afghanistan are digitally paid their salaries via a mobile phone. In turn they sent their pay to their families using the message service of mobile telephony. In Kenya, a company developed software for transferring money via mobile phone. (i.e., M-Pesa system for mobile payments). In Sweden and Denmark, most daily transactions of consumers/citizens are digital and tax services are connected digitally to the cash registers of most companies. In Northern Europe countries, digital transactions are routine (Gantzias 2012).

Fig. 6.2 Step-by-step
contactless payments

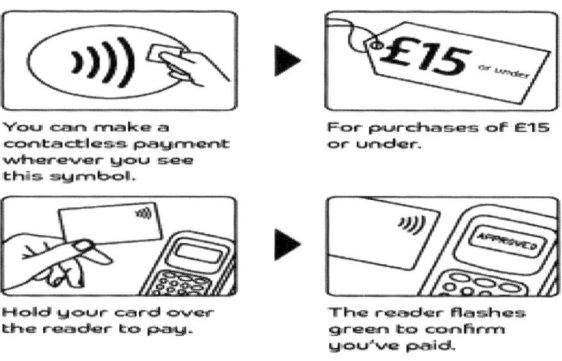

The recent rapid change in digital technology has contributed significantly to creative destruction of economic crisis in our capitalistic systems. Capitalism's vitality has come from the dynamic of what the Harvard economist Joseph Schumpeter called "creative destruction." He also defined it as the ability to adapt to changes in technologies and markets. The pressures are both domestic and global, as international trade increases and the digital technology are placing digital transactions in the free market economy (also see, McKnight et al. (2001)). Moreover, the emergence of info-communication devices (Info-Com devices) redefine wired and wireless communication systems by transforming mass communication systems from narrowband to broadband information, inspiring new methods of conducting business, making digital mobile transactions and placing cultures, communities and markets into info-communication globalization.

Nowadays, customers could have the info-communication right or a special permission from their banks to use their mobile phone as a digital wallet to buy a cinema ticket, a sandwich or a cup of coffee without the need for a card or cash (physical form of money). Google, PayPal, Visa, Master, Diners, and leading mobile operators are moving into the digital transaction free market economy. In 2011, Google launched its mobile wallet service in the USA, empowering people to pay for goods and services. Visa is very close to enter into digital wallet services this year, allowing users to make speedier payments online and over mobile phones. PayPal is in negotiations with retails to get them accept payments from its mobile Internet services in store. AT&T, Version, and T-Mobile in the USA are seriously considering to invest more than 90 billion dollars in building their own info-communication mobile payment platform (Taylor and Palmer 2011).

In the UK, there are different research projects to examine and analyze the role in using mobile phones as digital wallets. According to the BBC, "consumers can already take advantage of digital form of money in the UK, if their credit or debit card is enabled—designated on Barclaycards, for example, with a wireless symbol" (BBC 2011). The Barclaycard contactless Visa card issued as a quick and easy way to make everyday payments up to 15 pounds. Fig. 6.2 explains step-by-step how it works (also see, Gantzias Forthcoming).

The Payments Council, which oversees payments strategy in the UK, in a recent report has pointed out that using the physical form of money could be a minority activity by 2050 (BBC 2011). Mobile payments systems are reality! Moreover, the 2012 Olympics is expected to be a test bed for mobile payments, with the Samsung and Visa teaming up to allow visitors to pay with the NFC-enabled mobile handset (Taylor and Palmer 2011).

6.4   Conclusion: Action Programs for Global Info-Cash

Info-communication Industry and Code of Digital Transactions (CO.D.TRA) as a new system for producing, store and distributing money (i.e., Global Info-Cash) is a practical way for Greece to implement this idea in order to emerge from cultural and economic crisis after the Greek election 2012. The European leaders have recently put strong pressures on the Greek government and the Greek banks to implement fully their suggested policies or consider seriously alternative ways for Greek economy to emerge from crisis. Within this context, the Greek banks are heading towards that direction of using the methods of digital payment, using mobile phones as digital wallets. According to academic researches one out of ten Greek citizens uses debit or credit cards for payments in everyday payments transactions. Therefore, the Greek government introduced legislation so Greek citizens/users/costumers can make payments using cash (physical form of money) up to the amount of 1,500 Euros, above which Greek citizens/users/customers are obliged by law to use their bank accounts or their credit or debit cards in 2012. This is one of the methods that the Greek government has been employing in an effort to introduce transparency for everyday payment's transactions in the Greek free market economy (Gantzias Forthcoming).

Digital transactions may offer enormous opportunities to business people and consumers in free market economy. Interested parties need to be convinced that regulations of digital transactions are likely to set up a supportive flexible mechanism for empowering the use of the digital form of money (i.e., Global Info-Cash) both globally and locally. Within this context, *The Info-Communication Globalization, Participatory Freedom and the Global Info-Cash (GIC)* suggests "three dynamic action programs for introducing and implementing the 'Code of Digital Transactions' (CO.D.TRA) as a flexible mechanism that will work both locally and globally as a flexible self-regulatory system for activating the Global Info-Cash (GIC) in free market economy. The three action programs" are (Gantzias Forthcoming) as follows:

- "Legal Standards for Global Info-Cash" (LSGIC). This action program aims to create a globally compatible legislative framework in which all the interested parties when using the digital form of money (i.e., the Global Info-Cash) know that irresponsible behavior will be penalized by criminal and economical sanctions
- "Global Info-Cash Transactions Rights" (GICRT). This action program aims to create a network of hierarchical regulative bodies in order to introduce a set of public interest principles for digital transaction rights in which all interested parties know where to ask for support for their problems and where to complain at local/national, regional and global levels

- "Global Info-Cash Policies and Strategies" (GINCPL). This action program aims to develop a globally compatible framework of specific strategies and policies to switch on the digital form money both globally and locally. These types of strategies and policies are likely to be subject to transparency, public interest principle and participatory freedom.

References

BBC (2011) Orange customers of everything everywhere get mobile payments http://www.bbc.co.uk/news/technology-12287009. Accessed 27 Jul 2011

Bell E (2003) The blogs of war. The Observer, 30 March

Brown B (2010) Euro crash: the implications of monetary failure in Europe. Palgrave Macmillan, UK, p 4

Castells Manuel (2009) Communication power. Oxford University Press, New York

Castells Manuel (1996–1998) The information age: economy, society, and culture (1998). Volume I: the rise of the network society (1996). Volume II: the power of identity (1997). Volume III: end of millennium. Revised edition for volumes I and III (2000). Blackwell, Oxford

Crawford J, Marks S (1998) The global democracy deficit: an essay in international law and its limits. In: Archibugi D, Held D, Kohler M (eds) Re-imagining political community: studies in cosmopolitan democracy. Stanford University Press, Stanford

Dicker P (2007) Economic globalization: corporations. In: Ritzer G (ed) The Blackwell companion to globalization. Blackwell, Oxford, pp 291–306

Gantzias George K (Forthcoming) Info-communication globalisation, participatory freedom and the global info-cash (GIC) http://www.globalinfocash.com

Gantzias George (2012) Info-communication globalisation and the global info-cash (GIC): A Practical Way for Greece to Emerge from Crisis. In: Liargovas P. Greece: Economics, Political and Social Issues, Nova Publishers, USA

Gantzias George K (2010) The Crisis is an opportunity to Greece: from euro to info-cash, Kosmos of Ependitis, Economic Newspaper, 15 May, p 20

Gantzias GK (2001) The dynamics of regulation global control, local resistance: cultural management and policy. Ashgate, Aldershot, pp 37–44

Gantzias George K (2000) Communication systems in the 21st century: reform and public interest. In: George K, Gantzias, Dimitris Kamaras (ed) Digital communication, new media and the Greek information society: convergence, 'E-commerce and portals. Zenon publishers, London, p 11–56

Gantzias G (1998) The info-communication industry: digital markets global services. Zeno Publishers, London

Gantzias G, Kammaras D (2000) Media. In: Speake G (ed) Encyclopaedia of Greece and Hellenic tradition, vol 2. Fitzroy Dearborn, London, pp 1020–1023

GeBloch M, Fontela E (2003) Mobile communication from voice to data. Info 5(2):24–33

Herman ES (2005) The propaganda model: a retrospective. Cult Technol Policy J 1:5–22. doi:www.ctpj.info or http://www.eklogesonline.com/ctpj/en/articles.asp?state=articles

Lievrouw LA, Livingstone S (2002) Handbook of new media social shaping and consequences of ICTs. Sage Publication, London

Littlechild S (2000) Privatization, competition and regulation. IEA, London

Mavros George (2011) Digital Money will save us! Social Issues, Imerisia, Economic Newspaper, 12/13 Mar 2011, p. 38–39. (http://www.imerisia.gr/article.asp?catid=12333andsubid=2andpubid=102955157#). Accessed 13 Jul 2011

McKnight LW et al (2001) Creative destruction. MIT Press, Cambridge, p 3

Manolopoulos J (2011) Greece's 'ODIOUS' debt. Anthems Press, London

Nash K (2008) Global citizenship as show business: the cultural politics of Make Poverty History. Media Cult Soc 30(1):167–181

Negroponte N (1995) Being digital. Hodder ans Stroughton, London

Palmer Maija (2011) Racing to make mobile wallet pay. Financial Times, 27 December p. 21. www.ft.com

Pilbeam K (2010) Finance and financial markets, 3rd edn. Palgrave Macmillan, London, pp 457–481

Seaberg JG, Hawn J, Dincerler GE, Eugster CC, Rao N (1997) Attackers versus incumbents: the battle for value in an IP-networked world. McKinsey Quart 4:138–153

Selwyn LL and Laszlo JW (1997) The effects of internet use on the Nation's Telephone Network. Report prepared for the Internet Access Coalition, 22 July.

Tapscott D (1996) The digital economy: promise and peril in an age of networked intelligence. McGraw-Hill, New York

Taylor P, Palmer M (2011) Google reveals mobile payment plan. Financial Times, London. http://www.ft.com. Accessed 27 May 2011

Terranova T (2004) Network culture: politics for the information age. Pluto Press, London, pp 39–75

The Daily Mirror (2011) New mobile phone payment system. http://www.mirror.co.uk/news/latest/2011/05/20/new-mobile-phone-payment-system-115875-23142805/. Accessed 27 Jul 2011

Webster F (2005) Making sense of the information age: sociology and cultural studies. Cult Technol Policy J 1:49–66. doi:www.ctpj.info or http://www.eklogesonline.com/ctpj/en/articles.asp?state=articles

Webster F (2002) The information society revisited. In: Lievrouw LA, Livingstone S (eds) Handbook of new media social shaping and consequences of ICTs. Sage Publication, London, pp 22–34

Webster F et al (eds) (2003) The information society reader. Routledge Student Readers, Routledge

Urry J (2003) Global complexity. Polity, Cambridge

Part II
The Dilemma of Social Policy and Integration Process: Lessons and Prospects

Chapter 7
Building Bridges in South Asia: Regional Cooperation, Information Technologies and Opportunities for Integration

Kiran Prasad

7.1 Introduction

The end of World War II saw the birth and growth of several international political organizations to forge international and regional cooperation in solving international political, economic, social, cultural and humanitarian problems. While international organizations like the United Nations have member states from all over the world, regional political organizations like the European Union (EU) and South Asian Association for Regional Cooperation (SAARC) are aimed at achieving regional cooperation among its members. In recent years, international political organizations have occupied an important position to forge common links with countries that share similar values and interests.

International political organizations have entered a wide range of development areas to promote greater international understanding and cooperation. They are also concerned with promoting peace and security among different member states. They hold out a hope for negotiation, economic and social cooperation, conflict resolution and peace building among various member states. These organizations have become important forums for world leaders to address and engage with to improve regional and international cooperation and understanding. This chapter explores the prospects for regional cooperation through e-governance by SAARC in South Asia and the limits of social integration due to sociopolitical complexities in the region.

K. Prasad (✉)
Department of Communication and Journalism, Sri Padmavati
Mahila University, Tirupati 517502, India
e-mail: kiranrn_prasad@hotmail.com; kiranrn.prasad@gmail.com

E.G. Carayannis and G.M. Korres (eds.), *European Socio-Economic Integration*,   99
Innovation, Technology, and Knowledge Management 27,
DOI 10.1007/978-1-4614-5254-6_7, © Springer Science+Business Media New York 2013

7.2 Regional Cooperation and Economic Integration in South Asia

The South Asian Association for Regional Cooperation or SAARC was created in 1985 in Dhaka with seven members, as an expression of the region's collective decision to evolve a regional cooperative framework. India is the largest member country of SAARC which also comprises Maldives, Pakistan, Bangladesh, Sri Lanka, Bhutan and Nepal. Its headquarters is in Nepal. There are also cooperative joint mechanisms among the SAARC nations to step up monitoring of human trafficking of women and girls. Many Indo-Pak dialogues are held on the sidelines of the SAARC Summit. There are also several educational opportunities for mutual understanding and friendship under international exchange programmes funded by various international organizations.

In South Asia, India has a strategic geopolitical position as the largest country consisting of a population of over one billion and is credited as the largest, stable and functioning democracy. India is the second most populous country with great diversity of languages, geographical climates, religions and cultures. It has an area of approximately 3,287,263 sq. km making it the seventh largest in the world occupying 2.4% of the total land area of the world. The Indian economy ranks sixth in the world. The United Nations Conference on Trade and Development (UNCTAD) has credited India with a projected economic growth of 8.1%—the fastest rate of expansion in the world after China (Hindu 2011a).

Nevertheless, it is also a country of stark contrasts. South Asia including India is home to the largest rural-urban disparities. The National Council for Applied Economic Research (NCAER) estimates for 2001–2002 that India has an average 60.5 million households totalling to over 300 million individuals in the middle-income category, also called the middle class (Debroy 2001) who are the potential targets of global media and business conglomerates. This middle class is larger than the entire domestic market of the United States and even make up the combined population of two or three European countries (Tharoor 2005; Vineeth 2004:427) and constitute India's growing target for media advertising and consumer markets.

The sheer size of the market in the South Asian region makes economic integration an important factor in global stability. The SAARC regional grouping has achieved much in its 25 years of existence; starting from an intra-regional business of approximately $150 million, the last 5 years from 2005 to 2010 has seen business go up to $5 billion (Phadnis 2011). Nevertheless, during 2009, with a total trade volume of $628.9 billion, intra-regional trade in South Asia was a mere 5%. In comparison, East Asia's regional trade constituted 32% of its total trade in 2006. To make matters even worse, a Ministry of External Affairs concept paper points out that as much as 55% of the intra-regional trade potential remains largely untapped. Even though the need for intra-regional economic integration is greater than ever before in the present competitive environment, a 2006 World Bank report shows that South Asia is the least integrated region on the globe.

7.3 South Asia Forum (SAF)

The South Asia Forum (SAF) is an initiative that emanated from the Silver Jubilee Declaration of the SAARC Summit held in Thimphu, in April 2010. The governments and billions of people of the eight SAARC countries envisaged greater efforts at regional integration at the first meeting of the SAF in Delhi in September 2011. The regional grouping includes India, Sri Lanka, Pakistan, Nepal, Maldives, Afghanistan, Bhutan and Bangladesh. A meeting of business, think-tanks, academia, media and civil society, the main thrust of the meeting was to generate ideas, which could eventually lead to greater integration of the regional grouping, and help the region in moving towards an economic union (Phadnis 2011). SAF is seen as a unique concept because even though Track-II processes and people-to-people contacts are underway in the region, this is a first-of-its-kind forum, to be formally endorsed by the SAARC Summit.

The SAF initiative is being recognized across the globe as economic integration in this region will be an important factor for global stability. There is also a realization that in the changing environment, the service sector will play a greater role in integrating the economies of the region, instead of manufacturing. Hence, intra-regional trade in services, which was absent under South Asian Free Trade Area (SAFTA), is being considered. To take this path of cooperation forward, the Federation of Indian Chambers of Commerce and Industry (FICCI) has suggested a five-pronged strategy—providing freedom to trade without barriers, freedom to invest across borders, freedom of seamless travel, connectivity across the borders and creation of South Asian brand equity (Phadnis 2011).

7.4 Complexities of Economic Integration

The 17th Annual SAARC Summit held in Maldives in November 2011 with its theme "Building Bridges" was intended to make progress on several regional issues including improving the infrastructure of connectivity and trade and better people-to-people contact. Apart from increasing physical connectivity, the focus is also on political dialogue through bilateral meetings especially involving India and its neighbour member states. Despite these main objectives, as had happened at a few SAARC meetings, Indian bilateral meetings often dominated the SAARC. According to Radhakrishnan (2011), "the meetings at the sidelines between India and Pakistan, the two-nuclear powers in the region, have often overshadowed the modest agenda of SAARC."

The relations between Delhi and Islamabad had been frozen after the Mumbai 26/11 attacks in 2008. The bilateral meetings were also interesting in how both countries could take forward what's called the "Thimphu thaw" after the SAARC Summit held in Thimphu, in April 2010. This is significant in the light of the fact that India broke off talks with Pakistan twice, after the 2001 attack on the Indian Parliament and after 2008 Mumbai terrorist attacks. For a long time, Pakistan also held talks on the premise that it had to be Kashmir first or nothing. Beyond the contentious issue of Kashmir, the suspicion and mistrust that plagues India-Pakistan relations has extended to what each country is doing in Afghanistan (The Hindu 2011b). India attempts to ensure that the peace process with Pakistan stays on track and developments on the economic front between the two countries continue to step up trade and people-to-people contact.

Despite these political complexities in interregional relationships, Pakistan decided to acknowledge India as a most favoured nation (MFN) under World Trade Organization regulations. While India had already given Pakistan MFN status in 1996, the opposition in Pakistan has not died down. Denouncing the Pakistani cabinet's decision to grant MFN status to India, the leader of Lashkar-e-Taiba (LeT), a regional terrorist organization, was reported to have said, "The relationship between India and Pakistan is of guns and bullets and not of trade" (Mehra 2011). Under MFN status, India would enjoy the same trade advantages including lower tariffs that Pakistan grants its other trading partners. Pakistan is also expected to permit imports of many more Indian products than it does now, except for a small "negative" list, thus moving away from the current system where there is only a positive list of 1,934 items (Mehra 2011). There is also a gradual move between the two countries to move towards a Preferential Trade Agreement but in the shadow of the reality that terrorists can disrupt the slow gains made in furthering peace by both countries. Given the precarious state of relations between India and Pakistan, the two largest economies in the region, SAF can prove to be a non-starter while Bangladesh has leveraged the international system and has access to all international markets in Europe and America.

There is also another bone of contention between India and Pakistan regarding the need to induct more observers in SAARC. Australia, Japan and China were the observers in the 17th Annual SAARC Summit in November 2011. While Pakistan suggests lifting the moratorium on induction of observers and supports the inclusion of Turkey as observer, India believes that SAARC's internal processes and institutions must be stabilized before adding more observers (Dikshit 2011). India is particularly wary of adding more observers or increasing their role in a bid to curtail India's influence in the regional forum. It is perhaps one of regional groupings in which observers outnumber members; the eight-member SAARC forum now has nine observers.

India and Sri Lanka are concerned with the slow progress of the political solution to the aspirations of the Tamils in the Northern Province of Sri Lanka. Both countries were not pleased that the Tamil political group, the Tamil National Alliance (TNA) with whom the Sri Lankan government was holding talks took their cause to leaders and policy makers the United States, Canada and the United Nations. In spite of the political complexities between some of its neighbours, the India-China Model has been often invoked to demonstrate that "two not-too-friendly countries could succeed to interact in mutually beneficial ways. It does not imply that the contentious issues between them have vanished; rather, it means these issues can and should be resolved without foregoing the benefits of bilateral interaction" (The Hindu 2011b).

Table 7.1 Information and communication technology expenditure, worldwide by country 2003–2008 (% of GDP)

Country	2003	2004	2005	2006	2007	2008
India	3.2	3.8	4.4	4.1	3.9	4.5
Sri Lanka	2.4	2.7	3.3	3.8	4.6	4.3
Pakistan	3.2	3.3	3.9	4.2	4.4	4.4
Bangladesh	1.9	2.4	4.1	5.9	8.0	9.0
Indonesia	1.9	3.3	3.3	3.2	3.2	3.3
Singapore	10.1	9.7	9.6	8.7	7.5	7.1
Thailand	5.8	6.2	6.1	6.2	6.1	6.2

Source: The World Bank (2010)
Note: Information and communications technology expenditures include computer hardware (computers, storage devices, printers and other peripherals), computer software (operating systems, programming tools, utilities, applications and internal software development), computer services (information technology consulting, computer and network systems integration, web hosting, data processing services and other services) and communications services (voice and data communications services) and wired and wireless communications equipment

7.5 ICTs and Interregional Development

International communication policy debates which emphasize that creating digital opportunities is not something that happens after addressing "core" development challenges; it is a key component of addressing those challenges in the twenty-first century (G8 2002). Meanwhile, the developing countries continue to experience the commercial divide where e-commerce reaches only some and the digital divide is being regarded as one of the biggest non-tariff barrier to world trade today (Prasad 2009). South Asia has enormous potential for regional trade and economic integration which can be expanded using Information and Communication Technologies (ICTs). But the ICT infrastructure in the SAARC countries is not conducive for promotion of regional business and trade.

The low human development status of countries in South Asia has also been linked to their ICT poverty. The United Nations (2006) has identified a strong correlation between a country's information and communication technology diffusion index (ICTDI) and its income and level of human development as measured by the UNDP's Human Development Index (HDI). The top ranks are dominated by industrial countries from North America, Western Europe and the Asian Tigers, while many of the lower-ranking countries are from Africa. India and its neighbours Nepal, Bhutan, Pakistan and Bangladesh also fall into this group. The information and communication technology expenditure by countries during 2003–2008 as a percent of GDP shows that Bangladesh is far ahead of India (4.5%), Pakistan (4.4%) and Sri Lanka (4.3%) (see Table 7.1).

The Network Readiness Index rankings of 138 countries released by the Global Information Technology Report 2010–2011 assess the conduciveness of national

Table 7.2 The leading 20 countries worldwide with highest number of Internet users 2009 (millions and %)

Rank	Country or region	Population (million)	Internet users (million)	Penetration (% of population)	Growth 2000–2009	Share of world users (%)
1	China	1,339	360	26.9	1,500.0	20.8
2	United States	307	228	74.1	138.8	13.1
3	Japan	127	96	75.5	103.9	5.5
4	India	1,157	81	7.0	1,520.0	4.7
5	Brazil	199	68	34.0	250.2	3.9
6	Germany	82	54	65.9	126.0	3.1
7	United Kingdom	61	47	76.4	203.1	2.7
8	Russia	140	45	32.3	1,359.7	2.6
9	France	62	43	69.3	407.1	2.5
10	South Korea	49	37	77.3	96.8	2.2
11	Iran	66	32	48.5	12,780.0	1.9
12	Italy	58	30	51.7	127.5	1.7
13	Indonesia	240	30	12.5	1,400.0	1.7
14	Spain	41	29	71.8	440.0	1.7
15	Mexico	111	28	24.8	917.5	1.6
16	Turkey	77	27	34.5	1,225.0	1.5
17	Canada	33	25	74.9	97.5	1.4
18	Philippines	98	24	24.5	1,100.0	1.4
19	Vietnam	89	22	24.8	10,881.6	1.3
20	Poland	38	20	52.0	615.0	1.2
	Top 20 countries	4,375	1,325	30.3	359.9	76.4
	Rest of the world	2,393	409	17.1	461.5	23.6
	Total world	6,768	1,734	25.6	380.3	100.0

Source: Internet World Stats (2010)
Note: Population data are estimates

environments for ICT development and diffusion, including the broad business climate, regulatory aspects, the human and hard infrastructure needed for promotion, the degree of preparation for and interest in using ICT by key stakeholders and the extent of its use by them. India's Network Readiness Index stands at 48 out of 138 economies, while China was at the 36th spot.

The leading 20 countries worldwide with highest number of Internet users 2009 (millions and percent) can be seen in Table 7.2. It can be observed that the top 20 countries account for 76% of the world Internet users, while the rest of world accounts for only 23.6% of Internet users. India has only 7% of its billion-plus population using the Internet which accounts for a miniscule 4.7 share of the world's Internet users.

The ITU-sponsored Maitland Commission Report published in 1984 drew attention to the extreme inequalities of telephone access between rich and poor nations and argued that investment in telecommunications was not to be seen as luxury service for corporates and elites, but as an essential service that directly leads to economic growth. Telecommunication reforms were reinforced by structural adjustment programmes of the World Bank in India and in several other developing countries such as Brazil,

Kenya, Ghana and Chile. Despite being the world's fastest-growing cellular market in the world with around 1.5 crore new mobile subscribers being added every month, over 37,000 villages in India are still deprived of mobile telephony. As a result, rural tele-density has failed to match the growth of urban tele-density (Joshi 2011). While the tele-density in India is 11%, China has a tele-density of 29%. Rural tele-density in India stands at a meagre 2% compared with urban tele-density of 31% (Singh 2006). Despite the pace of reforms, tele-density in the rural areas is still very low leading to a big divide between urban and rural areas. The fixed tele-density in 2006 in India (4.58), Pakistan (4.16) and Sri Lanka (9.50) continues to be lower than the mobile tele-density of 8.82 in India, 25.22 in Pakistan and 27.1 in Sri Lanka. Most of the growth in tele-density in these countries is due to the growth in urban mobile tele-density. Although mobile phones are diffusing rapidly, fast, data-capable third-generation mobile networks are less common in low-income countries.

Mobile phones have an especially dramatic impact in developing countries—substituting for scarce fixed connections, increasing mobility, reducing transaction costs, broadening trade networks and facilitating searches for employment and new markets. Mobile telephones provide market links for farmers and entrepreneurs and are mainly used for communication and information services. "Much of the voice traffic over the cell phones is commerce directed. Access to agricultural market prices, access to agricultural trade information, facilitation of remittances from foreign workers, information on work opportunities using the phone can reduce substantial travel costs" (Richardson 1999).

The lack of available telephone lines and Internet service providers (ISPs) in many developing countries has been cited as a major barrier to ICT use among small and medium enterprises (SMEs) in Indonesia, the Philippines, Sri Lanka and Thailand. Availability outside major cities and the speed of connectivity were also a major concern (Asia Foundation 2002). Another major constraint is bandwidth for data traffic; slow and unreliable access limits ICT use. The percent of international capacity within the regions as a percentage of the total international capacity (within and outside the region) shows that 72% of European international capacity in 2005 is between European countries, while bandwidth among African countries only represents 1% of international capacity (United Nations 2006:12). The majority of interregional bandwidth of 35% in the Asian region is to Japan, Republic of Korea, Taiwan, Hong Kong, Singapore and Australia.

The shifting from traditional interactions to electronic transactions using ICTs leads to a number of legal and regulatory concerns. The lack of a satisfactory redress mechanism when things go wrong online may strongly discourage online transactions. Moreover, in the case of cross-border transactions, often there is no harmonized legal framework with rules that pertain to the determination of jurisdiction and applicable law, nor are there mechanisms that ensure the cross-border enforcement of legal rulings. Particularly in developing countries, access to reliable advice on appropriate security measures is often at a premium. In these countries, the cost of keeping abreast of rapid developments in the complex technological and legal issues involved in online transactions may be too high for many firms (Zhen-Wei Qiang et al. 2006:68).

The government's support of a regulatory framework for trust, security, enforcing authentication mechanisms and combating cyber-crime—combined with internationally accepted privacy and consumer protection protocols—is essential in encouraging the use of ICT applications in the economy. Of particular relevance for firms are low-cost online dispute resolution mechanisms both among firms and between firms and consumers. Countries are developing e-security policies and programmes, including public key infrastructure (PKI) and computer emergency response teams (CERT). These policies and programmes are often a combination of top-down, government-led initiatives together with bottom-up, industry-led programmes. PKI supports digital signatures and other public security services and is necessary in laying the foundation for e-applications such as e-signature, e-notarization and e-certification. The CERT program, a multi-agency information-sharing framework, aims at assessing and managing e-security risks, providing training and emergency alert and response services and offering backup to ensure the continuity of network systems and applications (Zhen-Wei Qiang et al. 2006:70). India has formulated cyber laws but a wider awareness about these laws has yet to be generated among the people.

7.6   Capacity Building for Citizens

India's experience in e-governance/ICT initiatives has demonstrated significant success in improving accessibility, cutting down costs, reducing corruption, extending help and increasing access to unserved groups (Das and Chandrashekhar 2007; Prasad 2009). Most of the State governments in India have gone in for e-governance initiatives through the use of information and communication technologies (ICTs) and are in the process of making the citizens Net-enabled too. With appropriate content, connectivity and capacity building measures, it is expected that regional cooperation can be improved through trade and communications.

In India, the e-governance initiatives of Kerala have been commended by international agencies and have also won admirers from outside the country. The World Bank delegation found the Kerala State IT Mission (KSITM) competent to perform the role of an international consultant, especially to developing countries in Asia Pacific and Africa. The KSITM had the added advantage of having practical experience in rolling out e-projects and is pioneer in the use of free and open software in e-governance (Praveen 2011). A delegation from Zimbabwe visited Kerala in December 2010 in study how to revive its economy through the application of ICT solutions. A delegation from Bangladesh visited Kerala in May 2011 to learn from the experience in mobile governance applications and the citizen-centric delivery of e-governance services undertaken by the State through the KSITM. Bangladesh is in the course of setting up 4,500 Net-enabled information centres similar to the Akshaya Common Service Centres (CSCs) of Kerala and wants an integrated application of ICTs in the delivery of e-governance services; it is presently scattered with the use of multiple networks and servers in Bangladesh.

7.7   Technological Implications for Regional Integration in South Asia

The policy challenges for e-governance lie in first bridging the digital divide and turning it into digital opportunities for development and in South Asia. The issues that need to be focused include the levels of technology, the penetration and access to ICTs, content creation, identifying areas for ICT intervention, legal and regulatory frameworks and the socio-economic impact of ICTs in scaling up regional cooperation in the region.

7.8   Levels of Technology

In the 1990s, globalization and the increasing information intensity of economic activity, coupled with rapid technological change and demand growth, made ICT critical to competitiveness and growth. But South Asia is faced with pressing concerns of infrastructure like hardware, connectivity and electricity. Connectivity is narrowly defined as the physical infrastructure available to a country, as distinct from broader factors determining access (e.g. literacy, cost). It represents the basic "limiting factor" regarding access to and use of ICTs—without the essential physical hardware, ICT use is not possible. UNCTAD defined narrow "connectivity" as the minimum set of measures necessary for ICT access, comprising Internet hosts per capita, PCs per capita, telephone mainlines per capita and mobile subscribers per capita. This excludes supporting infrastructure (such as electricity supply and transport), affordability and broadband access.

Even where PCs, mainlines and mobiles are available, they are not the same in high-income and low-income countries (United Nations 2006). Internet use is more likely to be in a shared facility in a low-income nation and less reliable and slower. A PC is likely to be older and less powerful in a low-income nation and more likely to be shared at work or school. Mainlines in high-income countries are, on average, more reliable than in low-income countries and are typically installed without delay.

The supporting infrastructure such as Internet servers are 100 times more in high-income countries than in low-income countries. The differences in the number of secure Internet servers, a proxy for the availability of e-commerce, are stark. While developed nations have more than 300 such servers per one million people, developing nations have fewer than two servers per one million people (United Nations 2006). Canada has more secure servers than all developing countries combined. Though broadband connectivity is expanding in the developing countries, most of the connections rely on telephony and dial-up access to the Internet. As the tele-density in South Asia is extremely low, particularly in rural areas, access to the Internet is concentrated in urban areas. The demand for power necessary to maintain networks and ensure their functioning often falls too short of supply in all developing countries of South Asia including India (Prasad 2008).

The lack of available telephone lines and Internet service providers (ISPs) has been cited as a major barrier to ICT use among small and medium enterprises (SMEs) in Indonesia, the Philippines, Sri Lanka and Thailand. Availability outside major cities and the speed of connectivity was also a major concern (Asia Foundation 2002). Another major constraint is bandwidth for data traffic; slow and unreliable access limits ICT use. The percent of international capacity within the regions as a percentage of the total international capacity (within and outside the region) shows that 72% of European international capacity in 2005 is between European countries, while bandwidth among African countries only represents 1% of international capacity (United Nations 2006:12). The majority of interregional bandwidth of 35% in the Asian region is to Japan, Republic of Korea, Taiwan, Hong Kong, Singapore and Australia.

ICT policies will have to address supporting infrastructure such as electricity, broadband access and ISPs in the developing countries if e-governance has to be sustained for regional cooperation in South Asia.

7.9 Penetration and Access

The penetration and access to ICTs is highly unequal across and within countries in South Asia. Although there is some progress being made in reaching out to rural areas and the urban poor, in many countries these groups still lag behind. While 50% of population in developed regions has Internet access, only 7% in the developing countries and <1% in the 50 least developing countries have Internet access. A person in a high-income country is 22 times more likely to be an Internet user than a person in a low-income country. Only 21% out of a 1,000 population in South Asia are Internet users, while most developed nations have connected nearly all their primary and secondary schools to the Internet; just 38% of developing countries have done so and <1% of many African countries (World Bank 2006).

Over the past 25 years, developing countries have considerably increased ICT access, especially for telephone services. Developing countries have accounted for more than 60% of the world's telephone lines (fixed and mobile) in 2005, up from <20% in 1980. During this period, population increased by half and real GDP more than doubled in these countries—while the number of telephone subscribers rose 28-fold (World Bank 2006:5). Between 2000 and the end of 2005, telephone access is estimated to have tripled from 129 in 2000 reaching almost 400 subscribers per 1,000 people in 2005. Despite rapid growth in the developing countries, mobile phones are 29 times more prevalent and land lines 21 times more prevalent in high-income countries than low-income countries.

Most of the recent growth has involved mobile phones which now outnumber fixed ones. Mobile phones have an especially dramatic impact in developing countries—substituting for scarce fixed connections, increasing mobility, reducing transaction costs, broadening trade networks and facilitating searches for employment and new markets. Mobile telephones provide market links for farmers and entrepreneurs and are mainly used for communication and information services. "Much of the voice traffic over the cell phones is commerce directed. Access to agricultural market prices, access to agricultural trade information, facilitation of remittances from foreign workers, information on work opportunities using the phone can reduce substantial travel costs" (Richardson 1999). Affordable access to telecommunications and the Internet will enable better trade, communication and information among people in the South Asian region.

7.10 Socio-economic Impact

There are fundamental questions of utilizing development funds on a priority basis for education and basic needs which have a direct effect on people's lives than incur huge spending on projects that will trickle benefits to them. For instance, the highly acclaimed Warana Wired Village Project in India covering 70 contiguous villages in Maharashtra cost $600,000. The costs of covering 600,000 villages in India can well be imagined. There is the question whether the solution to the digital divide lies not in principally in increasing hardware access but in some other area, such as education that could change priorities, save money and deliver better results (Chandrasekhar 2006). Financing affordable Internet access and ICT competence including investment and training to create, maintain and expand computer networks, will prove challenging to policy makers within developing countries and those in the field of global communication governance.

Telecommunications services are also much more expensive in developing countries than in developed countries, even without taking income level into account. Prices for broadband (defined by the ITU as a dedicated connection to the Internet of 256 kbs or faster) varied significantly between income groups and regions. In 2004, the monthly charge for a 256 kbs speed connection for high- and middle-income countries was on average $180. For low-income countries (with a GNI per capita of $825 or less), the charge was $1,976 (Zhen-Wei Qiang et al. 2006:63). Relative to income, the cost of Internet access in a low-income country is 150 times the cost of a comparable service in a high-income country (United Nations 2006). It is only in high-income countries that the cost of Internet service is low enough as to be broadly affordable for most households and small businesses.

There are concerns about the gender divide with women having lower access than men to the Internet but data on women's access in South Asia is scarce. The latest (Pew Global Attitudes Poll 2006) found that there is a sharp divide between men and women; men's use of computers exceeds that of women in 14 out of the 16 countries surveyed; only in Canada and Lebanon do the genders share the same amount of computer activity. Despite India's thriving computer-related industries, only 28% of men and 14% of women have access to computer either at home or at work. Access to the Internet is largely facilitated in India by cybercafes that are found across the country even in small towns.

A growing number of women in Asia where nearly three-fifths of the world's population lives in diverse, social, cultural, economic and political settings are creating and engaging various forms of ICTs as an outcome of international policy efforts to advance women's empowerment and development. The Meena Communication Initiative in South Asia developed by UNICEF (2002) and supported by the governments of Bangladesh, India, Pakistan and Nepal aim at changing the perceptions and behaviour that hamper the survival, protection and development of female children in the region. The initiative involves production of multimedia packages to put across gender, child rights and educational messages using the medium of popular entertainment. This project is based on a shared need for content creation in the region to promote gender equality and empowerment of women which is an important millennium development goal to be achieved in South Asia to improve the human development status in the region.

7.11   Content Creation

Basic literacy represents an important *ex ante* capability for Internet access, of which only a small subset may be realized as the proportion of Internet users. There is a linguistic and cultural divide that exists on the Internet as the language of the web pages is predominantly English and hence excludes a large number of people who lack formal education, especially in English. The use of English language as the dominant language of the Internet poses problems for majority of the Indians who have their early education in the regional languages. There are 27 major languages in India. Language diversity, particularly in rural areas, may not lead to a feasible application of ICTs as translation software is still in the nascent stage. Only an estimated 10% speaks fluent English, while the rest (more than 900 million Indians and about 1.2 billion South Asians) speak other languages. Thus, computer use and Internet access is effectively out of reach of those who do not know English. Training in English which can give people greater familiarity to the content on the Internet is a rare opportunity for majority of the poor in South Asia. According to Global Reach (United Nations 2006:47), 43% of online users and 68.4% web content use English. All the rest are in languages like French, Spanish, Japanese and recently in Chinese (see Table 7.3).

To add to the linguistic inaccessibility in South Asia is the added absence of culturally relevant content, and from this springs the dominance of "Anglo-Saxon" culture (Keniston 2004:16). Most of the websites in the world originate from the predominantly English-speaking countries like the USA, the UK, Canada, Australia and New Zealand, or from the city states like Singapore, Hong Kong and South Africa. This has led to an "Anglo-Saxon linguistic and cultural hegemony" (Keniston 2004:16) with many cultures and culturally relevant content absent on the Internet.

The Department of Information Technology of India has launched a Web-based translation facility in October 2008 which helps people to translate from English to regional languages and also edit scanned or handwritten documents on tablet personal computers. The facility includes development of machine translation from English to six Indian languages and bidirectional translation of nine Indian languages. It also includes "cross lingual information access," in which query results would be available in Hindi, English and one of the six Indian languages. With the help of the machine further

Table 7.3 Top ten main languages on the
Internet 2009 (millions of users)

Language	Users in million
English	478 million
Chinese	384 million
Spanish	137 million
Japanese	96 million
French	79 million

Source: Internet World Stats (2010)
Note: Data refer to the first half of the year

modules would be developed that would, with artificial intelligence technology, enable a person speaking one language to converse with a person with the knowledge of another language. This translation facility will enable Internet users to overcome their linguistic limitations and access web content in several languages (The Hindu 2007). Such initiatives are useful in South Asia which shares common languages and cultures.

7.12   Conclusion

The prospects for economic and social integration in South Asia are encouraging but political complexities continue to limit this integration. There is an encouraging advantage of a natural people-to-people bonding and cultural ties that have managed to thrive despite the state-manufactured animosity and mistrust. The increase in ICT infrastructure and uptake will impact trade and development positively in the region. The digital divide in South Asia has led to limited and fragmented participation in economic and social integration at the national and regional levels. The answer lay in capacity-building initiatives at the local and national levels and greater bilateral cooperation at the regional level. The SAARC forum has been able to create a climate of mutual trust leading to dialogue and understanding for moving South Asia towards economic integration, but this progress can be fragile if terrorism disrupts the gains being made in economic and social integration in the region.

References

Asia Foundation (2002) SME and eCommerce. http://www.asiafoundation.org/ICT/surveys.html. Accessed 16 Aug 2011
Chandrasekhar CP (2006) India is online but most Indians are not. The Hindu, 25 Sept 2006
Das SR, Chandrashekhar R (2007) Capacity building for e-governance in India. www.apdip.net/projects/e-government/capblg. Accessed 16 Aug 2011
Debroy B (2001) Class Conundrum. The Week, 30 Dec 2001
Dikshit S (2011) Ahead of summit, Pakistan wants more observers in SAARC. The Hindu, 10 Nov 2011, p 11

G8 (2002) Digital opportunities for all: meeting the challenge. Report of the digital opportunity task force (DOT Force). http://www.g7.utoronto.ca/summit/2002kananaskis/dotforce_report-card.pdf. Accessed 15 Aug 2011

Internet World Stats (2010) World internet population and usage statistics. http://www.internet-worldstats.com/stats.htm. Accessed 28 Aug 2011

Joshi S (2011) Remote villages yet to get mobile telephony. The Hindu. http://www.thehindu.com/news/national/article2424511.ece. Accessed 5 Sept 2011

Keniston K (2004) Introduction: the four digital divide. In: Keniston K, Kumar D (eds) IT experience in India: bridging the digital divide. Sage, New Delhi

Mehra Mishita (2011) MFN status to India: a small step for Indo-Pak trade. Economic Times. http://articles.economictimes.indiatimes.com/2011-11-06/news/30366560_1_mfn-status-pakistan-mfn-india-and-pakistan. Accessed 6 Nov 2011

Pew Global Attitudes Poll (2006) Truly a world wide web: globe going digital. http://pewglobal.org/reports/pdf/251.pdf. Accessed 8 Aug 2011

Phadnis Ashwini (2011) A meet that could raise SAARC hopes. Business Line. http://www.thehindubusinessline.com/opinion/article2424107.ece. Accessed 5 Sept 2011

Prasad K (2008) The digital divides: implications of ICTs for development in South Asia. Papers in International and Global Communication, No 3/08, ISSN 1752-1793, Centre for International Communication Research, Institute of Communication Studies, University of Leeds. http://ics.leeds.ac.uk/papers/cicr/exhibits/56/Leeds-CICRworkingpaper-Kiran.pdf

Prasad K (2009) Communication for development: reinventing theory and action, vol 2. BRPC, New Delhi

Praveen MP (2011) e-governance scheme gets global acceptance. The Hindu. http://www.hindu.com/2011/05/22/stories/2011052258340400.htm. Accessed 22 May 2011

Radhakrishnan RK (2011) Indian bilateral meetings set to dominate SAARC again. The Hindu, 8 Nov 2011, p 12

Richardson D (1999) The internet and rural development. FAO, Rome

Singh H (2006) Teledensity target to be revised for 2006, says DoT. The Financial Express. http://www.financialexpress.com/fe_full_story.php?content_id=113956. Accessed 9 Aug 2011

Tharoor S (2005) Who is this middle class? The Hindu, 22 May 2005

The Hindu (2007) Web-based translation facility from Oct '08. The Hindu. 26 Feb 2007. http://www.hindu.com/thehindu/holnus/001200702260311.htm. Accessed 9 Aug 2011

The Hindu (2011a) UNCTAD projects 8.1% GDP growth for India in 2011, next only to China. http://www.thehindu.com/business/Economy/article2430147.ece. Accessed 7 Sept 2011

The Hindu (2011b) The new India Pakistan plot. The Hindu, 12 Nov 2011, p 8

UNICEF (2002) Meena communication initiative. http://gkaims.globalknowledge.org. Accessed 2 Nov 2005

United Nations (2006) The digital divide report: ICT diffusion index 2005. United Nations, New York, NY

Vineeth VF (2004) Markets and mystics: how they look at our common heritage, the Mother Earth. J Dharma 29(4):421–436

World Bank (2010) Indicators. http://data.worldbank.org/indicator/IT.TEL.REVN.GD.ZS. Accessed 28 Aug 2011

World Bank (2006) Information and communications for development: global trends and policies. World Bank, Washington, DC

Zhen-Wei Qiang C, George RC, Naomi H (2006) The role of ICT in doing business. In: World Bank (ed) Information and communications for development: global trends and policies. World Bank, Washington, DC

Chapter 8
Education Policy and Regional Convergence in the European Union

Aikaterini Kokkinou, George M. Korres, Efstratios Papanis, and Panagiotis Giavrimis

8.1 Introduction

In the past three decades, important changes in the pattern of economic growth and productivity have been interpreted as a movement towards knowledge-based economy. Currently, output and employment are expanding fast in high-technology industries, as well as in knowledge-based services. More resources are spent on the production and development of new technologies, in particular on information and communication technology. At the same time, major shifts are taking place in the labour market, in particular, the increased demand for skilled labour. Globalisation and worldwide competition has shifted the comparative advantage of economies towards the factor of knowledge and innovation, where productivity based on the endogenous development capabilities plays a rather important role, as far as growth and competitiveness enhancement are concerned.

A. Kokkinou (✉)
Department of Economics, University of Glasgow,
Adam Smith Building, G128QQ Glasgow, Scotland, UK
e-mail: a.kokkinou.1@research.gla.ac.uk

G.M. Korres
Centre of Urban and Regional Development Studies (CURDS),
University of Newcastle, Newcastle, NE1-7RU, UK

Department of Geography, University of the Aegean,
Mytilene, Greece
e-mail: George.Korres@ncl.ac.uk; gkorres@geo.aegean.gr

E. Papanis • P. Giavrimis
Department of Sociology, University of the Aegean,
Mytilene 81100, Lesbos, Greece
e-mail: papanis@papanis.gr; giavrimis@soc.aegean.gr

E.G. Carayannis and G.M. Korres (eds.), *European Socio-Economic Integration*,
Innovation, Technology, and Knowledge Management 27,
DOI 10.1007/978-1-4614-5254-6_8, © Springer Science+Business Media New York 2013

Within this framework, the enhancement and convergence of growth are a major topic in the economic and social policy agenda of EU members, since governments seek to concentrate on problems not only related to growth, such as low employment growth, high unemployment, fiscal deficits and public debt, but also to national disparities and convergence attainment (Rebelo 1991).

In the modern knowledge economy, growth depends extensively on the presence or the formation of a network and environment favourable to innovation, which is based on the endogenous development capabilities. Even though the firm-specific factors are important determinants of innovation activity, technological opportunities and favourable entrepreneurial environment have a positive effect on innovation activity, as well. Technological change, innovation and technology creation and diffusion are an important factor to economic progress (Aghion and Howitt 1992; Grossman and Helpman 1991; Jones and Manuelli 1990).

At the national level, two complimentary sets of conditions need to be satisfied. The first is the existence of suitable endowment of both basic infrastructure (in the form of efficient transport, telecommunications and energy networks, good water supplies and environmental facilities and so on) and a labour force with appropriate levels of skills and training, strengthening of both physical and human capital, together with improvements in institutional support facilities and the administrative framework in place. The second set of conditions, which directly relates to the factors of regional competitiveness which are important in the knowledge-based economy, is that innovation should be accorded high priority, that information and communication technologies (ICT) should be widely accessible and used effectively and that development should be sustainable in environmental terms, a business culture which encourages entrepreneurship and the existence of cooperation networks and clusters of particular activities (Cohen and Levinthal 1989).

As is recognised, a lack of innovative capacity at regional level stems not only from deficiencies in the research base and low levels of R&D expenditure but also from weaknesses in the links between research centres and businesses, and slow take-up of information and communication technologies. Knowledge and access to it has become the driving force for growth in advanced economies, much more than natural resources or the ability to exploit abundant low-cost labour. Innovation, therefore, holds the key to maintaining and strengthening competitiveness which in turn inessential for achieving sustained economic development. The cost of not pursuing a vigorous cohesion policy to tackle disparities is, therefore, measured in economic terms, as a loss of the potential real income and higher living standards. Given the interdependencies inherent in an integrated economy, these losses are not confined to the less competitive states but affect every state in the Union (Malecki 1991; Malecki and Varaia 1986).

8.2 European Union: Looking at Regional Convergence

Since its establishment, the European Union has experienced wide ranging and in depth integration. Considering the deepening aspect, the European Economic and Monetary Union (EMU) in 1999 and the circulation of the new common currency—the euro—since 1.1.2002 are the most momentous achievements. Concerning the widening process, the 2004 enlargement was the most conspicuous in the EU's history. The ten new members are now adequately integrated in the single market, and some of them have already adopted the euro as well. The final goal of the EU—to be achieved through the common market and the economic and monetary union—also includes economic and social cohesion, both between members (as the mention of solidarity would indicate) and within themselves.

At this point, special attention is given to the connection between regional growth and spatial development both in the regional economic and the economic geography literature, with elements drawn from economic growth theories. The development of these geographic and economic patterns is closely linked to questions of economic con- or divergence as well as the reduction of regional disparities.

Endogenous growth theories on the other hand explain how rich economies (endowed with human capital and higher R&D activities) can sustain high rates of growth and generally predict divergence of regional growth, but less so with integration. Broadly speaking, one can identify two conflicting hypotheses in the theoretical literature on economic growth: the optimist one, claiming that technological improvements operate in such a way that, in the presence of free trade and relatively unrestrained market competition, economic convergence eventually takes place, and the pessimist one, claiming that the nature of modern technologies is such that market forces, when left to themselves, lead almost unavoidably to inequality and divergence (Fig. 8.1).

During the last years, regional development and convergence of the lagging regions in the European Union has been one of the main objectives of the European development strategy (European Union 2004 a, b). Development problems are more intense in lagging regions which present major differences in level of prosperity, economic performance, output, productivity and employment, compared to other EU regions. These disparities arise due to structural deficiencies in factors, which restrain economic activities and overall development. The imbalances in the EU, threatening the convergence path, are summarised in Table 8.1.

These territorial disparities affect the overall competitiveness of the EU economy. Covering costs of the consequences of disparities implies a suboptimal allocation of resources, as well as a lower level of efficiency and economic competitiveness. Within this framework, the enhancement and convergence of growth and productivity are a major topic in the economic and social policy agenda of EU members, since governments seek to concentrate on problems not only related to growth, such as low employment growth, high unemployment, fiscal deficits and public debt, but also to regional disparities and convergence attainment.

One of the focal points of the Treaty of the European Union is "to promote economic and social progress along with a high level of employment, as well as to achieve balanced and sustainable development ... through the strengthening of economic and social cohesion..." The framework of these policy objectives could be illustrated in Fig. 8.2.

On the other hand, strengthening regional competitiveness throughout the Union will boost the growth potential of the EU economy. Securing a more balanced

Fig. 8.1 European Union (25) after the 2004 enlargement (*Source*: European Union Web site)

spread of economic activity across the EU will reduce the risk of imbalances and divergence, making it easier to sustain the European model of economy and society (Fig. 8.3).

In policy terms, the objective is to help achieve a more balanced development by reducing disparities, avoiding regional imbalances, making policies more coherent, improving integration and encouraging cooperation between states and regions.

8.3 European Union: Regional Policy Objectives

Nowadays, economies all over the world are described taking part in a race seeking the most appropriate and effective ways that could provide them with the strengths and opportunities necessary to obtain and sustain a competitive advantage over their rivals. Due to this competitiveness race, productivity enhancement is of great

Table 8.1 Threats to EU regional convergence

Regional level	Threatens
• At EU level	• High concentration of economic activity and population in the central metropolitan areas, which account for the major percentage of population, GDP and R&D expenditure
• At national level	• Persistence of pronounced imbalances between the main metropolitan areas and the rest of the country in terms of economic development
• At regional level	• Persistence of territorial disparities beyond those measured by GDP or unemployment, such as, social exclusion, inadequate economic links and falling population
• Within regions and cities	• Development of poverty and social exclusion in areas with often only limited availability of essential services
• In areas constrained by geographical features (islands, sparsely populated areas and mountain areas)	• Declining population and ageing, while accessibility continues to be a problem and the environment remains fragile and threatened
• In outermost areas, with natural and geographical handicaps	• Continuation of severe social and economic problems which are difficult to tackle because of their remoteness, isolation, topological features, climate, small size of market and dependence on a small number of products

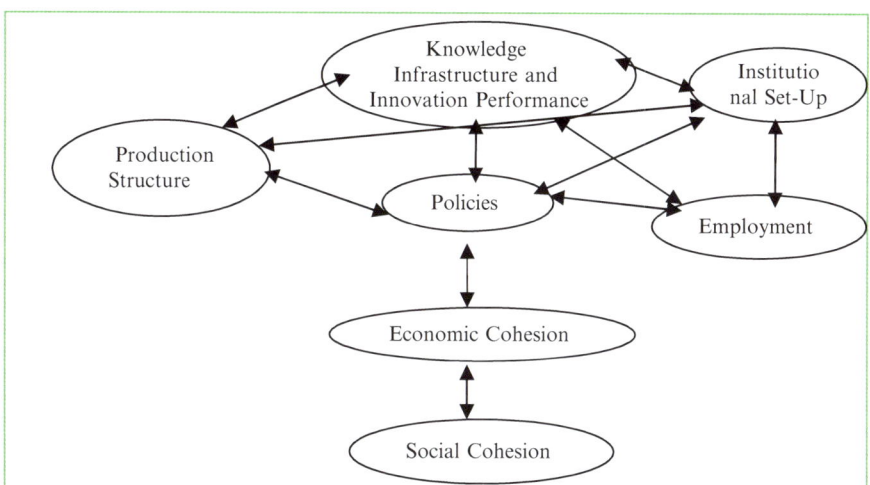

Fig. 8.2 Economic and social EU policy (*Source*: Own elaboration)

importance for the economic development in the face of uncertainties generated by international competition. That is the reason why countries are struggling to maintain and also accelerate their growth rates.

Within this framework, European Union set itself the goal of becoming the most competitive and dynamic knowledge-based economy in the world, capable of sustainable economic growth and closer regional as well as social cohesion.

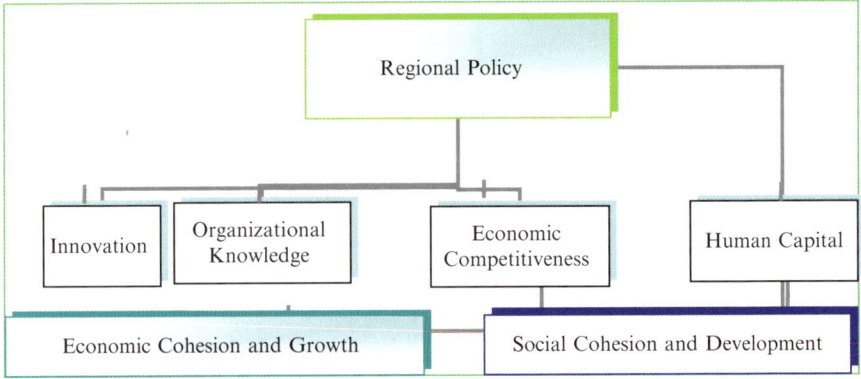

Fig. 8.3 Regional EU policy

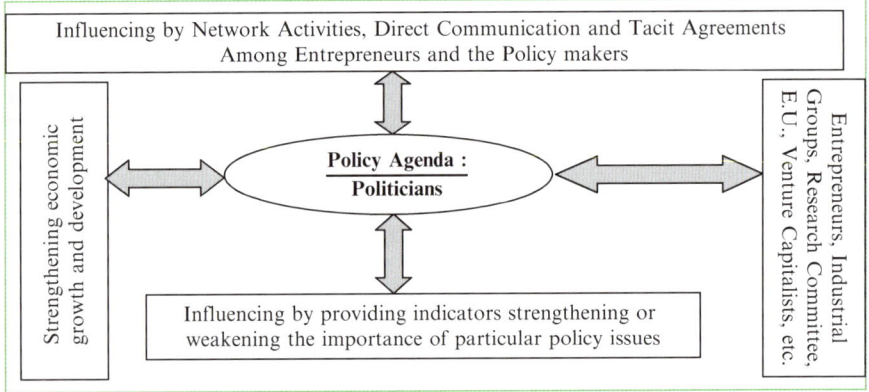

Fig. 8.4 Action framework of EU regional policy

At the Lisbon European Council, EU defined a comprehensive strategy aiming at long-term economic growth, full employment, social cohesion and sustainable development in a knowledge-based society. These mentioned priorities could be incorporated within an action framework, described in Fig. 8.4.

Within this framework, development and innovation consist two of the core subjects both in economic and political analyses. In EU, there is an increasing interest in the contribution of knowledge in the sustainable long-term economic growth, taking into consideration the need that competition forces technological innovations that increase productivity.

8.4   European Union: Economic Development and Innovation

The economic processes that create and diffuse the new knowledge are critical in the development process and there are powerful contacts between the investment in the human capital, the technological change and finally economic growth (Acs et al. 2002). The reason is that the new technologies lead to increase of productivity of factors of production, contributing in the long-term improvement of competitiveness (Griliches 1980). Technology and innovation play an important role in the creation of wealth and economic growth, and technology has become one of the most important factors in the models of growth (Geroski et al. 1993; Barro and Sala-i-Martin 1995, 1997; Freeman and Soete 1997; Sternberg 2000).[1] The role of innovation is multiple: as motive force, it directs the enterprises to ambitious and long-term objectives and it leads to the renewal of methods of production, supply and distribution, and management and marketing, as well as industrial structures and the appearance of new sectors of economic activity, achieving a wider spectrum of products and services, as well as relative markets. Inputs affect the intermediate inputs, which consequently affect and define the productivity and competitiveness level. Technology, also, contributes in the growth of economy, on the one hand because the new or improved products that result from innovations improve the level of existence and on the other hand, because, with regard to the international trade, the record of open economy depends also from the propensity to innovativeness (Fagerberg 1988a, b).

Developments in the theory of economic growth have renewed the interest for the role of innovation in the development process, underlining the interaction between the investment in innovative activities, technological change and economic growth. Technology and innovation play an important role in economic growth, and technology has become one of the most important factors in the models of growth (Geroski et al. 1993; Barro and Sala-i-Martin 1995, 1997; Freeman and Soete 1997; Sternberg 2000). The role of innovation is multiple: as motive force, it directs the enterprises to ambitious and long-term objectives and it leads to the renewal of methods of production, as well as industrial structures and the appearance of new sectors of economic activity.

The systematic analysis and the theoretical framework of the effects of innovation on the economic efficiency, productivity and growth is based on endogenous growth theory developed by Solow 1957; Arrow 1962; Romer 1986, 1990; Lucas 1990, 1993. In Solow (1957), technology is considered as a public good, which can be consumed free by everyone and nobody can be excluded by its consumption.

---

[1] Arrow (1962) was the first to systematically appreciate the importance of innovation and technological change in the capital formation and economic growth. He observed that increases in income per capita could not be explained by increases in capital to labour ratio and concluded that the power behind the increase in productivity is the acquisition of knowledge and learning experience created and acquired during the production procedure.

This good is an exogenously given factor explaining the economic development. Solow predicts that, in the long run, the differing national growth rates will converge in an international level, due to technology nature as a public good, which will be utilised by every country to enhance its economic capabilities. Arrow (1962) was the first to systematically appreciate the importance of innovation and technological change in the capital formation and economic growth. He observed that increases in income per capita could not be explained by increases in capital to labour ratio and concluded that the power behind the increase in productivity is the acquisition of knowledge and learning experience created and acquired during the production procedure.

Endogenous growth theory, as represented by Romer (1986), takes innovation as an endogenous variable which can explain the different national growth rates and why economies, even with different rates, do not converge to long-run steady state equilibrium. The reason is that the long-run productivity decrease is avoided, due to capital accumulation through the qualitative-technological improvements of natural and human capital. According to Romer (1986, 1990), knowledge and technological progress are the main engines of economic dynamism, and the economy grows endogenously through the accumulation and spillover of knowledge. Growth rate depends on the amount of technological activity within the economy and on the ability of the economy to exploit external technological achievements (Martin and Ottaviano 1999; Grossman and Helpman 1994; Coe and Helpman 1995). Increasing returns and technical change are incorporated within the production function as determinants of the endogenous growth rate (Romer 1986; Lucas 1988; Grossman and Helpman 1994; Barro and Sala-i-Martin 1997), and economic growth is sustained because of the continuous creation and diffusion of knowledge.

Endogenous growth theory claimed that not only the accumulation of capital but mainly the development and accumulation of knowledge and technological change leads to increased and sustainable growth. The reason is that the long-run productivity decrease is avoided, due to capital accumulation through the qualitative-technological improvements of natural and human capital. According to Romer (1986, 1990), knowledge and technological progress are the main engines of economic dynamism, and the economy grows endogenously through the accumulation and spillover of knowledge. Endogenous growth theory, as represented by Romer (1986), takes innovation as an endogenous variable which can explain the different national growth rates and why economies, even with different rates, do not converge to long-run steady state equilibrium. The reason is that the long-run productivity decrease is avoided, due to capital accumulation through the qualitative-technological improvements of natural and human capital. According to Romer (1986, 1990), knowledge and technological progress are the main engines of economic dynamism, and the economy grows endogenously through the accumulation and spillover of knowledge.

Growth rate depends on the amount of technological activity within the economy and on the ability of the economy to exploit external technological achievements (Martin and Ottaviano 1999; Grossman and Helpman 1994; Coe and Helpman 1995). Increasing returns and technical change are incorporated within the production function as determinants of the endogenous growth rate (Romer

1986; Lucas 1988; Grossman and Helpman 1994; Barro and Sala-i-Martin 1997), and economic growth is sustained because of the continuous creation and diffusion of knowledge.

An important contribution of the endogenous growth theory (Romer 1987, 1990) has been to identify the central role that knowledge and knowledge spillovers play in creating and sustaining growth. Pavitt and Soete (1982) examined growth as a result of the development of new knowledge in a country and the diffusion of knowledge between countries. According to Fagerberg (1987) there is a close relation between a country's economic and technological level of development. The rate of economic growth of a country is positively influenced by technological level of the country and its ability to increase it through imitation and exploitation of the possibilities offered by technological achievements elsewhere. Krugman (1991) identified the major role that knowledge spillovers play in generating increasing returns and higher growth. Geroski et al. (1993) asserted that innovations positively affect the development of enterprises and economies. Moreover, according to Silverberg and Verspagen (1995), technological change and diffusion constitute important factors in long-run macroeconomic growth and development. Moreover, Barro and Sala-i-Martin (1995, 1997) asserted that growth rate may increase in correlation with technological growth. Furthermore, Freeman and Soete (1997) focused on the importance of technology and innovation claiming that lack of innovation leads to economic death. At the same point of view Sternberg (2000) said that in industrialised economies, the rate of long-term macroeconomic growth depends on the ability of constant development of innovative products and processes.

Developments in the theory of economic growth have renewed the interest for the role of innovation in the development process, underlining the interaction between the investment in innovative activities, technological change and economic growth. Technology and innovation play an important role in economic growth, and technology has become one of the most important factors in the models of growth (Geroski et al. 1993; Barro and Sala-i-Martin 1995, 1997; Freeman and Soete 1997; Sternberg 2000). The role of innovation is multiple: as motive force, it directs the enterprises to ambitious and long-term objectives and it leads to the renewal of methods of production, as well as industrial structures and the appearance of new sectors of economic activity. Technological change, innovation and technology creation and diffusion are an important factor to economic progress, as illustrated in Fig. 8.5.

In the modern knowledge economy, growth depends extensively on the presence or the formation of a network and environment favourable to innovation, which is based on the endogenous development capabilities. Even though the firm-specific factors are important determinants of innovation activity, technological opportunities and favourable entrepreneurial environment have a positive effect on innovation activity, as well. Technological change, innovation and technology creation and diffusion are an important factor to economic progress. While innovation may lead to divergence between firms or nations, imitation through diffusion and dissemination tends to erode differences in technological competencies and hence leads to convergence (Fagerberg and Verspagen 2002).

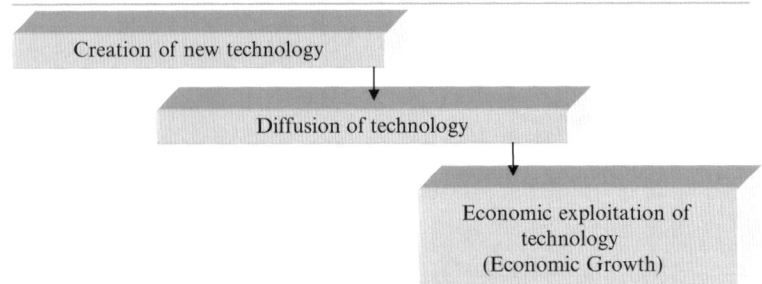

Fig. 8.5 Innovation and economic growth (*Source*: Own elaboration)

The enhancement and convergence of growth and competitiveness are a major topic in the economic and social policy agenda of EU members, since governments seek to concentrate on problems not only related to growth, such as low employment growth, high unemployment, fiscal deficits and public debt, but also to national disparities and convergence attainment. Within this framework, the European Union has defined a comprehensive strategy aimed at long-term economic growth, full employment, social cohesion and sustainable development in a knowledge-based society.

European cohesion policy makes a major contribution to these objectives, especially in those countries where there is unused economic and employment potential which can be realised through targeted cohesion policy measures. From a policy perspective, for national development to be sustained requires favourable conditions being established at the national level, in particular a macroeconomic environment conducive to growth, employment and stability and a tax and regulatory system which encourages business and job creation.

Knowledge lies at the heart of the European Union's Lisbon Strategy to become the "most dynamic competitive knowledge-based economy in the world." The "knowledge triangle"—research, education and innovation—is a core factor in European efforts to meet the ambitious Lisbon goals. Numerous programmes, initiatives and support measures are carried out at EU level in support of knowledge, whereas, "framework programmes" (FPs) have been the main financial tools through which the European Union supports research and development activities covering almost all scientific disciplines. FPs have been implemented since 1984 and cover a period of 5 years with the last year of one FP and the first year of the following FP overlapping (Table 8.2).

The current FP is FP7; however, it will run for 7 years, operational as of 2007, and will expire in 2013. It is designed to build on the achievements of its predecessor towards the creation of the European Research Area and carry it further towards the development of the knowledge economy and society in Europe. FP7 is also designed to respond to Europe's employment needs, competitiveness and quality of life.

Table 8.2 Budget breakdown of the Seventh Framework Programme of the European Community (EC) (2007–2013) and Euratom (2007–2011) (in EUR million)

	Themes	April 2005	May 2006	July 2006	December 2006
Cooperation	Health	8,317	5,984	6,050	6,100
	Food, agriculture and fisheries and biotechnology	2,455	1,935	1,935	1,935
	Information-communication technologies	12,670	9,110	9,110	9,050
	Nanosciences, nanotechnologies, materials and new production technologies	4,832	3,467	3,500	3,475
	Energy	2,931	2,265	2,300	2,350
	Environment (including climate change)	2,535	1,886	1,900	1,890
	Transport (including aeronautics)	5,940	4,180	4,180	4,160
	Socio-economic sciences and the humanities	792	607	610	623
	Security and space	3,960	2,858	Space 1,430 Security 1,350	Space 1,430 Security 1,400
Total cooperation		44,432	32,292	32,365	32,413
Ideas	European Research Council	11,862	7,460	7,460	7,510
People	Marie Curie Actions	7,129	4,727	4,728	4,750
Capacities	Research infrastructures	3,961	2,008	1,850	1,715
	Research for benefit of SMEs	1,901	1,266	1,336	1,336
	Regions of knowledge	158	126	126	126
	Research potential	554	350	370	340
	Science in society	554	359	280	330
	Coherent development of research policies			70	70
	Activities of international cooperation	358	182	185	180
Total capacities		7,486	4,291	4,217	4,097
Non-nuclear actions—Joint Research Centre		1,817	1,751	1,751	1,751
Total EU		72,726	50,521	50,521	50,521
Euratom for nuclear research and training activities		3,092	2,751	2,751	2,751

Source: European Union

The Seventh Framework Programme (FP7) bundles all research-related EU initiatives together under a common roof playing a crucial role in reaching the goals of growth, competitiveness and employment, along with a new Competitiveness and Innovation Framework Programme (CIP), Education and Training programmes and Structural and Cohesion Funds for regional convergence and competitiveness. It is also a key pillar for the European Research Area (ERA). The broad objectives of FP7 have been grouped into four categories: cooperation, ideas, people and capacities. For each type of objective, there is a specific programme corresponding to the main areas of EU research policy. All specific programmes work together to promote and encourage the creation of European poles of (scientific) excellence.

The commission calls upon member states to make the structural reforms necessary to deliver the results required. In the context of the Lisbon Strategy, the commission has adapted its regulatory framework on state aids to enable member states to develop new measures in favour of the support of innovation, taking into account the identified market failures of Europe in this domain. This should also encourage member states and regions to redirect state support, for instance, from structural funds, towards activities that are most directly correlated with the Lisbon Agenda.

8.5   Redefining the European Policy for Social, Economic and Territorial Convergence

Several dimensions should be promoted, in order to create a European Union of social and economic cohesion, driven by an integral policy on local and regional level. Special policy priorities could be summarised into the following points:

- European science policy: framework programme for research, technological development and demonstration activities
- European innovation policy: competitiveness and innovation framework programme with enlarged resources to support "strengthening Europe's strengths" on the global level
- Social, economic and territorial convergence policy
- Elaboration and implementation of a regional innovation strategy: elaboration of programmes and projects and mobilisation of actors in view to reinforce innovation in fields like information society, renewable energy, promotion of clusters, promotion of natural and historical heritage and technological prospective looking for new technologies suitable for the region
- Access of SME to advanced business services: creation of one-stop shop integrating available regional support services and consultants, advice to SME on new technologies ICT, management of knowledge and innovation, design and quality. Concentration of demand from SMEs in order to get a better supply from large firms, modernisation of administration and support to SME for grant application

- Clusters and promotion of cooperation: support for coordination structures in view of launching studies, innovation projects, marketing, audits and support to SME communications (seminars, travels, intranets)
- Risk capital: development of pre-seed and seed capital funds and promotion of business angels
- Entrepreneurship: organisation of competitions on innovative projects, practical guidance and assessment on enterprise and sponsorship of young entrepreneurs
- University-business cooperation: increase of parts of researches under contract by enterprise (partial time teaching?) and creation of specific university disciplines for business innovation
- Cross-border and transnational cooperation (not much developed so far): joint technological research centres, universities and research institute networking, transfer of know-how and technology, joint training and exchange of students and trainers
- Innovation: centres of excellence, clusters, new standards and platforms
- Social and territorial cohesion: IT accessibility, battle against content illiteracy, services for the elderly, creativity and entrepreneurship, civic society and innovation-absorbing society issues
- Quality of life: quality of food, health care, clean water, clean air and clean energy
- Access to natural resources and the global price of abusing environment
- Human resources for creating, implementing and experiencing
- Knowledge economy needs a knowledge-absorbing society
- Digital literacy and content literacy

Social cohesion should remain a matter for the European Union as a whole in securing an "innovation/knowledge absorbing society." Main challenges within this area are:

- Digitalization of the elderly and initiation of online market services/health care services/leisure time services/administrative services for the elderly
- Improving the flexibility of the labour market by creating local and regional education and employee exchange platforms
- Strengthening the role of NGOs in local social development to integrate those who cannot cope with the speed of changes (cultural and social changes, content illiteracy, inability to cope with complex problems, intolerance towards the "new workers from outside")

The balance and synergies between cohesion and Lisbon Agenda cannot be done automatically. Since one of the main priorities of Lisbon Agenda is a higher rate of aggregate economic growth in the EU, it should be achieved under the shied of promoting cohesion and reduction of the regional economic disparities within the Union. This means that a shift in regional policy has to be made in order to satisfy both needs.

As it has been asserted in this chapter, globalisation and worldwide competition has shifted the comparative advantage of economies towards the factor of knowledge and innovation, where productivity based on the endogenous development capabilities plays a rather important role, as far as growth and competitiveness enhancement are concerned. In order to promote innovation activities and technological opportunities, productivity enhancement seems to have a significance to the long-run performance of the economy as a whole.

Under this perspective, growth policies should focus on creating favourable environment for the cooperation between firms and institutions that support the development and exploitation of knowledge and innovation. Furthermore, policies should promote the entrepreneurial relations between firms and institutions, fostering the development and dissemination of the expertise, the mobility of human and physical capital and the enhancement of the relationships between business and research entities. Specifically, they should encourage actions such as, promoting innovation, technology transfer and interactions between firms and higher education and research institutes, networking and industrial cooperation and support for research and technology supply infrastructure.

As it has already been mentioned, innovation and technology are an important source of regional competitiveness through facilitating cooperation between the various parties involved in both the public and private sectors. In particular, they can improve collective processes of learning and the creation, transfer and diffusion of knowledge and transfer, which are critical for innovation. Such cooperation and the networks that are formed help to translate knowledge into economic opportunity, while at the same time, building the relationships between people and organisations which can act as a catalyst for innovation. Such actions should extend to all the policy areas relevant for economic, scientific and social development and should ideally establish a long-term policy horizon.

This, however, needs to happen not just in central parts where productivity and employment are highest and innovative capacity most developed but throughout the Union. Countries and regions need assistance in overcoming their structural deficiencies and in developing their comparative advantages. This means, among others, that encouraging the development of knowledge-based economic activities and innovation and that particular attention needs to be given to:

- Developing new innovation promotion policies which focus much more on the provision of collective business and technology services to groups of firms which can affect their innovative behaviour, rather than direct grants to individual firms which tend only to reduce costs temporarily
- Developing new policies to strengthen the capacity of SMEs to innovate through business networks and clusters and improving their links with the knowledge base, including with universities and research centres
- Encouraging the development of the indigenous R&D potential of weaker regions and their capacity to adapt technological advances made elsewhere to local circumstances and needs
- Facilitating access of researchers, businesses and others in less favoured regions to international networks of excellence, sources of new technology and potential R&D partners

These conditions are largely related to economic competitiveness and include, among others, the capacity of a regional economy to generate, diffuse and utilise knowledge, in order to maintain growth and prosperity.

References

Acs ZJ, Anselin L, Varga A (2002) Patents and innovation counts as measures of regional production of new knowledge. Res Policy 31:1069–1085

Aghion P, Howitt P (1992) A model of growth through creative destruction. Econometrica 60(2): 323–351

Arrow KJ (1962) The economic implications of learning by doing. Rev Econ Stud 29(3):155–173

Barro RJ, Sala-i-Martin X (1995) Economic growth. McGraw-Hill, New York, NY

Barro R, Sala-i-Martin X (1997) Technological diffusion, convergence and growth. J Econ Growth 2:1–26

Coe D, Helpman E (1995) International R&D spillovers. Eur Econ Rev 39:859–887

Cohen WM, Levinthal DA (1989) Innovation and learning: the two faces of R&D. Econ J 99: 569–596

European Union (2004a) Third report on economic and social cohesion

European Union (2004b) Treaty of the European Union

Fagerberg J (1987) A technology gap approach to why growth rates differ. Res Policy 16:87–99

Fagerberg J (1988a) International competitiveness. Econ J 98:355–374

Fagerberg J (1988b) Why growth rates differ. In: Dosi G, Freeman C, Nelson RR, Silverberg G, Soete L (eds) Technical change and economic theory. Pinter, London, pp 432–457

Fagerberg J, Verspagen B (2002) Technology-gaps, innovation-diffusion and transformation: an evolutionary interpretation. Res Policy 31:1291–1304

Freeman C, Soete L (1997) The economics of industrial innovation, 3rd edn. Pinter, London

Geroski P, Machin S, Van R, Geroski J (1993) Innovation and profitability. Rand J Econ 24(2): 198–211

Griliches Z (1980) R&D and the productivity slow down. Am Econ Rev 70:2

Grossman GM, Helpman E (eds) (1991) Innovation and growth in the global economy. MIT Press, Cambridge, MA

Grossman G, Helpman E (1994) Foreign investment with endogenous protection. NBER Working Paper, No. 4876

Jones LE, Manuelli R (1990) A convex model of equilibrium growth: theory and policy implications. J Polit Econ 98:1008–1038

Krugman P (1991) Geography and trade. MIT Press, Cambridge, MA

Lucas RE Jr (1988) On the mechanics of economic development. J Monet Econ 22:3–42

Lucas RE (1990) Why doesn't capital flow from rich to poor countries? Am Econ Rev 80(2): 92–96

Lucas RE (1993) On the determinants of foreign direct investment: evidence from East and Southern Asia. World Dev 21(3):391–406

Malecki EJ (1991) Technology and economic development: the dynamics of local regional and national change. Longman Scientific and Technical, Harlow

Malecki EJ, Varaia P (1986) Innovation and changes in regional structure. In: Nijkamp P (ed) Handbook of regional and urban economics, vol I. Elsevier Science Publishers, Amsterdam

Martin P, Ottaviano GIP (1999) Growing locations: industry location in a model of endogenous growth. Eur Econ Rev 43:281–302

Pavitt K, Soete L (1982) International differences in economic growth and the international location of innovation. In: Giersch H (ed) Emerging technologies: the consequences for economic growth, structural change and employment. Mohr, Tubingen

Rebelo S (1991) Long run policy analysis and long run growth. J Polit Econ 99:500–521

Romer PM (1986) Increasing returns and long-run growth. J Polit Econ 94:1002–1037

Romer P (1987) Growth based on increasing returns due to specialization. Am Econ Rev 77(2):56–62

Romer PM (1990) Endogenous technological change. J Polit Econ 98:71–102

Silverberg G, Verspagen B (1995) Long term cyclical variations of catching up and falling behind. An evolutionary model. J Evol Econ 5:209–227

Solow R (1957) Technical change and the aggregate production function. Rev Econ Stat 39: 312–320

Sternberg R (2000) Innovations networks and regional development—evidence from the European regional innovation survey (ERIS): theoretical concepts, methodological approach, empirical basis and introduction to the theme issue. Eur Plan Stud 8:389–407

Chapter 9
Innovation Process in the European Union: The Case of the Galileo Project

Gloria Pirzio Ammassari and Maria Cristina Marchetti

9.1 Introduction

The new trends related to globalization, imply the increase of social and economic complexity, as well as higher rates of change and competitiveness. New, concrete, and serious management problems have recently triggered partnerships, fusions and *join venture*, with the aim to cope with these changes. In such circumstances, financial elites show high dynamicity and international orientation; they are acting within different social–political contexts, to seize in time the direction to the changes in progress, and to react consequently.

On the political side, the literature on globalization[1] has often assessed the end of the Nation–State, due to the emergence of a few supranational realities that limit the power of single states. This theoretical scope implies the risk of "mainly focusing on phenomena of power *displacement*—i.e., the dispersion and the transfer of the state's power—ignoring the new emerging *networks* of power, i.e., the links with transnational and supranational subjects."[2]

Although supranational institutions are turning more and more powerful, national and transnational webs, are linking and strengthening each other. European Union

---

The Introduction and Paragraphs 1 and 5 are written by Gloria Pirzio; paragraphs 2, 3, 4 are written by Maria Cristina Marchetti

[1] See Robertson (1992); Albrow (1997); Beck (1999); Beck (2000).

[2] Weiss (2005), p. 398.

G.P. Ammassari (✉) • M.C. Marchetti
Department of Political Sciences, Sapienza University of Rome,
Rome, Italy
e-mail: gloria.pirzio@uniroma1.it; mc.marchetti@uniroma1.it

E.G. Carayannis and G.M. Korres (eds.), *European Socio-Economic Integration*,
Innovation, Technology, and Knowledge Management 27,
DOI 10.1007/978-1-4614-5254-6_9, © Springer Science+Business Media New York 2013

is an interesting example of this long-period trend, since its basic, institutional ambiguity just turns into a "strong weaving with national webs of power."[3]

Within this framework, the innovation processes are a test for the political and financial elites' capability of facing the changes in progress. The need for quick reactions, especially in the field of technological progress, is highlighting a gap, that cannot last without jeopardizing the whole process. In other words, elite's possibility of implementing the innovation process, basically depends of their ability to "make webs," triggering cooperation processes, rather than individual actions. It is just in this context, that the State–nation prevails again, by weaving its action with the involved, financial actors.

As a consequence, The Galileo Project is an interesting example of a complex process, where different political–institutional levels of action—local, national, supra-national (EU), global/international—meet the action of the involved industrial groups. The political and financial elites are supposed to cooperate for a project that meets those industries' needs, and, at the same time, has a strong political meaning.

In fact, Galileo project matches two main interests: on the one side, an industrial sector that, after the end of Cold War, has turned crucial for the global, geopolitical balance; on the other, the aims of European Union, which uses economic integration as a tool for political unification. From the point of view of the big industrial groups, the integration is a reality that can even overcome the state protectionism typical of some countries, such as France; however, at the same time, state protectionism is basic to play a role in the global context with a high "bargaining power".

This paper shows the results of a research, that the Italian Ministry of University and Research (MIUR) financed together with the Department of Political Studies of the University of Rome "La Sapienza". The research consist of the decision process reconstruction, that has started and implemented Galileo Project; this was possible through the administration of interviews to opinion-leaders, both institutional and industrial, involved in the project.

9.2 The European Space Policy

The interest of European Union in space policy is recent, and so is the awareness of member States of space's strategic importance, within the globalization scenario.[4]

Of course, in the past several European countries developed their own space policy, even by making reciprocal agreements—France is the main example, though a Community-level interest for this issue was still missing.

The prospect change is due to two causes: on the one hand, the high, international political value[5] of space; on the other, the will of Europe to achieve political autonomy in the world scene. In fact, the European space issue is deeply linked to

---

[3] *Ibidem*, p. 411.

[4] Valori (2006).

[5] See Di Nolfo (2004).

the Common Foreign and Security Policy, and involves Europe's political future and its ambition in the new geo-political scenarios.[6]

Through the years, the space policy itself has undergone several changes, according to the different historical phases. During the Cold War, it was a field of fight between the two blocks, in the name of a power policy, for which the conquest of space would symbolically be the most relevant achievement. After the fall of the Berlin wall, within a context of redefinition of geopolitical scenarios, the space becomes a tool of data collection and territory control, crucial in the era of globalization.

In the USA, the effort of theorization of space usage with political aims has produced the most significant results. Doubtless, the American space doctrine is a model to base upon to start this debate in Europe: first country in the world to have acknowledged the strategic value of space; nowadays the USA covers about 95% of the space investments worldwide, while Europe only 4 %[3]. Thus, the USA has achieved a global monopoly, of which the Global Positioning System (GPS) is the main example.

On the other side, two main issues have so far characterized European space policy.

1. It began for initiative of France that very soon seized the political meaning of space both for prestige reasons and the peculiar foresightedness of its political and financial elites. In a scenario marked by Cold War and the beginning of USA/USSR rivalry in the space conquest, in 1961 general de Gaulle started the CNES (Centre National d'Etudes Spatiales), that, since, has been the base of French lead in the space policy.[7] Afterwards, the idea of making of the French example the standpoint for European space policy, clashed against the resistance of France itself to share the achieved experience with the other European countries; in addition some European countries showed a strong mistrust to public intervention in the industrial field, which is typical of the state French centralism. Within this framework, European space policies linked to the different phases of communitarian integration process.

2. As a direct consequence of the point 1, European space policy was based upon a crucial contradiction: before joining European institutions, it grew up within a parallel institution, the European Space Agency (ESA), which is an intergovernmental, atypical agency, both for its functioning and its political legitimacy.

On the institutional side, ESA does not belong to European Union: some States are a part of ESA and not of EU (Norway and Switzerland) and vice versa (Greece and Luxembourg). Of course, this implies a lack of balance between UE and ESA members. ESA's budgets depend upon the contribution, that the single states belonging to Space Agencies provide, according to their Internal Gross Product.[8] Within ESA, the principle of "geographical return" is valid; this means that each States should receive back a sum,

---

[6] Nicolas Werner (2004).

[7] Casini (2004).

[8] 2006 ESA's budget amount 2,904 million euros.

more or less amounting to its contribution, in terms of contracts for Space Programs. The Council is the controlling body of ESA; it represents all the member States that have the right to one vote each, regardless the amount of their contributions.

This feature will appear crucial in the different phases of Galileo Project. Every 5 years, the Council elects a General Director.

The following step towards a European Space Policy was an always increasing cooperation between ESA and EU; in fact European Union acknowledged that ESA could be the privileged partner.

In March 2000, Mr. Antonio Rodotà, at that time the general Director of ESA, commissioned a Report on the possible evolution of the Agency. This Report, known as "Wise Men Recommendations," considered the possible outcomes of a cooperation between ESA and European Union. In November 16th of the same year, ESA council and European Union adopted a common resolution basing upon that document, that lay the foundations for a tighter, future cooperation.

In January 2003, European Commission issued the Green Book on "European Space Policy," in cooperation with ESA, and in November 2003 the White Book "Space: a new frontier for an expanding Union. An action plan for implementing the European Space Policy." Also in November, the Council of ESA adopted the "Frame Agreement," formerly approved by European Council (October 2003), in which the cooperation between ESA and European Union received an institutional acknowledgment. ESA becomes EU's privileged partner in constructing a space policy, although keeping its full independence.

Even if the relationship between ESA and European Union have become more formal, some questions are still open; first, the so called "geographical return," which denies competitiveness and free market competition, that are typical European values. In addition, the voting rules within the Council provide each country with an actual veto right, since, for example, even Luxembourg has the same power as Germany. Finally, since ESA and UE membership do not perfectly overlap, the overall consequence is very slow decision-making, which does not fit with the change rate of technology field.

9.3   The Galileo Project

In the framework of European space politics, the Galileo Project, together with the Global Monitoring Earth System (GMES), is a basic test of cooperation ESA/UE.

In the middle of the 1990s, in Europe the possibility arose of realizing a system of satellite navigation alternative to the American GPS and the Russian GLONASS. The debate went on at different levels—political/strategic, economic, scientific, in order to start a European system of satellite navigation.

The satellite radio navigation is an advanced technology that bases upon the emission of a signal from satellites; this signal can assess the position of any object. This fits with the needs of a global position, in which space/time definition is basic in several fields (security, finance, law enforcement, mobility, health-science, etc.).

Galileo Project implies a set of 30 satellites and earth-stations that provide information on the users' position in all those fields.[9]

In the conclusions of the Minister Council of March 17, 1998, on the communication of European Commission "Towards a Trans-European Positioning and Navigation Network," the Council openly requested the Commission to arrange a recommendation on the future of the European satellite navigation.

Since this declaration, in 1998 several international meetings and conferences occurred among the main actors in this field, aiming to assess the realization modes of a European navigation system; this system was also supposed to fit with the wider project (GNSS—Global Navigation Satellite System), that was starting in the meantime.

During those meetings, some issues arose, that would affect the future development of Galileo:

1. The relationship with other international partners, the USA and Russia, which already had their own satellite navigation systems.
2. The internal European relationships, namely, the balances among the major countries in the aerospace market (Italy, Germany, France, Spain, the UK).
3. The project funding.

On January 1999, European Parliament adopted a resolution according to the Communication of the Commission, in which the member States were invited to hold a European Council on Space and the Commission was asked to fix a strategy for the future creation of a Trans-European navigation system.

The report of Commission work is available in the communication "Galileo. Involving Europe in a New Generation of Satellite Navigation Services," of February 10, 1999. This communication contains both *strategic* and *financial* studies, and especially a cost-benefit analysis, according to the possible income from the usage of satellite navigation.

The councils of Colonia, Feira, Nice (December 7–8, 2000). Stockholm, Laeken (December 14–15, 2001) and Barcelona always stressed out the strategic importance of Galileo Project for Europe. The White Book on the European policy of Transportation until 2010, reaffirmed the importance for the Union of an autonomous system of satellite navigation.

The Commission's *strategic* remarks mainly focused on the European Union's need to acquire its own navigation system, to stop the dependence from Russian and—namely, American systems (GPS). The Galileo's main difference from those two systems is that they are basically military. On the opposite, Galileo has started

---

[9] The functioning is quite simple: the satellites are provided with a clock, that can measure time very accurately. The satellites emit personalized signals, of which it is possible to assess the exact moment of emission. The reception-device is on earth, for example within a self-phone, and its memory contains the exact reference of each satellite's orbits. By reading the signal, the reception-device can recognize which satellite has sent it, assess how long the signal took to arrive, ad calculate the distance from the satellite. If the reception-device has received the signals from at least four satellites simultaneously, it can calculate the right position.

with civilian purposes, which guarantee signal regularity and reliability,[10] as well as a bigger precision.[11] Furthermore, Galileo is complementary to GPS, which means that it is possible to use both systems co-ordinately (double sourcing). This is one more advantage, since it is possible, having two independent, compatible systems, for them to control each other. It is also strategic the European will to achieve its autonomy from the USA.

The acknowledgment of the strategic importance of space for the contemporary international politics, is not foreign to the birth of Galileo, even is this feature has always been the background of the project, with no explicit declaration. On this subject, the European Commission's report states that "Galileo gives Europe clear opportunities for strengthening political ties with other countries"; in addition, Commission openly rejects the so called "zero option," i.e., Europe's withdrawal from having a role in the realization of the GNSS, on behalf of the USA or any other State that might start an autonomous system. Those issues were the thread of a long debate between Europe and the USA, whose conclusion was the agreement of May 28, 2004. In fact, the USA, after an early skepticism on the actual capability of UE members of making an agreement on Galileo, have taken a position of defense, since the early steps of the projects took place. In fact, the USA hold a monopoly in the field of the satellite navigation, due to the advantage acquired with the creation of GPS; even USSR's competition, with GLONASS system, could overcome this supremacy. Nowadays, all those that aim to join the market of territory localisation can only use GPS technology.

The bad side is that GPS is under control of American Department of Defense, which can black out the signal for security reasons (e.g., military attack) or start a jamming mechanism. Those problems are crucial for a system, which is supposed to localize things or people in the earth surface, as well as give a precise definition of time.

Crucial was the role of the American, industrial lobbies for the change of the America's position on Galileo. In fact, those groups have always been interested in Galileo's applications, and favorable to the improvement of its signal reception. Then, Galileo's realization is of interest also for the American market that, although larger than the European, has a boundary in the military origin of GPS.

On the opposite, Galileo's force is that it has civilian aims; of course, this does not exclude military use, though who will control the signal emission will be a public agency, i.e., European Union itself.

About the *financial* side, in January 1998 the Communication of the Commission highlighted that the application market of Galileo amounts potentially 80 billion euros just for the first 20 years. However, it is from Galileo's satellite infrastructure—the satellite setting and the earth-emplacements—that the application market will arise. Furthermore, the ultimate outcome of this market is impossible to foresee, since the cost recovery plan only bases upon the application, with no regard to the structure itself.

---

[10] Galileo is provided with a "message integrity" signal that informs the users of any error.

[11] In the last years, GPS has been out of order, both for planned and unplanned reasons; no early communication was given to users.

Of course, compelling is the comparison with GPS applications: in Europe, GPS hardware market in 1997 was 2,287 million dollars, with a foreseen increase to as 960 million dollars on 2004.

European Commission has estimated Galileo's cost—including making and launching 30 satellites and setting earth stations—as about 3.2 billon euros, mainly covered by EU and ESA funds.[12] However, private fundings are also admitted, with the Public Private Partnership (PPP) contracts already tested in other occasions.

As we are going to see later, PPP formula faces problems when the "public partner" is made of several countries, which can slow down decision making and implementation.

From a wider scope, Galileo is European contribution to the GNSS, which will be able to make all the satellite navigation system already existing, work together. With this aim, EU stated a two phase strategy:

• GNSS 1: EGNOS (European Geostationary Navigation Overlay Service) is the first European experience in the field of satellite navigation.
• GNSS 2: Galileo.

As already stated, it is important to make a distinction between Galileo's implementation (sending satellites into orbit and building earth bases), from applications into other fields. Five service areas are assessed:

• Open Service (OS): About personal mobility.
• Commercial Service (CS): Based upon a crypted signal, useful in trading (signal *liability*). This signal is certified.
• Safety of Life Service (SOL): Sea and air navigation.
• Search and Rescue (SAR): Air aid.
• Public Regulated Service (PRS): Signal jamming-free, for government, police, etc. use.

Thus, we have a complex structure that involves several actors, both institutional and economic, sometimes with opposite interests, though they need to balance among them to equally share commitments and advantages.

9.4   The Project Partners

This project is so important both strategically and financially, that a few institutions are in charge of checking both its implementation and its political implications. In fact, Galileo is an interesting experiment of cooperation among different institu-

---

[12] The study commissioned to PricewaterhouseCoopers, has produce very similar conclusions: they have assessed that, within 20 years, the cost/benefit rate will be 4.6, the highest of any other European, infrastructural project. Other initial studies have assessed that, in the early 20 years, Galileo project will create, for European firms, a market of devices and services of about 80 billion euros.

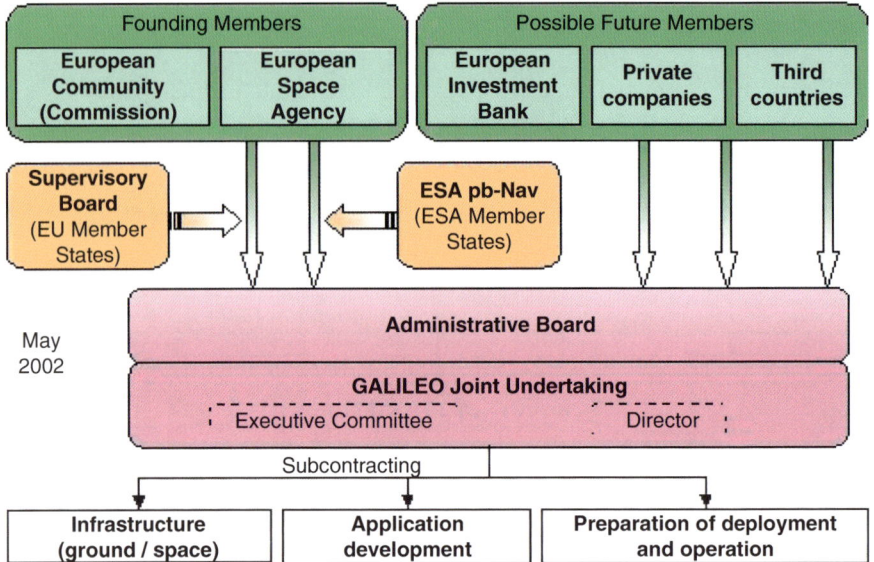

tional levels; in addition, we are facing a strong cooperation between the public and private sectors, whereas, the aerospace funding has always been only public.

A specific actor is in charge of each different phase.

The partners of the project are: (1) European Commission, (2) ESA, (3) Galileo Joint Undertaking (GJU), and in the future (4) the Concessionary.

European Commission and ESA just carry out activities, that Commission has already considered as necessary to start the European space policy. Though, what is really new is GJU.[13] This is a joint venture between ESA and the European Commission, though the European Bank of Investments and private companies—as well as single States available to financing GJU with at least five million Euros.[14]

The following organs are part of GJU (1) the Board of Directors, consisting of the representatives of GJU members. This body takes all strategic decisions of financial and budgeting areas; (2) the Executive Committee, consisting of one representative of European Commission, one representative of ESA and one representative—from the private sector—of the Board of Directors; (3) the Director, i.e., the legal representative of GJU. The admission of new members needs 75 % of boards' votes.

GJU's purposes are: (1) controlling the project implementation, (2) setting the following steps of the program, especially setting the conditions for the private companies' participation.

In fact, Galileo project implies several phases:

---

[13] Galileo Joint Undertaking' Statute is contained in the Council Resolution No. 876/2002.

[14] This share of participation has been reduced to 250,000 euros for SME's.

1. *Development and Validation Phase*. Consists in the definition of the system and its manufacture components. It implies sending into orbit the first four satellites that will validate the signal. (IOV). This phase implementation is still in progress under GJU's supervision; GJU is also coordinating the Galileo-related activities for the 6° (Framework Program).
2. *Deployment*. Implies sending into orbit the whole constellation (30 satellites) and building all the earth structures. The Concessionary will manage this phase.
3. *Implementation (Operation)*. Deeply linked to the former phase, it implies managing the commercial side of the system.

On December 28, 2006, with a considerable delay, the launch of the first satellite occurred—Jupiter A—with the main purpose to occupy the frequencies that the International Telecommunication Union (ITU) assigned to Galileo.

Since 1st of January 2007 all the powers of Galileo Join Undertaking have been replaced by the *Galileo Supervisory Authority*, a special Agency created with the Council Resolution of July 12, 2004 in order to represent the public interest in the project.[15]

9.4.1 The Public Private Partnership

The three phases above stated imply several actors, which is critical for the project because of the difficult balance between public and private interests. As above stated, Galileo is a PPP, which is a kind of very innovative contract, mainly in the space sector. With a PPP contract, the first part of investments is public; in the other phases of the project implementation and management, a private investment follows.

The initial study, that PriceWaterHouseCooper issued in November 2001 states that "The principal objective of a PPP should be to achieve value for money for the public sector by transferring appropriate risk and responsibility to the private sector in a way which creates incentives to optimize the technical solution and cost of the system".[16] Through the PPP formula, the system can guarantee the "value for money" principle that is necessary to attract private capitals.

As a consequence, public capitals (ESA, EU) could fund the *Development* phase, while private capital (the *Concessionaire*) the *Deployment* phase. Those phases do

---

[15] Council Resolution (EC) 1321/2004. The document affirms this: "Given the strategic nature of the European satellite positioning and navigation programmes and the need to ensure that essential public interests in this field are adequately defended and represented, it is imperative to supervise the next phases of the system and the use of Community funds allocated to the programmes in accordance with the relevant political orientations of the Council and financial decisions of the budgetary authorities: a European Global Navigation Satellite System (GNSS) Supervisory Authority (hereinafter referred to as the Authority) should be set up."

[16] PriceWaterHouseCoopers (2001), p. 9.

not run in a strict temporal order: in fact, while the *Development* phase will be still in progress, the call for tenders will be already happened. Though, this implies that the private sector will be in need for a stricter control over the *Development* phase, in order to reduce the rate of risk. In fact, private partners are so far supposed to invest high sums in a project, whose the former phases are unknown, because the public sector has been managing them. "The issue of control is particularly important, because the price for investing while assuming a risk that industry cannot control will be high and if the private sector does not control key parts of the process, it will be much less able to bring efficiencies to bear. This calls for an early award of the Concession".[17]

Possible delays, due to agreement problems between European institutions and industrial lobbies, would imply a loss of income for the involved companies and a too high risk.

Actually, the *Development* phase was already implying the presence of private partners—as possible, future GJU members. Nowadays, the *Development* phase seems likely to receive full coverage only from public funding (ESA/EU); private investors, as Concessionaires, will join the project only in a following time.

9.4.2 The Concession Process

Deeply linked to PPP formula is the Concession contest, as well as the contract bargaining with the winners; GJU manages both those issues.

Galileo's Concessions is one of the crucial issues of the project, and among the most interesting for the operational and relational consequences. In fact, the initial study that PricewaterhouseCoopers issued in November 2001 stated that the Concession was the best kind of project managing, as the one that could keep the income rate high enough to attract investors.

At the beginning, the European commission had decided the creation of a private/public *joint venture*; this could confer to the Commission the control over the whole system, and, at the same time, provide all the financial advantages of the private investors' presence. However, the initial study assessed that "Industry does not understand how there can be a return from participation in the Development phase: and in the Deployment and Operations phases it remains concerned about insufficient profitability (…), high levels of revenue risk, very long time horizons and a potential conflict of interest for the public sector if it is both equity investor and public sponsor of the project. We do not believe this is a viable model for attracting investment".[18]

Then the following option was the model of Concession that could ensure a clear division between the public sector, responsible of the Development phase, and the private, responsible of the following ones.

---

[17] PriceWaterHouseCoopers (2003), p. 7
[18] PriceWaterHouseCoopers (2001), p. 11.

In October 2003, the GJU announced a "call for tenders," to select one or more consortia, interested in the Concession. Three consortia passed the selection: "EURELAI," consisting of Finmeccanica, Alcatel, and others; the INARSAT consortium, mainly consisting of EADS and THALES; the EUTELSAT consortium that actually deals with satellite services; this last one decide to withdraw. The two competitors consortia left also represented two political partners: the first consisted of Italy, part of France and the UK and others; in the other one were Germany and the rest of France.[19] "Entrusting the concession always matters both at the political–institutional level and the financial one; splitting Europe was not politically *polite*, thus the two consortia matched together and, on October 21, 2006, they submitted a common offer; immediately after, they were bargaining the contract conditions with GJU. Now there are seven relevant partners—Alcatel, Finmeccanica, EADS, THALES, ISPASAT and others—that are bargaining. The role division—Who does what? How? When? etc.—is quite strict. The game is quite complex".[20]

The political–institutional level consisting of the balance among different interests within ESA and EU overlaps the financial level, i.e., the matters on industrial policy among the great companies of the space sector.

Actually, a kind of control over the phase of *Development* by industrial groups already exists de facto, since those groups, that will win the competition for the concession, are often linked to the groups that have a contract with ESA for the implementation of the phase of *Development*.

Galileo Industries, now European Satellite Navigation Industries (ESNIS)—a *joint venture* created in 2000 from Alcatel Alenia Space SAS (France), Alcatel Alenia Space SpA (Italia), EADS Astrium Ltd (UK), Galileo Sistemas y Servicios (Spain), (which is a consortium consisting in seven Spanish companies, three firms close to Thales and others), on January 19, 2006 signed a contract with ESA for 950 million euros, for sending into orbit the first four satellites of the constellation and for the signal validation (IOV).[21]

As a consequence, we are facing a contradiction: the project competitiveness, that the private investors' participation should have assured, is clashing, on one side, with the principle of "geographical return," and on the other, with bargains among big, industrial companies, aiming to ensure to all the partners the participation to all the project phases.

---

[19] For a description of the Concession contest see interview to Finmeccanica published in the volume Pirzio Ammassari (2007).

[20] *Ibidem.*

[21] This way, Galileo Industries is ready to offer to ESA a fully operative system within 2009 (IOV included) and to become the first contractor for the FOC phase (Full Operational Capability), in which the 26 left satellites will be put into orbit.

9.5 Italy's Participation to Galileo Project

One should acknowledge to Italy to have immediately seized the strategic relevance, both political and economic, of this project; though, Italy was unable to take advantage from this initial situation, and showed an always growing gap between political and financial sides.

The first steps occurred late in the 1990s, thanks to an important synergy between political elites, institutions—namely Italian Space Agency and the big companies of the space sector. For Italy, it was a difficult time financially: the entry in the Euro zone necessarily implied austerity; in addition, ASI was owing to ESA a considerable sum.

The turn point is the law no. 10, of January 29, 2001, that allocated 600 billion liras "aiming to develop Italian initiatives in the sector of satellite navigation, strengthen industry and services' competitiveness, to promote research and to allow an adequate participation to European programmes." This bill "not only allowed the Space Agency to join the board of ESA with capitals provided by the law—unique in Europe, but also granted funds for national projects before the European project started so that they would improve the national, industrial, and scientific fabrics and face Europe from a very strong position. A clear, political plan provided the funds, without which the project would only be an empty box".[22]

Though, this law is quite obscure and nowadays, the allocated fund was not completely used and ENAV has even returned its part to the Ministry del Treasury.[23] The most likely explanation is that the switch from the Center–Left, Europe oriented administration to the Center–Right one, aiming to strengthen the ties with the USA, have reduced the Italian participation; this allowed the other countries to increase their decision power, by calling the "principle of geographical return".

Several are the features of the Italian participation to Galileo project that would be an interesting object of analysis, though two of them standout for highlighting the limits of Italian intervention: (1) the multiplication of single initiatives, and (2) the lack of continuity, which allowed the other countries to recover the initial Italian advantage.

About the first issue, it is important to point out the proliferation of committees and bodies, that are supposed to start initiatives linked to the project implementation. The Province of Rome set up a Scientific Board, consisting of nine experts, coming from big companies, Small Medium Size Enterprises, Universities, and Institutions. Afterwards, a Coordination Centre for research and Development arose, in cooperation with Regione Lazio. The first is supposed to seize the main fields for the application of the Galileo's signal and to stimulate the Small Medium Enterprises lying in the Roman area; the latter should have a function of initiative coordination.

Furthermore, we have the projects, that Regione Lazio and the Society of the Technological Pole of Tiburtino started on their own. It is unclear if those initiatives are coordinated with each other, or if they imply a loss of energy and funds, as being likely no to go further the first phase.

---

[22] See interview to Cfr. De Julio, President of ASI from1996 through 2001.

[23] The fund was bound to ASI and ENAV for the initiative mentioned.

The institution of a National Coordination for the Galileo Project at the Presidency of the Council of Ministries could fulfil only partially this lack of coordination and could just carry out a function of representation—actually most important with European institutions.

Just to show some specific initiatives, we have the "promotional activities," such as the "Eneide Mission," that Mr. Storace, the president of Regione Lazio, promoted to show that the region not the country! was able to flight to the moon! From a middle-period perspective, this mission was supposed to be a "visit card," to propose Rome's candidature, to host some of the project's institutional seats (Satellite Agency, Galileo Supervisory Authority, the seat of the Concessionary, which in the meantime settled in Toulouse).

About this peculiar issue, some observers think that Rome's candidacy would be an advantage; others believe that no real financial benefit could arise, but only a better public image, while it could be much better to claim on the opposite, they claim for more and bigger contracts for space industry. In this case, the limits of Italian intervention are that a possible success on the first front would be the result of an intense, political bargaining carried out in the European institutions. About the second front, because of the "principle of geographical return," the possibility of success for Italy depends on its capability of setting up a "Country—offer," that can never neglect the overall amount of funding for this project.

As for the second issue, on the one hand the lack of continuity in the intervention has allowed the other European countries to regain ground with regard to the initial Italian advantage; on the other hand, this has made the involved Italian industrial groups realize that they had to act independently by creating partnerships, consortia at the trans-national level; but it is to be stressed that Finmeccanica, among these agreement, has transferred 67 % of Alenia Spazio to the French Alcatel. If the large industry withdraws because it is not supported by the country system, there are still, as indicated in an interview: "a series of small enterprises, since, even in this sector, we have the problem of a lack of critical mass, so that we have more or less 80 enterprises in the air-space sector, but the only one which is important at the international level is Finmeccanica (…) We cannot keep 80 small enterprises without any importance in the international context; they have at most a "niche" business, but they don't make critical mass, they have no capacity of dialogue with the large European space groups."[24]

Therefore, within the European Union appears the differentiation between the "country-systems" coordinated at the central level, like France, and a system, such as the Italian one, where the enterprises are integrated in the European system, but partly losing their national specificity.[25]

---

[24] Interview with Mr Alfredo Roma.

[25] Even then it was pointed out that the transformations induced by globalization maintain and almost increase the need for a strategy of the country system. This aspect had appeared very clearly in the interview with Alenia Spazio: "It is not only a problem of Alenia going to Asia, Africa, South America, to supply some systems. All this has to be followed, or preceded, by a capacity of the Country, by a political capacity, since to be able to supply this kind of system to South Africa or to Israel or to Saudi Arabia implies a political penetration. In the context of globalisation, what is absolutely necessary, in addition to technical capacity, is the political capacity to enter these markets." Cf. Pirzio Ammassari (2004), p. 15.

9.6 Galileo: A Challenge for European Union

In conclusion, Galileo Project is an interesting object of analysis, to seize a complex project realization's path, in which different institutional levels overlap and opposite interests clash. At the same time, Galileo is an important test for the European integration, namely in the field of industrial system.

In other words, Galileo project's shows several sides, one for each political or financial act of the elite that is involved in the implementation.

1. *The international level* is inborn in the project that implies a satellite navigation system, potentially world-wide. This feature implies bargaining international agreements that involve both political and financial elites. That also refers to the geopolitical setups, arisen from the end of Cold War, and evident in the USA–UE clash for the frequency assignation. Furthermore, the project's capability of attracting state partners (any single state can decide to fund the project) or foreigners, industrial groups, contribute to redefine the contemporary set-ups. Within this framework, the agreements with Israel and China are basic steps.

2. The *European level* is crucial even if it shows some contradictions, as the former level did. The literature on Globalization and European integration share the idea that the two processes would imply the end of the Nation/states. In fact, Galileo Project shows clearly how even in a supra-national context, such as the European context, one has the same influence as one's own country of origin. The very idea that the economic elites can act as completely separated from their country of origin clashes with a reality within which the economic and political dimensions are much more strictly related than one could think at first. The growing interrelation between the two spheres of action—political and economic—follows two directions: on the one hand, mergers, partnerships, joint ventures between European enterprises cannot be independent from the negotiation capacity of their national states; on the other hand, those changes represent as many ways to implement the European integration process. People meet, work together, exchange information and skilled personnel, recognizing that a complex project requires cooperation, rather than competition. On the other hand, no country could have been able to implement Galileo project all alone, both because space sector, by definition, has no borders, and because the skills required have made it necessary to enter into agreements. The economic will to participate in the realization of a big satellite infrastructure, has required an otherwise difficult dialogue between the national states. Lobbying by the various industrial groups has also played a decisive role as to the political agreements between the different countries. In fact, on the industrial plan, European integration is a reality. As argued in a 2002 interview by the Engineer Viriglio, then Managing Director of *Alenia Spazio*, "In practice, at the industrial level we will by far anticipate the United Europe. *Finmeccanica* is now realizing an integration of its enterprises with the rest of European enterprises".[26] Such integration has turned into reality thanks to Galileo

---

[26] Interview with the Managing Director of Alenia Spazio (16.1.2002) in Marchetti (2004), p. 250.

project, but following two opposed perspectives: the French one, where the industrial groups, supported by state protectionism, are able to acquire important parts of the block of shares of other European industries (after merger, Alcatel controls more than 60 % of Alcatel Alenia Space shareholding)[27]; and the Italian model (if it is possible to speak of model in this case) according to which the industrial groups, without any state support, enter the market and sell important shares of the industrial wealth of the country to foreign groups. These can even be considered the two faces of the globalization process: "for us, globalisation is in itself an extremely close opportunity; to take this opportunity, we should either have an official policy of the country aiming at this, or make alliances that will be more or less close depending on the force of the national role. If the national role is such that we feel politically supported, we will make a "positioning" alliance: we divide a slice of the world and decide who goes on the one hand and who on the other. If my country is too weak, we have to provide for stronger protections".[28]

3. The *national level* refers to the state capacity to defend the national interests where it is necessary. This aspect concerns the capacity to act as a "Country-System," through the joint action of all the institutional levels involved. This means the adoption of a specific action program joining, as in a single process, research, industrial and manufacturing sectors, large industries and small and medium enterprises. The lack of support by the institutions inevitably resulted in a reduction of the efforts made by the industrial groups. There are markets, like that of space, where the political factor is still very important; industrial groups face this situation through strategic alliances, that have to be stronger if they receive less support from their country of origin.

4. The *local level* is particularly important since some local contexts have a high concentration of space sector enterprises. It is the case of *Regione Lazio* and, in particular, of the *Provincia di Roma*, hosting the headquarters of the main enterprises of the sector (Finmeccanica, Alenia Alcatel Space, Telespazio) as well as a series of small and medium-sized enterprises, specialized in the production of specific parts.

The interesting aspect of a complex project, such as Galileo, is that the four above-mentioned levels interact. This implies an internal coordination and a global vision that have been lacking in the Italian action. A project like Galileo needs a remarkable capacity to work in the long run, acting not only on the institutional plan but also on the plan of financing research and new entrepreneurial activities, stimulating the creation of synergies able to multiply the effects. However, it is equally worth stressing that, when innovation processes are at stake, the slowdown inherent to the European decision-making processes risks to produce unintentional effects: Galileo, meaning to overcome American GPS has brought about an innovation process involving also the US navigation system, which is going towards its third phase

---

[27] In April 2007 Alcatel transferred its participation in Alenia to Thales, another French group and one of the world biggest in the aerospace sector.

[28] *Ibidem*, p. 243–244.

(GPS III). Further slowdown in the implementation phases would make Galileo obsolete even before starting to work at full capacity.

Such contradictions have led complex negotiations to a stalemate and to delays on the part of the consortium, which gathers, however, the best of the European industry (Eads—the group controlling Airbus, Thales and Alcatel—for France, Finmeccanica for Italy, TeleOp for Germany, Inmarsat for Great Britain and Hispasat and Aena for Spain). So, following the alarm given by the Commissioner Jacques Barrot, the Council of the 27 European Ministers of Transports voted unanimously an ultimatum to respect by 10th May the engagements undertaken (since July 2005), otherwise the Council could envisage "alternative solutions in terms of costs, risks and feasibility".

As a matter of fact, the combining of the two consortia in one was subject to the condition that the eight firms would grow in a single company able to proceed with shared purposes, following the timed plan according to which the European satellite system should start working in 2008, expiration adjourned to 2010 and now, realistically, not before than 2012, quite late to face the new generation of the American GPS and maybe even the competition of the Chinese Beidou.[29]

Therefore, the EU Commissioner for transports Jacques Barrot has proposed to charge to the Union budget the putting into orbit of all the 30 satellites, cancelling the 2005 contract with the consortium and then providing for other calls for tender for the management of the system. This solution would charge all the costs and risks of the first phase to the public party, which is certainly a profitable result for the industrial groups.

Finally, the Transport Council Meeting of June 6–8, 2007 in Luxembourg adopted the following resolution:

- The current concession negotiations have failed and should be ended.
- The deployment of the Galileo system is stated by the end of 2012.
- The implementation of a deployment of Galileo and EGNOS by the public sector would need additional public funding.

The breakdown of concession contract negotiations with the private consortium prevented the introduction of the European GNSS by the date originally scheduled. However, early January 2010, the European Commission announced the award of three of the six contracts for the procurement of Galileo's initial operational capability.

- The contract for the system support services was awarded to ThalesAleniaSpace and covers the industrial services needed to support the ESA for the integration and the validation of the Galileo system.
- The contract for a first order of 14 satellites was awarded to OHB System AG. The first satellite is expected to be delivered in July 2012 and the last one in March 2014. The remaining 12–14 satellites needed to reach the Full Operational

---

[29] A. Cerretelli, "Ultimatum Ue per Galileo. I ministri dei trasporti immaginavano possibili scenari alternativi," *Il Sole-24-Ore*, 23 March 2007, N.81.

Capability will be procured in subsequent work orders from either OHB or EADS Astrium GmbH under the framework contract signed with both manufacturers.

• The contract for the launch services was awarded to Arianespace and covers the launch of five Soyuz launchers, each carrying two satellites. The launch of the first two operational satellites of the EU's GNSS took place on October 21, 2011.

The contracts were signed on 26 January between the ESA, acting on behalf of the European Commission, and the companies involved.

On 25th October 2010, the contract for the operations was signed with SpaceOpal GmbH (an Italian–German joint venture) and the ESA on behalf of the European Commission.

The final two procurement contracts for the ground mission infrastructure and the ground control infrastructure were awarded in June 2011.

In conclusion, the case of Galileo Project has been an interesting test of the difficulties of a common project in the sector of high technology.

References

Albrow M (1997) The Global Age. London, Polity Press

Beck U (1999) Che cos'è la globalizzazione. Roma, Carocci

Beck U (2000) I rischi della libertà. L'individuo nell'epoca della globalizzazione. Il Mulino, Bologna

Casini S (2004) In nome dell'Europa: la grandeur spaziale della Francia, vol. 5. In Le mani sullo spazio, Limes

Di Nolfo E (2004) Dagli imperi militari agli imperi tecnologici. La politica internazionale nel XX secolo. Bari, Laterza

Werner N (2004) L'avenir de l'Europe Spatiale. Fondation Robert Schuman, Paris, France

Marchetti MC (2004) Attori economici e mutamento sociale. Un'indagine nell'area romana. Franco Angeli, Milano

Pirzio Ammassari G (ed) (2007) Politica ed economia: strategie di un capitalismo maturo. Il caso del Progetto Galileo. FrancoAngeli, Milano

Pirzio Ammassari G (2004) Gli attori economici di fronte al mutamento: un'indagine sul sistema produttivo romano. In: Marchetti MC (ed) Attori economici e mutamento sociale. Un'indagine nell'area romana. Franco Angeli, Milan

Price Water House Coopers (2001) Inception study to support the development of a business plan for the Galileo Programme

PriceWaterHouseCoopers (2003) Galileo Study. Phase II. Executive. Summary, 17 Jan 2003

Robertson R (1992) Globalization, social theory and global culture. Sage, London

Valori GE (2006) Geopolitica dello spazio, Potere e ricchezza nel futuro del pianeta. Rizzoli, Milano

Weiss L (2005) L'integrazione globale accresce il potere degli Stati. In Rivista Italiana di Scienza Politica, Anno XXXV

European Union Documents

European Commission, Galileo—Involving Europe in a new Generation of Satellite Navigation Services. Brussels, 10 Feb 1999 COM (1999) 54 Final

European Commission. White paper, space: a new European frontier for an expanding Union An action plan for implementing the European Space. Brussels, 11 Nov 2003, COM (2003) 673 Final

European Commission. Green paper, European space policy. Brussels, 21 Jan 2003, COM (2003) 17 Final

Council Resolution (EC) 1321/2004

Council resolution on Galileo (2007) 2805th Transport, Telecommunications and Energy Council Meeting, Luxembourg

Siti Internet

http://www.asi.it
http://www.comune.roma.it
http://www.esa.int
http://www.esnis.net
http://www.europa.eu.int
http://www.filas.it
http://www.gpsworld.com
http://www.provincia.roma.it
http://www.regione.lazio.it
http://www.romaeconomia.it
http://ec.europa.eu/transport/gsa/index.htm
http://www.galileoju.com

Chapter 10
A Benchmarking Study for Human Capital in Europe

Aikaterini Kokkinou, George M. Korres, Efstratios Papanis, and Panagiotis Giavrimis

10.1 Innovation and Economic Growth: An Interrelation Analysis

Since early, economic theory dealt with the innovation as basic factor of economic development and technical change. The first approach in defining innovation has been made by Schumpeter (1934), which first focused on innovation factor as one of the core sources of dynamism in the capitalistic social and economic growth, asserting that innovation is one of the centred activities towards economic change and growth.

In modern economy, technology and innovation possess an important role in the models of growth. The developments in the theory of economic growth have renewed the interest for the role of innovation in the development process, underlining the contacts between investment in innovative activities, technological change and economic growth (Acs et al. 2002).

A. Kokkinou (✉)
Department of Economics, University of Glasgow,
Adam Smith Building, G128QQ Glasgow, Scotland, UK
e-mail: a.kokkinou.1@research.gla.ac.uk

G.M. Korres
Centre of Urban and Regional Development Studies (CURDS),
University of Newcastle, Newcastle NE1-7RU, UK

Department of Geography, University of the Aegean,
Mytilene, Greece
e-mail: George.Korres@ncl.ac.uk; gkorres@geo.aegean.gr

E. Papanis • P. Giavrimis
Department of Sociology, University of the Aegean,
Mytilene 81100, Lesbos, Greece
e-mail: papanis@papanis.gr; giavrimis@soc.aegean.gr

E.G. Carayannis and G.M. Korres (eds.), *European Socio-Economic Integration*,
Innovation, Technology, and Knowledge Management 27,
DOI 10.1007/978-1-4614-5254-6_10, © Springer Science+Business Media New York 2013

Table 10.1 Innovation determining factors

- Educational level of population, which determines the educational level of human capital
- The infrastructure level, including road and telecommunication networks
- Investment conditions and possibilities and access to investment capital
- Legislative and macroeconomic regulations, as are licence laws, royalties, law, taxation, subsidies, investment and competition policy
- Entrepreneurship investment and activities, market size and market access
- Competitive environment
- Entrepreneurship and entrepreneurial culture
- Demographics and population trends

Source: Own elaboration

The main underlying reason is that new technologies lead to enhanced productivity of production factors, contributing in the long-run competitiveness (Griliches 1980; Fagerberg 1988). Innovation, as a motive force, prompts the renewal of productive structures and lies behind the appearance of new forms of economic activity (Barro 1991, 1997, 1999; Barro and Sala-I-Martin 1991, 1995).

This approach leads to the shift from the economy based to the productive factors to an economy based to innovation and knowledge creation and diffusion. The main scope is the promotion of innovation, through the production of new or improved products, services and productive processes with economic value, which are in strong position to be successfully introduced in the market. In general, one may distinguish the following determining factors towards innovation production (Table 10.1).

Summarising the above elements in two general categories, Porter and Stern (1999) support that the basic factors which determine innovation activities are, in one hand, the general macroeconomic and productive environment, and on the other hand, the particular microeconomic environment comprising factors which promote and strengthen innovative activities as well as the particular conditions developed in networks of enterprises, and finally the kind and intensity of relations between these elements. Of particular importance is the connection between investment in human capital and technological change and economic growth (Freeman 1987; Lundvall 1992; Metcalfe 1995; Furman et al. 2002; Nelson 1993). According to production theory, there can be distinguished the following basic growth determining factors, which contribute actively in the development process, as presented in Fig. 10.1.

The interaction of these factors, as well as the effectiveness with what these factors are connected for the production of an economic product, represents the productivity of economy, a country or even a group of countries, like European Union. The productivity differences in national or regional economy level reflect also differences in the level of prosperity of economy compared to others (Hall and Jones 1999).

10.2 Innovation and Human Capital: Women Participation

One of the basic assumptions of modern economic growth theory is that investment in human capital greatly influences technological change and, consequently, economic growth level (Romer 1986, 1990; Lucas 1988). Lucas (1988) suggested that

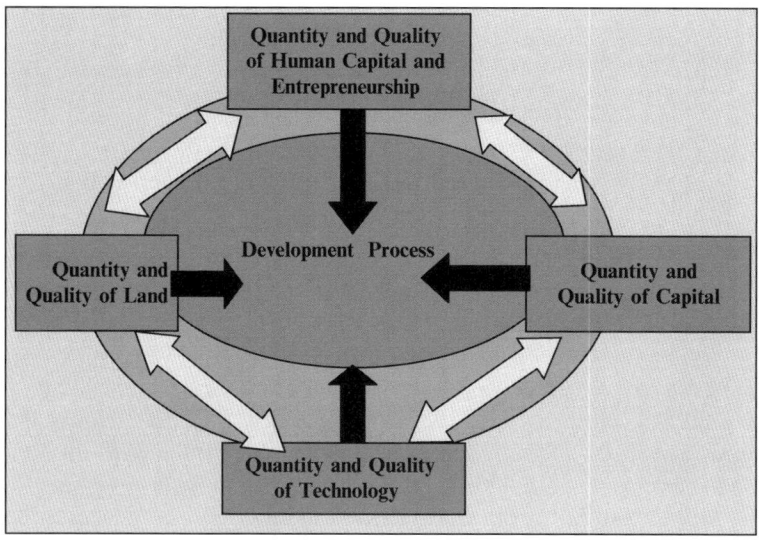

Fig. 10.1 Economic systems: main flows. *Source*: Own elaboration

if an economy invests a sufficient amount of production factors in the accumulation of human capital, then the economy will enjoy a long-term sustainable growth. Within this framework, considering also the Lisbon goals (the goal for the EU to become, until 2010, the most competitive and dynamic economy in the world, regarding knowledge, new technology and innovation), the policies of social and economic cohesion within European Union are unbreakably connected with economic and social development.

Equality within the EU is strengthened institutionally by the provisions of the European Union Constitution. More specifically, gender equality is one of the main ethics and objectives, already declared in the Treaty of Amsterdam. One of the most important European Constitution novelties is the incorporation of the Chart of Fundamental Rights, which contributes considerably in the promotion of women rights. Moreover, the gender equality and discrimination exclusion are also constitutionally guaranteed, applying in the whole frame of the EU policies.

In the past few years, equality between men and women in the level of the EU has also economic interest, as human capital is closely connected to demographic trends and labour market. The Employment Summit in November 1997 in Luxembourg first formed the European Strategy for the Employment and recognised for the first time in political level that the gender equality constitutes not only a social justice matter but also a matter of great economic interest, regarding women participation in employment and labour market, as an element of competitiveness of the European economy and as means towards economic and social development (OECD 1993, 1997).

Taking into consideration the latest demographic data, the economically active population of the EU permanently shrinks, which implies that, for the EU to remain competitive, it should effectively utilise the labour force and human capital, through policies that will particularly facilitate those with problems in labour market participation, as women. Moreover, with regard to the objectives placed in Lisbon in 2000, the goal is to reach the 60% of women participation in labour force by 2010, as a means of total employment increase. Via this objective, it was judged that there would be significant contribution in total employment rate enhancing social and economic development and wider social cohesion (European Communities 2008b).

10.3 Gender Equality and Innovation: What Is the Situation?

Regarding the case of Greece, during the last decades, there has been important progress on gender equality in social and economic activities. The Constitution of 1975 first guaranteed gender equality as a special expression of general equality, in legislative fields that concern family, education, labour relations and social and economic activities. The constitutional revision of 2001 established specifically positive measures for the obliteration of any gender discriminations. However, reality records certain refuted elements. As it is observed in international level, thus and in Greece, at the last decades, the rate of employment of women has been increased considerably. In regard to the case of Greece, however, this development does not mean also reduction of inequalities in the employment between the two genders, as it is presented in Table 10.2.

From the data presented in the table, it is observed that the participation of men in workforce amounts in the percentage of 79.2, against 55.1 for women. On the other hand, the indicator of employment of men amounts in the percentage of 75.4, compared to 49.0 for women. Important differentiation is also observed regarding the rate of unemployment of women (11.1%), concerning 4.8% for men that are unemployed.

On the other hand, there are no particular differences observed concerning the percentage of women and men that study in the tertiary education. According to Table 10.3, in Greece, the young persons which study in institutions of tertiary education represent almost the same percentage for both genders.

Nevertheless, despite the almost equal percentages of men and women students, it is realised that the professional segregation because sexes has direct relation with the educational choices of the two. Even though educational level of women and men has been almost evened, different educational choices of the two genders, as for the type of education or specialisation, influence directly also their professional choices, with maintenance of professional gap because sex.[1]

Table 10.4 presents students in doctoral programmes in the scientific field of natural sciences, information technology, engineering, science, mathematics and computing, manufacturing and construction, fields that can be considered technological.[2]

---

[1] According to European Commission (2008).

[2] According to the definition by the International Standard Classification of Education (ISCED97) and the Eurostat Manual of Fields of Education and Training (1999).

Table 10.2 Employment index (population above 15 years of age, 2008)

Total		Women			
Women		Employment index			
Age groups	Total	Working force participation	Employment rate	Unemployment rate	Non-economically active
15–19	100	7.2	4.6	36.3	92.8
20–24	100	45.3	33.3	26.4	54.7
25–29	100	76.4	63.5	17.0	23.6
15–29	100	46.3	36.7	20.7	53.7
30–44	100	73.0	65.5	10.3	27.0
45–64	100	45.4	42.8	5.6	54.6
65+	100	2.0	2.0	0.0	98.0
Total (15–64 years)	100	55.1	49.0	11.1	44.9

Total		Men			
Men		Employment index			
Age groups	Total	Working force participation	Employment rate	Unemployment rate	Non-economically active
15–19	100	10.4	8.4	18.9	89.6
20–24	100	55.4	47.4	14.5	44.6
25–29	100	91.5	82.8	9.6	8.5
15–29	100	57.8	51.1	11.5	42.2
30–44	100	97.2	93.8	3.5	2.8
45–64	100	77.9	75.9	2.5	22.1
65+	100	7.1	7.0	1.0	92.9
Total (15–64 years)	100	79.2	75.4	4.8	20.8

Source: National Statistical Service of Greece

The above table shows that there exists supremacy of men with regard to their direction to the specialisation on technology and innovation fields, with the corresponding low percentage of women, who are directed in more traditional sectors.

Corresponding, and more intense picture, is also presented with regard to the attendance of women in activities of research, technology and innovation, where it is observed that while women constitute the 50% of European students, they only possess the 10% of superior places in academia and still smaller percentage in industry.[3]

Human capital in research and development denotes the share of the workforce with a tertiary education degree in the fields of science and technology, or is occupied in workplaces, which require such type a degree. Human capital in research and development plays a fundamental role in growth and competitiveness enhancement. The investment in human capital has a direct positive effect in technological change.

---

[3] According to European Commission (2008).

Table 10.3 Women participation among students in tertiary education

	1998	1999	2000	2001	2002	2003	2004	2005	2006
EU (27)	52.8	53.2	53.5	53.9	54.4	54.5	54.8	54.9	55.1
EU (25)	52.7	53.1	53.5	53.9	54.4	54.6	54.8	55.0	55.1
EU (15)	–	–	–	–	–	–	53.4	53.5	53.7
EU (13)	52.0	52.3	52.5	52.7	53.2	53.3	53.4	53.5	53.7
Belgium	–	52.1	52.3	52.8	53.1	53.3	53.8	54.4	54.7
Czech Republic	48.1	49.7	49.8	50.1	51.2	50.7	51.2	52.6	53.8
Denmark	55.5	56.3	56.9	56.5	57.5	57.9	57.9	57.4	57.4
Germany	46.5	47.4	48.1	48.7	49.0	49.5	49.4	49.6	49.7
Estonia	56.8	57.8	58.5	60.1	61.5	61.5	61.8	61.5	61.6
Ireland	52.7	53.5	54.1	54.7	55.1	55.7	55.2	54.9	55.1
Greece	50.1	50.3	50.0	51.1	51.2	51.0	51.7	51.1	50.9
Spain	53.0	53.0	52.9	52.5	53.1	53.1	53.8	53.7	53.9
France	54.7	54.4	54.2	54.1	54.8	55.0	55.0	55.2	55.3
Italy	54.7	55.2	55.5	56.0	56.2	56.2	56.2	56.6	56.9
Cyprus	–	56.0	57.1	58.0	54.8	49.5	47.9	52.0	50.9
Latvia	58.9	61.6	63.4	61.8	61.5	61.7	62.3	63.2	63.3
Lithuania	60.3	60.0	60.0	59.8	60.5	60.0	60.0	60.1	59.9
Luxembourg	51.7	51.7	–	–	–	53.3	–	–	51.6
Hungary	54.0	54.2	53.9	54.8	55.3	56.7	57.3	58.4	58.5
Malta	–	51.5	53.3	54.8	56.9	56.9	55.9	56.3	57.0
Holland	48.6	49.3	50.0	50.5	50.7	51.0	50.9	51.0	51.1
Austria	49.2	50.0	51.0	51.8	52.7	53.0	53.3	53.7	53.8
Poland	56.8	57.0	57.5	58.0	57.9	57.8	57.6	57.5	57.4
Portugal	56.0	55.9	56.5	57.0	57.0	56.6	56.1	55.7	55.2
Romania	49.9	51.0	51.8	53.5	54.4	54.3	54.8	54.6	55.4
Slovenia	55.2	56.0	56.1	56.1	57.5	56.2	56.9	57.8	58.4
Slovakia	51.0	51.7	50.4	51.3	52.1	53.1	54.1	55.3	57.7
Finland	53.5	54.0	53.7	53.9	54.1	53.5	53.4	53.6	53.9
Sweden	56.2	57.6	58.2	59.1	59.5	59.6	59.6	59.6	59.6
Great Britain	52.7	53.2	53.9	54.5	55.2	55.9	57.0	57.2	57.3
Croatia	–	–	–	–	–	53.2	53.7	53.8	54.1
FYROM	54.6	55.1	55.0	55.8	55.2	56.2	57.0	56.7	56.7
Turkey	–	39.6	39.8	40.8	41.4	41.3	41.4	41.9	42.4
Iceland	60.0	62.2	61.9	62.7	63.2	63.7	64.5	64.9	64.3
Liechtenstein	–	–	–	–	–	27.0	26.7	28.8	30.3
Norway	56.7	57.4	58.4	59.2	59.6	59.7	59.6	59.6	59.7
Switzerland	–	–	–	–	43.3	44.2	44.9	46.0	46.9
USA	55.6	52.8	55.8	55.9	56.3	56.6	57.1	57.2	57.4
Japan	44.6	44.7	44.9	44.9	45.1	45.6	45.8	45.9	45.7

Source: Eurostat

Moreover, the percentage of technological change is influenced immediately by the rate of improvement of quality of workforce, investment in human potential, training and education. Development policies are related immediately with the policies of growth of human capital, as well as with the improvement of technological progress

Table 10.4 Ph.D. students in research and development, as percentage of total population, age 20–29

	1998	1999	2000	2001	2002	2003	2004	2005
Men								
EU (27)	–	–	–	–	–	–	–	–
Belgium	–	–	0.31	0.28	0.30	0.30	0.32	0.34
Bulgaria	–	–	0.13	0.15	0.16	0.18	0.21	0.23
Czech Republic	0.56	0.57	0.66	0.80	0.85	0.96	1.05	1.11
Denmark	0.00	0.29	0.37	0.27	0.37	0.39	0.43	0.38
Germany	–	–	–	–	–	–	–	–
Estonia	0.26	0.28	0.31	0.32	0.34	0.38	0.42	0.47
Ireland	0.31	0.32	0.33	0.32	0.33	0.37	0.42	0.43
Greece	–	–	–	–	0.63	–	0.94	1.08
Spain	0.26	0.26	0.26	0.28	0.24	0.30	0.34	0.34
Italy	0.06	0.06	0.07	0.12	0.15	0.19	0.26	0.26
Cyprus	–	–	–	0.03	0.04	0.04	0.11	0.14
Latvia	0.18	0.17	0.17	0.19	0.15	0.14	0.16	0.15
Lithuania	0.15	0.18	0.19	0.19	0.20	0.21	0.26	0.27
Luxemburg	–	–	–	–	–	–	–	–
Hungary	0.14	0.14	0.15	0.21	0.01	0.53	0.24	0.23
Malta	–	–	0.01	0.01	–	0.00	–	0.02
Holland	–	–	–	–	–	–	–	–
Austria	0.96	1.05	1.09	1.12	0.71	0.65	0.67	0.66
Poland	0.15	–	0.19	0.22	0.24	0.25	0.23	0.23
Portugal	0.39	–	0.25	0.25	0.28	0.35	0.41	0.41
Romania	–	–	–	–	–	0.41	0.13	0.27
Slovenia	–	–	–	–	–	–	–	0.22
Slovakia	0.39	0.45	0.45	0.46	0.47	0.51	0.54	0.58
Finland	1.69	1.68	1.78	1.79	1.79	1.64	1.75	1.75
Sweden	0.81	1.02	1.05	1.06	1.08	1.12	1.16	1.12
Great Britain	0.58	0.71	0.65	0.65	0.64	0.69	0.73	0.76
Croatia	–	–	–	–	–	0.03	0.04	0.07
Iceland	–	–	0.01	0.04	0.02	0.02	0.04	0.10
Norway	0.34	0.30	0.06	0.28	0.27	0.45	0.47	0.49
Switzerland	–	–	–	–	0.84	0.90	0.95	1.00
Women								
EU (27)	–	–	–	–	–	–	–	–
Belgium	–	–	0.14	0.13	0.14	0.15	0.16	0.18
Bulgaria	–	–	0.10	0.12	0.13	0.15	0.16	0.17
Czech Republic	0.17	0.18	0.23	0.29	0.33	0.38	0.41	0.46
Denmark	0.00	0.14	0.13	0.11	0.15	0.17	0.18	0.16
Germany	–	–	–	–	–	–	–	–
Estonia	0.12	0.14	0.16	0.20	0.24	0.26	0.30	0.32
Ireland	0.21	0.21	0.22	0.23	0.25	0.26	0.27	0.28
Greece	–	–	–	–	0.34	–	0.50	0.62
Spain	0.16	0.17	0.17	0.14	0.18	0.21	0.24	0.23
Italy	0.06	0.06	0.07	0.08	0.10	0.15	0.20	0.20
Cyprus	–	–	–	0.03	0.02	0.02	0.08	0.11

(continued)

Table 10.4 (continued)

	1998	1999	2000	2001	2002	2003	2004	2005
Latvia	0.09	0.10	0.10	0.13	0.11	0.10	0.11	0.11
Lithuania	0.07	0.10	0.12	0.12	0.13	0.15	0.19	0.20
Luxemburg	–	–	–	–	–	–	–	–
Hungary	0.06	0.05	0.06	0.09	0.00	0.42	0.11	0.11
Malta	–	–	–	–	0.00	0.01	–	0.01
Holland	–	–	–	–	–	–	–	–
Austria	0.26	0.31	0.34	0.36	0.26	0.27	0.27	0.28
Poland	0.08	–	0.10	0.11	0.13	0.14	0.15	0.15
Portugal	0.23	–	0.19	0.22	0.23	0.29	0.34	0.34
Romania	–	–	–	–	–	0.28	0.14	0.19
Slovenia	–	–	–	–	–	–	–	0.12
Slovakia	0.18	0.20	0.19	0.19	0.22	0.25	0.26	0.27
Finland	0.67	0.76	0.81	0.86	0.87	0.81	0.89	0.90
Sweden	0.33	0.45	0.48	0.50	0.54	0.59	0.61	0.61
Great Britain	0.26	0.32	0.31	0.32	0.33	0.31	0.33	0.33
Croatia	–	–	–	–	–	0.01	0.03	0.05
Iceland	–	–	0.01	0.03	0.02	0.03	0.03	0.09
Norway	0.10	0.10	0.04	0.09	0.10	0.17	0.19	0.21
Switzerland	–	–	–	–	0.32	0.36	0.42	0.45

Source: Eurostat

and the modernisation of productive base, as well as conditions of flexibility of labour market (Breschi and Lissoni 2001; Almeida and Kogut 1999).

The number of persons occupied in sectors of research and development presents an important augmenting tendency from 1993 onwards, which reaches also up to the increase at 80%. Germany, Great Britain and France have well above ten millions of persons occupied in research and development, and these three countries occupy globally almost half of the 85 millions of human capital of European Union.

Figures 10.2, 10.3, 10.4 and 10.5 illustrate researchers by R&D performing sector per 1,000 employment, the graduation rates at doctorate level as a percentage of population in reference age, the higher education expenditure on R&D as a percentage of GDP and the difference in median gross annual earnings of doctorate holders working as researchers and as non-researchers as a percentage of median gross annual earnings of doctorate holders not working as researchers, respectively. All sectors include the business enterprise, government, higher education, other education and private non-profit sectors. For Belgium, the Netherlands and Spain, data relate to graduates from 1990 onwards only. For Spain, the sample has limited coverage of doctorate holders for the years 2007–2009.

Regarding the expenditure on human capital, specifically public expenditure in education as percentage of GDP, the benchmarking is as follows: Denmark presents percentage 8.3%, Sweden 7.4%, Portugal 7.3%, France 6.4%, Belgium 6.2% and Estonia 6.2%, correspondingly. The average percentage of EU–25 is 5.4%, while Greece has the last ranking with 3.5%. Especially low percentages correspond also to Slovakia 3.6%, Romania 3.9%, Germany 4.0% and Spain 4.4%.

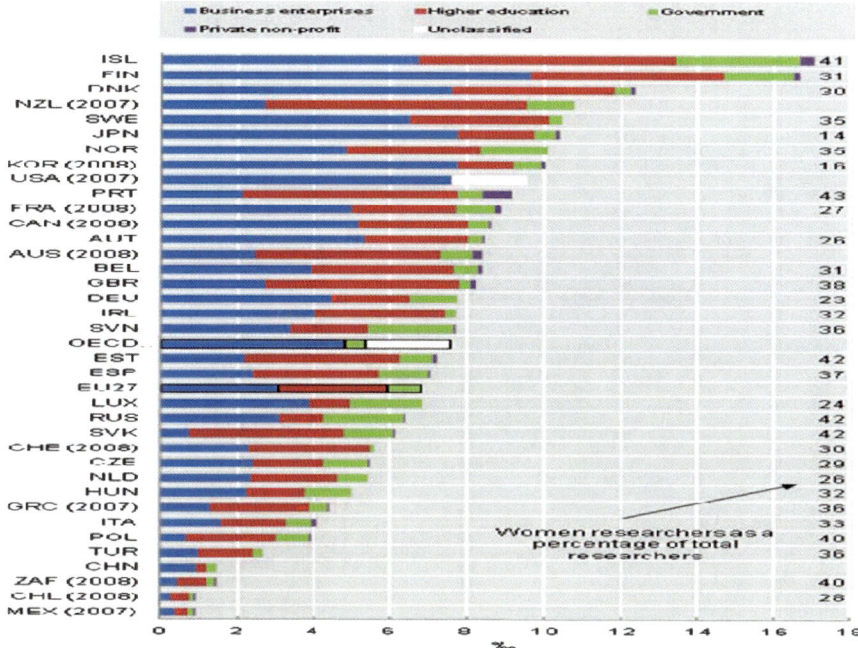

Fig. 10.2 Researchers by R&D performing sector per 1,000 employment (2009). *Source*: OECD, Main Science and Technology Indicators Database, June 2011

Human capital which is occupied in professions related to research and development activities represents the individuals who participate actively in the production and distribution of activities of research and development and technological innovations. In the EU roughly 59 million individuals are occupied in professions related to research, innovation and technology, roughly 1/3 of the economically active population. The participation of women amounts to 51% of total employment, showing equal gender participation. Remarkable it is that, in Lithuania, the corresponding rate of attendance of women reaches the 72%.[4]

Regarding the percentage of human capital that is occupied in the research and development, as percentage of total employment, the corresponding percentage of 2005 in European Union–25 was 16.8%. In the first places, Norway presents percentage 26.8%, Denmark 26.5%, Finland 23.4%, Sweden 23.9% and Belgium 21.6%, while in the opposite side with the lowest percentages correspond to Portugal with 10.7%, Czech Republic 11.1%, Poland 13.5%, Italy 11.1% and Austria 12.9%, while also Greece presents the corresponding percentage of 16.3%.

Regarding national distributions in the member states, in five of them the participation of women exceeded the percentage of 45%, specifically, Latvia (49.8%),

---

[4] European Communities (2008a).

Fig. 10.3 Graduation rates at doctorate level as a percentage of population in reference age, 2000 and 2009. *Source*: OECD (2011), *Education at a Glance 2011: OECD Indicators* and (2009) *Education at a Glance 2009: OECD Indicators*, OECD, Paris

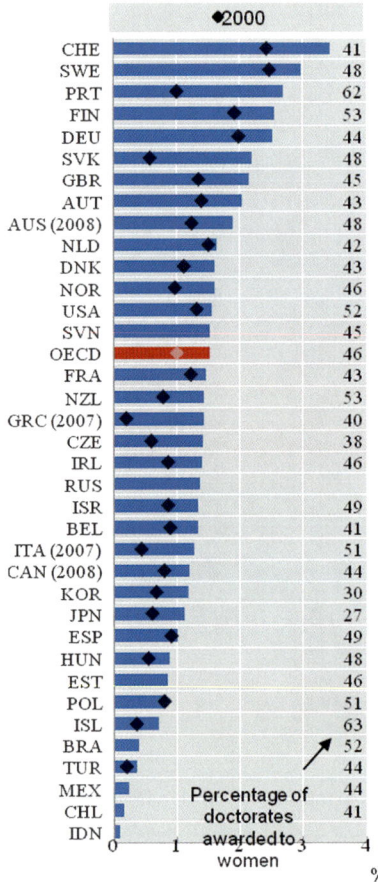

Lithuania (48.5%), Bulgaria (46.5%), Romania (46.2%) and Portugal (45.1%). This tendency is also observed in Croatia with percentage of 45.6%. Apart from Portugal (45.1%) and Spain (37%), the tendency in the old member states with regard to women participation in the professions related of research and technology is under the European Union average (27%). The lower percentages (under 20%) are observed in Austria, Luxembourg and Germany. The same picture presents also the women participation in professions of research and technology in the private sector. The private sector in Bulgaria occupies above the 50% of workplaces with women, followed by Latvia (49.4%), Romania (42.7%) and Croatia (42.5%). On the other hand, the percentage of women that was occupied in professions related to research and technology in private sector is 31.7% in Lithuania and 26.9% in Portugal. This differentiation implies that women occupied in research and development are mainly occupied in public sector or educational institutions. Regarding the European Union average, women participation represents the 23% of workplaces in professions related to research and development in the private sector. Scandinavian countries, like Sweden and Denmark, are closer to EU average, while Austria (11.5%) and Germany (11.0%) are well behind.

Fig. 10.4 Higher education
expenditure on R&D as
percentage of GDP, 1999 and
2009. *Source*: OECD, Main
Science and Technology
Indicators Database, June 2011

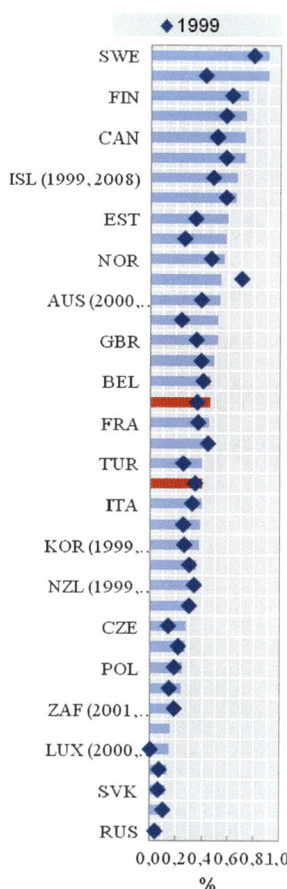

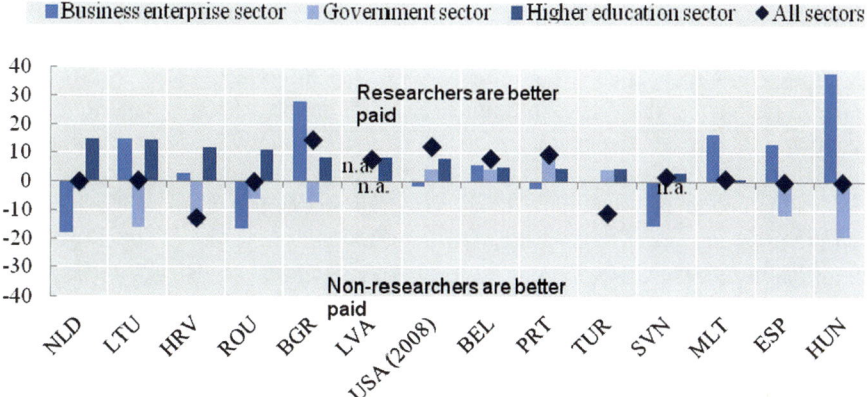

Fig. 10.5 Difference in median gross annual earnings of doctorate holders working as researchers
and as non-researchers as a percentage of median gross annual earnings of doctorate holders not
working as researchers, 2009. *Source*: OECD, based on OECD/UNESCO Institute for Statistics/
Eurostat data collection on careers of doctorate holders 2010, June 2011

Table 10.5 Seventh Program for Research and Development (2007–2013)

Programmes	Seventh programme budget provisions	Programme description
Cooperation	61%	Main goal: cooperative research 1. Competitiveness 2. Strategic cooperation 3. Employment
Ideas	16.3%	Main goal: research and knowledge creation 1. Research 2. Knowledge-based economy
People	9.8%	Main goal: human capital 1. Researcher networks (Marie Curie Networks) 2. Individual fellowships, co-financing of regional/national/international programmed 3. Industry-academia scheme 4. International linkages 5. Excellence award
Skills	10.3%	Main goal: research activities 1. Research infrastructure 2. Innovation in small and medium enterprises 3. Knowledge regions 4. Research personnel 5. Information society 6. International research cooperation

Source: European Union

Even though total human capital in research and development in European Union is increasing continuously from 2000 onwards, however, corresponding women participation remains low. The reasons for the low participation of women in professions related to research and development may be attributed to certain stereotypes with regard to the role of woman in the society and the so-called "women" and "men" professions, the absence of supportive structures for the woman in labour market and the legislative and legal frame, along with the general underlying conditions in labour market.

European Union, within the framework of Lisbon Strategy, gives priority, inter alia, in supporting the access to training and lifelong programmes, contributing to competition and efficiency of European Union economy in the world market. According to "Progress towards the Lisbon objectives in Education and Training-Indicators and Benchmarking" (2008), Greece remains last in all of the initiative programmes, as well as the expenditure for programmes of work training. Regarding Greece, the percentage of workers who participate in programmes of training is the lowest in the EU (14%).

Today, promotion of research and development and innovation is mainly realised through the 7th Program Framework of Research and Technological Growth. The 7th Program (2007–2013) constitutes the basic tool of European Union for financing and promoting of research and technological growth. The structure of 7th Program includes four special development programmes, as presented in Table 10.5.

Inter alia, the main objective remains the creation of workplaces, with the promotion of entrepreneurship, the promotion of research and development and innovation, as well as with a more dynamic relation between public and the private sector. Particularly in Greece, women (which is 52% of the total population) participate in political, economic, professional and social activities with terms of equal rights, access and opportunities ensuring and contributing in growth and achieving social cohesion.

The initiative for aid in the sectors of research and development should be focused in the following points:

- In the creation of "internal market" for the research, as a space of free dissemination and diffusion of knowledge, researchers and technology, aiming at the promotion of collaborations, the increase of competitiveness of European innovation system and the achievement of synergies and exploitation of allocated resources
- In the re-organisation of European innovation system and in the more efficient coordination of national innovation activities and policies, in regional and national level

10.4 Concluding Remarks and Policy Implications

As it was analysed above, in the modern knowledge-based economy, innovation activities have a distinguished role as an important factor for economic growth, at micro- and macro-level, both at regional and national level.

More specifically, supporting actions could be located in the following points:

- Employment enhancement and promotion of labour market access, through active policies of equal access in the labour market and increase of women participation in workforce with parallel action towards social inclusion for special categories of women.
- Promotion of business entrepreneurship, as factor of employment creation and promotion of economic and social development.
- Promotion and improvement of systems of education, training, lifelong learning programmes and inclusion of women in the labour market. Promotion of women inclusion should be not only in quantitative terms (increase of indexes) but also in qualitative terms (reduction of wages gap, confrontation of obstacles and stereotypes in education and work) through employment policies.
- Enhancement of research and development activities and production and distribution of innovation, with exploitation of human capital in the sectors of research and technology.
- Enhancement of information society, which offers great possibilities in reducing economic and social inequalities and encouraging of learning and knowledge.

In conclusion, there is great need of entrepreneurship promotion, focused on knowledge creation and diffusion, contributing to economic growth and development.

Moreover, considering the high number of individuals participating in tertiary education, there should be a strong relationship between education and labour market. The core point could focus, initially, in more general economic environment and policy. Of fundamental importance is the implementation of macroeconomic policies that contribute in the creation of business and entrepreneurial environment and facilitate the access in the market of technology and in the production, diffusion and exploitation of knowledge. At the same time, long-term economic and development policies should be focused in the establishment of growth and innovations incentives, creation of new knowledge, as well as effectiveness of related expenditures and investments, through creation of information centres, technological centres, innovation financing programmes and transfer of technology.

References

Acs ZJ, Anselin L, Varga A (2002) Patents and innovation counts as measures of regional production of new knowledge. Res Policy 31:1069–1085

Almeida P, Kogut B (1999) Localization of knowledge, and the mobility of engineers in regional networks. Manage Sci 45:905–916

Barro RJ (1991) Economic growth in a cross section of countries. Qual J Econ 106:407–443

Barro RJ (1997) Determinants of economic growth: across-country empirical study. MIT Press, Cambridge, MA

Barro RJ (1999) Human capital and growth in cross-country regressions. Swedish Econ Policy Rev 6(2):237–277

Barro RJ, Sala-i-Martín X (1991) Convergence across states and regions. Brooking Pap Econ Act, Vol. 22(1), p. 107–182

Barro RJ, Sala-I-Martin X (1995) Economic growth. McGraw Hill, New York, NY

Breschi S, Lissoni F (2001) Knowledge spillovers and local innovation systems: a critical survey. Ind Corp Change 10:975–1005

European Communities (2008a) Human resources employed in science and technology occupations—issue number 77/2008. European Communities, Luxembourg

European Communities (2008b) Progress towards the Lisbon objectives in education and training-indicators and benchmarks. European Communities, Luxembourg

European Commission (2008) Benchmarking policy measures for gender equality in science. European Commission, Brussels

Eurostat (1999) Manual of fields of education and training. Eurostat, Brussels

Fagerberg J (1988) Technical change and economic theory. Pinter Publishers Ltd, London

Freeman C (1987) Technology policy and economic performance: lessons from Japan. Pinter Publishers, London

Furman JL, Porter ME, Stern S (2002) The determinants of national innovative capacity. Res Policy 31(6):899–933

Griliches Z (1980) R&D and the productivity slow down. Am Econ Rev 70:2

Hall R, Jones CI (1999) Why do some countries produce so much more output per worker than others. Qual J Econ 114(1):83–86

Lucas RE (1988) On the mechanics of economic development. J Monet Econ 22(1):3–42

Lundvall BÅ (ed) (1992) National systems of innovation: towards a theory of innovation and interactive learning. Pinter, London

Metcalfe JS (1995) The economics foundations of technology policy: equilibrium and evolution-
    ary perspectives. In: Stoneman P (ed) Handbook of the economics of innovation and techno-
    logical change. Blackwell, Oxford, pp 409–512
Nelson R (1993) National innovation systems. A comparative analysis. Oxford University Press,
    New York, NY
OECD (1993) Frascati manual, 5th edn. OECD, Paris
OECD (1997) International Standard Classification of Education (ISCED97). OECD, Paris
Porter M, Stern S (1999) The new challenge to America's prosperity: findings from the innovation
    index. Council on Competitiveness, Washington, DC
Romer PM (1986) Increasing returns and long-run growth. J Polit Econ 94:1002–1037
Romer PM (1990) Endogenous technological change. J Polit Econ 98:71–102
Schumpeter JA (1934) The theory of economic development. Harvard Economic Studies,
    Cambridge, MA

Chapter 11
Social Policy and Socio-economic Integration in Europe

Aikaterini Kokkinou, George M. Korres, Efstratios Papanis, and Panagiotis Giavrimis

11.1 EU Regional Policy Objectives

Nowadays, economies all over the world are described taking part in a race seeking the most appropriate and effective ways that could provide them with the strengths and opportunities necessary to obtain and sustain a competitive advantage over their rivals. Due to this competitiveness race, productivity enhancement is of great importance for the economic development in the face of uncertainties generated by international competition (Acs et al. 2002; Aghion and Howitt 1992; Coe and Helpman 1995; Cohen and Levinthal 1989). That is the reason why countries are struggling to maintain and also accelerate their growth rates.

One of the focal points of the European Union cohesion policy is "to promote economic and social progress along with a high level of employment, as well as to achieve balanced and sustainable development ... through the strengthening of economic and social cohesion..." The framework of these policy objectives could be illustrated in Fig. 11.1.

The chart presents development as described by the interlinkages among the economic and social policies aiming to achieve and sustain positive results towards development and

A. Kokkinou (✉)
Department of Economics, University of Glasgow,
Adam Smith Building, G128QQ Glasgow, Scotland, UK
e-mail: a.kokkinou.1@research.gla.ac.uk

G.M. Korres
Centre of Urban and Regional Development Studies (CURDS),
University of Newcastle, Newcastle NE1-7RU, UK

Department of Geography, University of the Aegean,
Mytilene, Greece
e-mail: George.Korres@ncl.ac.uk; gkorres@geo.aegean.gr

E. Papanis • P. Giavrimis
Department of Sociology, University of the Aegean,
Mytilene 81100, Lesbos, Greece
e-mail: papanis@papanis.gr; giavrimis@soc.aegean.gr

E.G. Carayannis and G.M. Korres (eds.), *European Socio-Economic Integration*,
Innovation, Technology, and Knowledge Management 27,
DOI 10.1007/978-1-4614-5254-6_11, © Springer Science+Business Media New York 2013

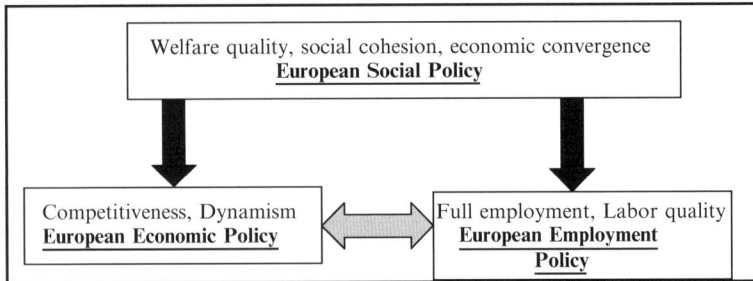

Fig. 11.1 Strategic policies, flows and socio-economic development

Table 11.1 Economic development priorities

Priority	Means and actions
• Give priority to innovation and entrepreneurship	• Creating closer links between research institutes and industry, developing conditions favourable to R&D, improving access to finance and know-how and encouraging new business ventures
• Ensure full employment	• By emphasising the need to open up employment opportunities, to increase productivity and quality at work and to promote lifelong learning
• Ensure an inclusive labour market	• Unemployment is reduced, and social and regional disparities in access to employment are narrowed
• "Connect" Europe	• Closer integration and by improving transport, telecommunications and energy networks
• Protect the environment	• Stimulating innovation and introducing new technologies, for example, in energy and transport

Source: Adaptation from the European Union 2004a

growth. The combination of the three policies targets to the enhancement and convergence as far as productivity, competitiveness and development process are concerned (Table 11.1).

Within this framework, at the Lisbon Summit (2000), European Union set itself the goal of becoming the most competitive and dynamic knowledge-based economy in the world, capable of sustainable economic growth and closer regional as well as social cohesion. At the Lisbon European Council, the EU defined a comprehensive strategy aiming at long-term economic growth, full employment, social cohesion and sustainable development in a knowledge-based society. Into doing, it has identified a number of priorities. The above-mentioned priorities could be incorporated within an action framework, in which development and innovation consist two of the core subjects both in economic and political analyses. In the EU, there is an increasing interest in the contribution of knowledge in the sustainable long-term economic growth. Development process is supported henceforth in the strategic planning, which constitutes a process of long-term objectives and policies based on scientific analysis, international experience, participative processes and the special

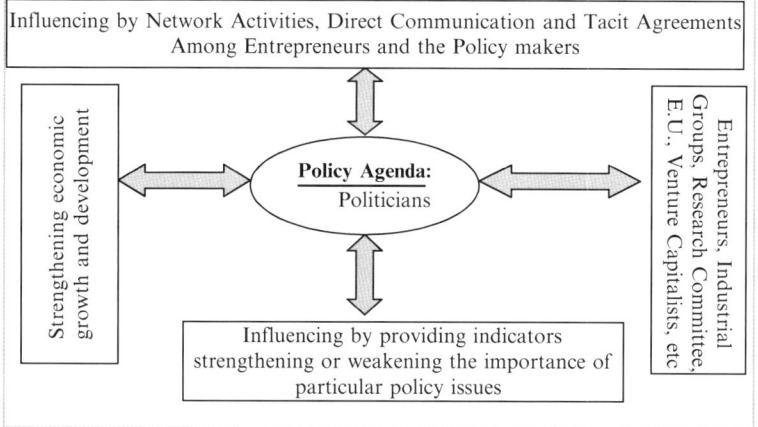

Fig. 11.2   Action framework of the EU regional policy

conditions that prevail in each economy (Fagerberg (1988a, b); Griliches 1980; Grossman and Helpman 1991, 1994; Jones and Manuelli 1990). In the frame of configuration of developmental priorities, the exploitation of comparative advantages should be mainly taken into account, combining the exploitation of developmental possibilities and the reduction of regional inequalities (Lucas 1988, 1990, 1993; Malecki 1991; Malecki and Varaia 1986; Martin and Ottaviano 1999; Solow 1957). The above-mentioned priorities could be incorporated within an action framework, described in Fig. 11.2.

Into this framework, the aid of growth and productivity constitutes main subject in the European economic and social policy. The EU is focused more not only in the problems of employment, unemployment, budget deficit, and public debt but also in the problems of national differences and achievement of convergence and cohesion on issues of technology and innovation (European Union 2004b).

The technological policy of European Union aims immediately in the aid of role of competitiveness of Europe, as well as in the aid of cohesion of community and in balancing of regional differences between the member states. The contribution of research and technology in the regional growth as well as in the cohesion of European community is considered particularly important, and the economic competitiveness of European Union depends, to a great degree, on research and innovation (Rebelo 1991; Romer 1986).

In this aspect, the SWOT analysis (Strengths, Weaknesses, Opportunities and Threats) is used in order to diagnose the main characteristics of internal and external environment of European Innovation process, as analysed in Table 11.2.

The treaty of Rome had not given extensive competences in the European Community for the exercise of effective and dynamic technological policy, based only on fragmentary and on certain decisions by the Council of Ministers. However, the European Council of Lisbon in March 2000 placed the objective that Europe becomes the most competitive and dynamic knowledge economy in the world, capable of a sustainable

Table 11.2 SWOT analysis

(a) Strategic goal and development pillar: competitiveness enhancement

Strengths	High-skilled human resources
Weaknesses	Large number of small and medium enterprises (SMEs), low productivity of public sector, imbalances in labour supply and demand
Opportunities	Modern administrative and law framework, technology and knowledge diffusion, clustering enhancement, education
Threats	Delays in market liberalisation, labour market rigidities

(b) Strategic goal and development pillar: productivity enhancement

Strengths	Convergence under Lisbon strategy goals, modern European technological policies
Weaknesses	Bureaucracy, credit market rigidities, weaknesses of SMEs to support knowledge creation and accumulation, low value added
Opportunities	EU enlargement with countries with developing economies, low labour cost, high productivity and value added
Threats	Dualism in entrepreneurial activity and development

(c) Strategic goal and development pillar: investment enhancement

Strengths	Mobility and diffusion of entrepreneurial and investment capital, credit market liberalisation
Weaknesses	Large number of SMEs, low degree of specialisation, limited productive network, low connection of education with market needs
Opportunities	EU enlargement with developing economies and markets, European development and innovation programmes
Threats	Trade and transport infrastructure weakness, limited business services

(d) Strategic goal and development pillar: R&D infrastructure enhancement

Strengths	Increase of the technology-based firms, increase in the technology and innovation expenditure, connection of knowledge creation with economic results and economic products
Weaknesses	Low level of R&D expenditure, low technological infrastructure
Opportunities	International trade trends, tax regimes, European development funds
Threats	Regional disparities in technological expenditure and knowledge diffusion, imperfect competition in energy market

(e) Strategic goal and development pillar: environment protection enhancement

Strengths	New energy resources, clean environment practices
Weaknesses	Insufficient administrative framework
Opportunities	Development funds, innovation policies
Threats	Global warming, polluting agents

(f) Strategic goal and development pillar: human resources and employment enhancement

Strengths	High-skilled human capital, education enhancement, high education expenditures, higher education participation, international research activities
Weaknesses	Small percentage of skilled R&D personnel, limited lifelong learning, low human capital mobility
Opportunities	Education infrastructure, regional education and innovation activities
Threats	Brain drain towards USA, labour market rigidities

economic growth, accompanied by employment enhancement and social cohesion in the next 10 years. In the European Council of Lisbon, the EU determined a strategy that aimed in the long-term economic growth, employment, social cohesion and sustainable

Table 11.3 Regional convergence policy, financing of the programming period 2007–2013

	Total (billion €)	Convergence (billion €)	Regional competitiveness and employment (billion €)	Territorial cooperation (million €)
Bulgaria	6.9	6.7		179
Estonia	3.45	3.4		52
Cyprus	0.64	0.213	0.399	28
Lithuania	6.9	6.78		109
Letonia	4.6	4.5		90
Poland	67.3	66.55		731
Spain	35.2	26.2	8.5	559
Sweden	1.9		1.6	265
Portugal	21.5	20.47	0.938	99
Ireland	0.901		0.751	151
France	14.3	3.2	10.2	872
Netherlands	1.9		1.6	247
Luxemburg	0.065		0.05	15
Denmark	0.613		0.51	103
Malta	0.855	0.84		15
Czech Rep.	26.7	25.9	0.419	389
Italy	28.8	21.6	6.3	846
Slovakia	11.6	10.9	0.449	227
United Kingdom	10.6	2.9	6.9	722
Belgium	2.3	0.638	1.4	194
Slovenia	4.2	4.1		104
Hungary	25.3	22.9	2	386
Germany	26.3	16.1	9.4	851
Romania	19.7	19.2		455
Austria	1.46	0.177	1.03	257
Finland	1.7	1.6		120
Greece	20.4	19.6	0.635	210

Source: Eurostat

development based on knowledge society, underlining a broad spectrum of priorities, as displayed in Table 11.3.

11.2   EU Economic and Social Development

Within this framework, development and innovation consist two of the core subjects both in economic and political analyses. In the EU, there is an increasing interest in the contribution of knowledge in the sustainable long-term economic growth, taking into consideration the need that competition forces technological innovations that increase productivity.

Developments in the theory of economic growth have renewed the interest for the role of innovation in the development process, underlining the interaction between the investment in innovative activities, technological change and economic growth. Technology and innovation play an important role in economic growth, and technology has become one of the most important factors in the models of growth (Geroski et al. 1993; Barro and Sala-i-Martin 1995, 1997; Freeman and Soete 1997; Sternberg 2000).[1] The role of innovation is multiple: as motive force, it directs the enterprises to ambitious and long-term objectives, and it leads to the renewal of methods of production, as well as industrial structures and the appearance of new sectors of economic activity.

An important contribution of the endogenous growth theory (Romer 1987, 1990) has been to identify the central role that knowledge and knowledge spillovers play in creating and sustaining growth. Pavitt and Soete (1982) examined growth as a result of the development of new knowledge in a country and the diffusion of knowledge between countries. According to Fagerberg (1987), there is a close relation between a country's economic and technological level of development. The rate of economic growth of a country is positively influenced by technological level of the country and its ability to increase it through imitation and exploitation of the possibilities offered by technological achievements elsewhere. Krugman (1991) identified the major role that knowledge spillovers play in generating increasing returns and higher growth. Geroski et al. (1993) asserted that innovations positively affect the development of enterprises and economies. Moreover, according to Silverberg and Verspagen (1995), technological change and diffusion constitute important factors in long-run macroeconomic growth and development. Moreover, Barro and Sala-i-Martin (1995, 1997) asserted that growth rate may increase in correlation with technological growth. Furthermore, Freeman and Soete (1997) focused on the importance of technology and innovation claiming that lack of innovation leads to economic death. At the same point of view, Sternberg (2000) said that in industrialised economies, the rate of long-term macroeconomic growth depends on the ability of constant development of innovative products and processes.

In the modern knowledge economy, growth depends extensively on the presence or the formation of a network and environment favourable to innovation, which is based on the endogenous development capabilities. Even though the firm-specific factors are important determinants of innovation activity, technological opportunities and favourable entrepreneurial environment have a positive effect on innovation activity, as well. Technological change, innovation and technology creation and diffusion are an important factor to economic progress. While innovation may lead to divergence between firms or nations, imitation through diffusion and dissemination tends to erode differences in technological competencies, and hence lead to convergence (Fagerberg and Verspagen 2002).

---

[1] Arrow (1962) was the first to systematically appreciate the importance of innovation and technological change in the capital formation and economic growth. He observed that increases in income per capita could not be explained by increases in capital to labour ratio and concluded that the power behind the increase in productivity is the acquisition of knowledge and learning experience created and acquired during the production procedure.

Table 11.4 Framework of productivity and competitiveness

Phases	Inputs/outputs	Policy directions
First phase	Inputs (productivity enhancement)	• Macroeconomic entrepreneurial and work environment • Economic and technological infrastructure • Education and skills • Entrepreneurship and business development • Innovativeness and creativity
Second phase	Intermediate output (productivity enhancement)	• Productivity • Production factors cost • Prices and wages
Third phase	Final output (competitiveness enhancement)	• Development • Employment • Living standards • Quality of life • Competitiveness

Social disparities cannot be ignored, since they affect the overall competitiveness of the EU economy. Covering costs of congestion or treating the social consequences of disparities implies a suboptimal allocation of resources, as well as a lower level of efficiency and economic competitiveness than could potentially be attained in the regions affected. To combat territorial disparities and achieve a more spatially balanced pattern of economic development requires some coordination of development policies if they are to be coherent and consistent with each other.[2] Under these circumstances, growth rate is one of the main points in the EU political and economic agenda.

European cohesion policy makes a major contribution to these objectives, especially in those regions where there is unused economic and employment potential which can be realised through targeted cohesion policy measures, so adding to the growth of the EU economy's a whole. From a policy perspective, for regional development to be sustained requires favourable conditions being established at the national level, in particular a macroeconomic environment conducive to growth, employment and stability and a tax and regulatory system which encourages business and job creation (Table 11.4).

At the regional level, two complimentary sets of conditions need to be satisfied.[3] The first is the existence of suitable endowment of both basic infrastructure (in the form of efficient transport, telecommunications and energy networks, good water supplies and environmental facilities and so on) and a labour force with appropriate levels of skills and training, strengthening of both physical and human capital, together with improvements in institutional support facilities and the administrative framework in place. The second set of conditions, which directly relates to the factors of regional competitiveness which are important in the knowledge-based econ-

---

[2] Third Cohesion Report, 2004.

[3] Third Cohesion Report, 2004.

omy, is that innovation should be accorded high priority, that information and communication technologies (ICT) should be widely accessible and used effectively and that development should be sustainable in environmental terms; a business culture which encourages entrepreneurship; and the existence of cooperation networks and clusters of particular activities.

11.3 Conclusions and Prospects

In the past decades, important changes in the pattern of economic growth in countries worldwide have taken place. Recent improvements in productivity and employment have been interpreted as a movement towards a knowledge-based economy. Currently, output and employment are expanding fast in high-technology industries such as computers and electronics, as well as in knowledge-based services such as financial and other business services. More resources are spent on the production and development of new technologies, in particular on information and communication technology. Computers and related equipment are now the fastest growing component of tangible investments. At the same time, major shifts are taking place in the labour market in particular the increased demand for skilled labour whereas demand for low-skilled workers is falling across the OECD.

As it has been asserted in this chapter, globalisation and worldwide competition has shifted the comparative advantage of economies towards the factor of knowledge and innovation, where productivity based on the endogenous development capabilities plays a rather important role, as far as growth and competitiveness enhancement are concerned. In order to promote innovation activities and technological opportunities, productivity enhancement seems to have a significance to the long-run performance of the economy as a whole.

European cohesion policy makes a major contribution to these objectives, especially in those regions where there is unused economic and employment potential which can be realised through targeted cohesion policy measures, so adding to the growth of the EU economy's a whole. From a policy perspective, for regional development to be sustained requires favourable conditions being established at the national level, in particular a macroeconomic environment conducive to growth, employment and stability and a tax and regulatory system which encourages business and job creation. At the regional level, two complimentary sets of conditions need to be satisfied. The first is the existence of suitable endowment of both basic infrastructure (in the form of efficient transport, telecommunications and energy networks, good water supplies and environmental facilities and so on) and a labour force with appropriate levels of skills and training, strengthening of both physical and human capital, together with improvements in institutional support facilities and the administrative framework in place. The second set of conditions, which directly relates to the factors of regional competitiveness which are important in the knowledge-based economy, is that innovation should be accorded high priority, that information and communication technologies (ICT) should be widely accessible and used effectively and that development should be sustainable in environmental terms; a business culture which encourages entrepreneurship; and the existence of cooperation networks and clusters of particular activities.

Under this perspective, growth policies should focus on creating favourable environment for the cooperation between firms and institutions that support the development and exploitation of knowledge and innovation. Furthermore, policies should promote the entrepreneurial relations between firms and institutions, fostering the development and dissemination of the expertise, the mobility of human and physical capital and the enhancement of the relationships between business and research entities. Specifically, they should encourage actions such as promoting innovation, technology transfer and interactions between firms and higher education and research institutes, networking and industrial cooperation and support for research and technology supply infrastructure.

Innovation and technology is an important source of regional competitiveness through facilitating cooperation between the various parties involved in both the public and private sectors. In particular, they can improve collective processes of learning and the creation, transfer and diffusion of knowledge and transfer, which are critical for innovation. Such cooperation and the networks that are formed help to translate knowledge into economic opportunity, while at the same time building the relationships between people and organisations which can act as a catalyst for innovation. Such actions should extend to all the policy areas relevant for economic, scientific and social development and should ideally establish a long-term policy horizon.

This, however, needs to happen not just in central parts where productivity and employment are highest and innovative capacity most developed but throughout the Union. Countries and regions need assistance in overcoming their structural deficiencies and in developing their comparative advantages. This means, among others, encouraging the development of knowledge-based economic activities and innovation and includes, among others, the capacity of a regional economy to generate, diffuse and utilise knowledge and so maintain an effective regional innovation system. In policy terms, the objective is to help to achieve a balanced sustainable development by reducing disparities, avoiding regional imbalances, making policies more coherent, improving integration and encouraging cooperation between states and regions.

References

Acs ZJ, Anselin L, Varga A (2002) Patents and innovation counts as measures of regional production of new knowledge. Res Policy 31:1069–1085

Aghion P, Howitt P (1992) A model of growth through creative destruction. Econometrica 60(2):323–351

Arrow KJ (1962) The economic implications of learning by doing. Rev Econ Stud 29(3):155–173

Barro RJ, Sala-i-Martin X (1995) Economic growth. McGraw-Hill, New York, NY

Barro R, Sala-i-Martin X (1997) Technological diffusion, convergence and growth. J Econ Growth 2:1–26

Coe D, Helpman E (1995) International R&D spillovers. Eur Econ Rev 39:859–887

Cohen WM, Levinthal DA (1989) Innovation and learning: the two faces of R&D. Econ J 99:569–596

European Union (2004a) Third report on economic and social cohesion

European Union (2004b) Treaty of the European Union, 1992

Fagerberg J (1987) A technology gap approach to why growth rates differ. Res Policy 16:87–99

Fagerberg J (1988a) International competitiveness. Econ J 98:355–374

Fagerberg J (1988b) Why growth rates differ. In: Dosi G, Freeman C, Nelson RR, Silverberg G, Soete L (eds) Technical change and economic theory. Pinter, London, pp 432–457

Fagerberg J, Verspagen B (2002) Technology-gaps, innovation-diffusion and transformation: an evolutionary interpretation. Res Policy 31:1291–1304

Freeman C, Soete L (1997) The economics of industrial innovation, 3rd edn. Pinter, London

Geroski P, Machin S, Van R, Geroski J (1993) Innovation and profitability. Rand J Econ 24(2):198–211

Griliches Z (1980) R&D and the productivity slow down. Am Econ Rev 70:2

Grossman GM, Helpman E (eds) (1991) Innovation and growth in the global economy. MIT Press, Cambridge, MA

Grossman G, Helpman E (1994) Foreign investment with endogenous protection. NBER Working Paper No. 4876

Jones LE, Manuelli R (1990) A convex model of equilibrium growth: theory and policy implications. J Polit Econ 98:1008–1038

Krugman P (1991) Geography and trade. MIT Press, Cambridge, MA

Lucas RE Jr (1988) On the mechanics of economic development. J Monet Econ 22:3–42

Lucas RE (1990) Why doesn't capital flow from rich to poor countries? Am Econ Rev 80(2):92–96

Lucas RE (1993) On the determinants of foreign direct investment: evidence from East and Southern Asia. World Dev 21(3):391–406

Malecki EJ (1991) Technology and economic development: the dynamics of local regional and national change. Longman Scientific and Technical, Harlow

Malecki EJ, Varaia P (1986) Innovation and changes in regional structure. In: Nijkamp P (ed) Handbook of regional and urban economics, vol I. Elsevier Science Publishers, North Holland

Martin P, Ottaviano GIP (1999) Growing locations: industry location in a model of endogenous growth. Eur Econ Rev 43:281–302

Pavitt K, Soete L (1982) International differences in economic growth and the international location of innovation. In: Giersch H (ed) Emerging technologies: the consequences for economic growth, structural change and employment. Mohr, Tübingen, pp 105–133

Rebelo S (1991) Long run policy analysis and long run growth. J Polit Econ 99:500–521

Romer PM (1986) Increasing returns and long-run growth. J Polit Econ 94:1002–1037

Romer P (1987) Growth based on increasing returns due to specialization. Am Econ Rev 77(2):56–62

Romer PM (1990) Endogenous technological change. J Polit Econ 98:71–102

Silverberg G, Verspagen B (1995) Long term cyclical variations of catching up and falling behind. An evolutionary model. J Evol Econ 5:209–227

Solow R (1957) Technical change and the aggregate production function. Rev Econ Stat 39:312–320

Sternberg R (2000) Innovations networks and regional development—evidence from the European regional innovation survey (ERIS): theoretical concepts. Methodological approach, empirical basis and introduction to the theme issue. Eur Plan Stud 8:389–407

Chapter 12
Conversations with Civil Servants: East European Public Administration Reform in Search of Socioeconomic Development

Roswitha M. King

12.1 Introduction

Countries of central and eastern Europe find themselves in a position of making important choices about design and organization of their civil service. In many cases public administration reform was delayed, because it was judged to be of lesser urgency than the creation of a market economy. It is, however, increasingly recognized that an effective and professional civil service is an important precondition for a sustainable market economy as well as for socioeconomic development in general, and the opinion is gaining ground that civil service and market economy should coevolve.

Redesigning public administration has been a challenging task. The high degree of politicization under the Soviet regime had placed civil service in an entirely subservient position relative to political forces. Given these initial conditions, the transformation of civil servants into creative policy makers and professional policy implementers does not come easily, and it is not yet completed. This means that the way in which civil service will organize itself remains an open issue in many countries. This suggests that if trends for the future are to be detected, they may be best obtained through conversations with civil servants and politicians.

The interviews, which form the basis of this study, were conducted in 2001/2002. At that time, the aspiring EU member candidate countries were in hyper-drive to satisfy the requirements for the EU entry—including requirements for public administration. After the countries became EU members in 2004, an apparent reform fatigue set in—understandable for anyone who witnessed the enormous energy output prior to the EU entry. Judging from subsequent research by other

R.M. King (✉)
Østfold University College, N-1757 Halden, Norway

Centre for European and Transition Studies, University of Latvia, Riga, Latvia
e-mail: roswitha.king@hiof.no; roswitha.king@gmail.com

E.G. Carayannis and G.M. Korres (eds.), *European Socio-Economic Integration*, Innovation, Technology, and Knowledge Management 27, DOI 10.1007/978-1-4614-5254-6_12, © Springer Science+Business Media New York 2013

authors, the key points of our findings remain valid[1] to this date[2]—not only for the target countries of our paper, but also (and prominently) for the 2007 EU entrants Romania[3] and Bulgaria, as well as the Balkan countries that formed after the break-up of Yugoslavia, and the Central and East European countries outside the EU. As a consequence little has changed in the public administration landscape since the time of the interviews—preserving the relevance of the findings to this date. In addition EU entry prompted an exodus of many of the countries' most experienced civil servants toward Brussels to fill commission and committee posts as representatives of their countries at the EU table—leaving behind a gap not so easily filled in some of the smaller countries.

In this contribution I am reporting on the findings collected during 56 conversations with civil servants and politicians in Estonia, Lithuania, Czech Republic and Poland. In particular I am reporting on the following important classes of relations:

---

[1] See for example:

For Russia: Nistotskaya (2009).

For Poland: Tatiana Majcherkiewicz (2006), in particular page 2 and 3.

For Estonia: Keris and Jako (2006), in particular page 7.

For Romania: Ioniţă (2006), in particular pages 6–8.

For the former Yugoslav states: Rabrenovic and Verheijen (2005), in particular pages 2 and 3.

For Post-communist Europe on the whole: Meyer-Sahling (2004).

For Hungary: Meyer-Sahling (2006).

[2] See UNDP/RCPAR (2011) midterm evaluation report of an ongoing development project for a demonstration that the concerns addressed in this paper have not gone away.

[3] Consider, for example the following quotes from Ioniţă (2006) on the state of public administration in Romania:

p. 6. "Generally speaking, the problems that were present during communist times did not disappear; some of them were not even openly addressed, leaving also political-administrative relations largely unreformed. Positions in the upper levels of the civil service continued to be distributed based on party loyalty, a practice known as 'political clientelism'."

p. 6-7 "A related weakness of post-communist political-administrative relations has been the exclusion of the civil servants from the policy development process. The potential role of civil servants as professional advisors on policy matters has been disregarded, as politicians have relied heavily on political advisers from outside the civil service when it came to policy development. Although the communist period has appropriate for the new circumstances, the true main cause for keeping the civil servants away from policy formulation was political clientelism. Administrators were granted positions of influence on the basis of their likely future use to a party or interest group powerful enough to maintain them, regardless of their managerial skills or other professional qualifications."

p. 7 "A general problem affecting the reform of political-administrative relations throughout the CEE is that of trust. Are new governments willing to work with the same civil service that they find in place once they gain power, or do they feel threatened by it, as they perceive it a Trojan horse of the former government that will systematically undermine their governance?"

12.1.1   Internal Relations

- Employment Relations/Internal Labor Market.
- Evaluation of performance and outcomes.
- Centralized versus decentralized decision making.
- Rules versus discretion.

12.1.2   External Relations

- Relations between the public sector and the private sector.
- Relations between civil servants and politicians.

One interesting finding is the relatively small variation in response profiles across the researched countries. This suggests that starting from common initial conditions of extremely centralized decision making, as well as political dominance over public administration, countries are pursuing similar goals along similar trajectories. A strong equalizing force has been the countries' intensive preparation for joining the European Union (EU)—which they did on May 1, 2004. By imposing a common set of qualification criteria, including criteria for public administration capacity, the European Commission has focused the reform efforts of East European countries on a common, narrowly defined set of goals and objectives. Seen in this light, the similarity in response profiles to the interview questions should not come as a surprise. As a consequence, this contribution is centered on features that are common to the research target countries, with only occasional remarks directed at their differences.

12.2   Interview Methodology

During 2001/2002 56 conversations took place, each conversation lasting between 1 and 2 h. The protocol called for a standardized structured interview (each interviewee was presented the same list of questions), and a subsequent unstructured conversation. Around 61% of interviewees agreed to a meeting upon first contact. The remaining 39% agreed to be interviewed after several iterations of follow-up mail and telephone calls. This mix of people with initial high, and initial low enthusiasm mitigates possible self-selection bias.

The final selection of interviewees was taken from four groupings of the ministerial hierarchy in the following proportions:

- Vice-Minister, Secretary of State, Secretary General, Deputy Secretary General, and Director General: 28%.
- Directors of Departments: 42%.
- Heads of Subdivisions of Departments: 15%.
- Officials, Analysts, and Advisors of Civil Service Offices and other supra-ministerial units directing and monitoring civil service reform: 15%.

In accordance with the orientation of the research project the majority of interviewees, 85% were civil servants.[4] The remaining 15% were political people. The definition of civil service positions and political positions follows the respective civil service legislation.

While incumbents of political posts are subject to replacement after a formation of a new government,[5] incumbents of civil service post are not to be replaced as a consequence of a change in government, in order to provide continuity of the state.[6] This is in accordance with the respective countries' civil service legislation. However, it was reported that in practice civil servants often are replaced after changes in government.

Politicians are included in the interviews because, although civil service legislation makes clear distinctions between political posts and civil service posts, in practice this line is blurred. Furthermore, a number of interesting developments are evolving at the dividing line between civil service and politicians. It also is of interest to learn how politicians perceive civil service, and compare it to civil servants' own perception.

The following institutions were visited:

- Ministry of Foreign Affairs.
- Ministry of Agriculture.
- Ministry of Labor and Social Affairs.
- Ministry of Environment.
- Ministry of Economy.
- Ministry of Culture.
- Office of Public Administration/Office of Civil Service/European Committee.

To preserve confidentiality of sources this report avoids any links between statements and the individuals issuing or supporting the statements. Tape recorders were not used, in accordance with the interview protocol. The interview protocol was distributed to interviewees well in advance.

---

[4] In this paper we define a civil servant to be a civilian career public sector employee working in a department of government. This category always includes such public employees at the level of national government, and may, depending on the country, also include those working at the regional or municipal level of government. By "civil service" we then mean a certain branch of governmental service, whose employees are hired and promoted on the basis of merit, and who are expected to deal with the public according to a code of ethics which includes impartially, transparency, accountability and professionalism. By comparison we define public administration more broadly as the design, implementation and management of government policy or branches of government policy. Public administration is meant to pursue the public good by bringing about and guarding social justice and by enhancing civil society.

[5] However, a number of instances were reported, where political people stayed on after a change in government.

[6] For example the "classical model" of public administration calls for a civil service, which is professional, independent of political parties, and responsible for the implementation of state policy. Whereas governments may change frequently, career civil servants remain, accumulate experience and skills, and guarantee continuity of the state.

The texts of respective countries' civil service laws served as an additional, and corroborating, source of information. With the exception of Czech Republic, the visited countries had, at the time of the interviews, enacted comprehensive civil service laws.

12.3   Interview Results

12.3.1   Internal Relations

A large part of public administration reform concerns relations, and modes of operation, inside individual institutions. It includes issues such as policies and practices of hiring and firing employees, career development opportunities, and other personnel policies. Furthermore, the degree of centralization or decentralization of decision-making, as well as rules versus discretion, belongs to this category. Employee motivation, incentives, and quality control are further important concerns of internal relations. This is by no means an exhaustive list of internal relations themes; rather, it is determined by the scope of this project.

12.3.1.1   Employment Relations/Internal Labor Market

Definitions of clear human resource strategies are in an early development stage. Recruiting is, on average, conducted relatively passively, and often lacks proactive initiatives to attract talented candidates.

There is a lack of mechanisms for allocating staff to areas with the greatest needs. This leads to observed mismatches. Some departments are overstaffed, while some are understaffed. All-too-often it is the understaffed departments that are charged with the most urgent tasks.

While civil service legislation provides the necessary legal framework for civil service reform, it is the organization, strategy, quality of personnel, and leadership that drive the reform. Therefore, recruiting, retaining, and developing good staff is of great importance.

Finding Qualified Staff

The majority of interviewees reported a shortage of qualified applicants for civil service positions. 69% of all interviewees[7] had repeatedly experienced serious difficulties in finding qualified staff. Vacant positions were reported to persist over

---

[7] When the term "x% of interviewees" is used, it means that all interviewees responded, i.e., No. of interviewees = No. of respondents = 56.

significant periods of time. There was little variation between countries. There was, however, substantial variation between different types of ministries across the target countries. Of the 31% of interviewees, who reported no problems in recruiting staff, representatives of the Ministry of Foreign Affairs formed the majority. Applicants are attracted to this ministry through a combination of factors, such as opportunity of foreign assignments, the status that this ministry enjoys, and the successful cultivation of a certain esprit de corps.

Representatives of the Ministry of Culture accounted for the second group of respondents that reported to have no problems in recruiting staff. Here the explanation lies in the severe scarcity of private sector employment opportunities for arts graduates, which drives large numbers of applicants toward every job opening at the Ministry of Culture.

Overall one of the most serious difficulties was reported to be the recruiting of lawyers, stemming from the salary differential between private and public sector lawyer positions. In the Czech Republic this shortage, reportedly, at times has been so severe that the Ministry of Foreign Affairs "rents out" its lawyers to other ministries.

Personnel Departments

Personnel departments were, on average, reported to be weak, inadequately staffed, under-utilized, and the object of complaints. This is unfortunate, given the difficulty in recruiting qualified staff.

Particularly in Poland and Lithuania the personnel departments were reported to do only what is required by law. This typically means that they are not vigorously competing for talent in the job market. Furthermore, once employees are hired, they typically receive little assistance from the personnel department in matters of career development.

If personnel departments are to engage in setting incentives to attract and retain capable personnel, they need to know what motivates people to enter public administration, and what motivates them to stay

What Motivates People to Enter the Public Administration Profession?

70% of interviewees reported the *opportunity* for educational programs, and interesting contacts to be the main motivator for people to enter into public administration. This also points to a potential problem: high turnover rate at entry level positions. Many newcomers consider an entry level public administration position to be a good jumping board for subsequent application to private sector positions, which, on average, offer higher salaries.

14% of interviewees thought that the *challenge* of working on interesting and important matters was the key attractor for people to enter the profession. Many respondents reported a noticeable shift over the past decade. The challenge of "doing something for one's country" was an important motivator in the early years after political independence of the target countries. In the meantime more pragmatic personal reasons motivate job applicants.

9% of respondents listed the prospect of involvement in *policy design* as the principal attractor of their employees—emphasizing the creative element.

3% listed the *status* that a public administration position carries as the biggest attractor, and 3% listed *job security* as the principal motivator.

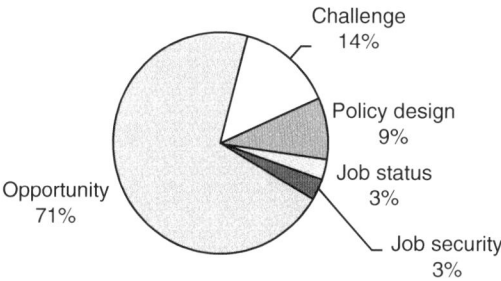

Reasons for Joining Civil Service

What Motivates People to Stay in the Public Administration Profession?

Long-term career prospect was listed as the main motivator by 80% of respondents. This points to an important, but currently unfulfilled role to be played by personnel departments. Designing alternative career paths and providing career counseling would go a long way to meet career expectations of employees, while at the same time increasing stability and administrative capacity of the public institution, and reducing the reported high personnel turnover.

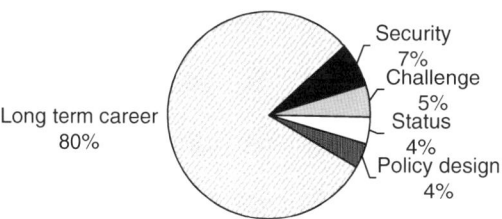

Reasons to stay in Civil Service

7% of respondents reported that *job security* was the main motivator, 5% named *challenge*, 4% *status* and 4% *policy design* as principal factors to motivate people to stay in public administration.

12.3.1.2 Evaluation of Performance and Outcomes

Evaluation mechanisms are in their infancy, both with regard to evaluation of outcomes and evaluation of individual employee performance.

On the employee evaluation side a comprehensive performance management system is still lacking in most cases. In conjunction with weak accountability systems this means that quality of results and performance are only weakly linked with remuneration. As a consequence motivation systems are non-transparent and highly discretionary. Furthermore, a dependence between evaluation, remuneration and budget, in most cases, is completely lacking.

Among the target countries of this research Estonia appears to have gone the furthest in matters of evaluation of performance and outcomes. A set of evaluation criteria and indicators have been developed. But statistics are, often, collected without being processed. So they have little effect on subsequent decisions.

To get an impression of the weights that are placed on different classes of indicators, interviewees were asked to rank the following criteria according to their importance:

– On-time performance.
– True-to-plan implementation (rather than "watered down").
– Cost-effectiveness
– Widely accepted (policy approval)
– Percent of target group reached.

80% of interviewees responded to this question and gave a ranking. Of this group of respondents 53% stated that the most important criterion was that a policy was widely accepted. 25% stated that an implementation that was true-to-plan was the most important thing. 13% considered that reaching the largest possible number of people in the relevant target group was number one concern, and 9% listed cost effectiveness as the highest priority. None of the respondents listed "on-time" as the highest priority.

Evaluation Criteria for Judging Outcomes

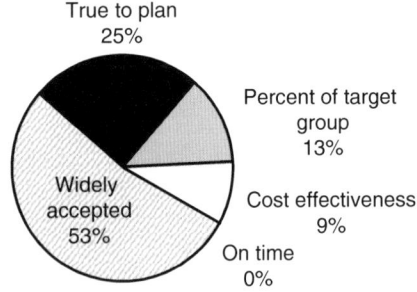

12.3.2 Centralization Versus Decentralization of Decision-Making

Given the initial condition of extreme centralization of public administration under the Soviet System, the post-soviet trend clearly has been toward decentralization.

Interviewees were asked whether they considered decision-making at their institution to be centralized or decentralized. 91% of interviewees responded to this question. Of this group of respondents 20% thought that decision-making was centralized, while 80% described it as decentralized.

The high response rate describing the conditions as "decentralized" has to be kept in perspective. It is to be expected that many respondents use the extreme centralization of administrative relations of the past as a reference point. Against such an extreme point of reference the tendency to overstate the current situation as "decentralized" should not be ignored.

When asked, whether decision-making was too centralized, too decentralized, or just right, responses were as follows: 19% of respondents considered it to be too centralized, 2% considered it to be too decentralized, while the majority, 79%, considered it to be just right. (Reference group for this question: 52 respondents; 93% of interviewees). Several comments are in order: Among the group, who considered the degree of decentralization "just right" was a sub-group, which qualified the response in an interesting way. They considered the situation "just right for the moment, given the capacity limitations of lower-tier staff." According to their description, delegation of decision authority to lower levels had come to a halt, necessitated by the lack of staff with the requisite qualifications. But in the absence of this binding constraint, further decentralization was considered desirable. Particularly in Poland and Lithuania a number of senior officials, as well as department heads, reported aggravation about work overload that should (but at the moment could not) be delegated to lower level staff.

12.3.3 Rules Versus Discretion

It is difficult to disagree with the view that there should be rules as well as room for discretion. There is, however, perennial disagreement on the "right" proportions of rules versus discretion.

While rules, at the minimum, set the legal framework for the policy environment, discretion is credited with providing necessary variation for different human and social situations, as well as providing creative space.

There was wide agreement, expressed by 91% of respondents, that there is sufficient room for creativity. (Reference group: 55 respondents; 98% of interviewees). Furthermore, 97% of interviewees reported that they did not feel too restricted by rules, leaving only 3%, who had experienced rules to be too restrictive.

It is, however, interesting to note that 41% of interviewees expressed a desire for more rules, while 59% did not want more rules. Among the reasons behind a desire for more rules are the perception of too much discretion given to people with insufficient competence and experience. In the eyes of respondents there is a direct link between too much discretion given to inexperienced officials and erratic policies, aborted policies and other indicators of an immature policy-making and implementing process. Another reported reason for wanting more rules is the perceived inefficiency of having to "re-invent the wheel" again and again, in matters that should be treated as routine. Furthermore, inconsistency in the treatment of similar cases was identified as a major reason for customer dissatisfaction with public sector services, leading to alienation of citizen from the public sector in general.

By "more rules" respondents typically meant a more systematic way of formulating policy goals and the means to achieve them, and more cooperation on identifying best practices. Tools and processes for systematic knowledge sharing and transfer of best practices are typically absent or in the early stage of development. This is a serious obstacle to organizational learning.

12.3.4 External Relations

12.3.4.1 Public Sector–Private Sector Relations

What tasks in a society should be performed by the public sector, and what tasks by the private sector? Different countries at different times have attempted to answer this question based on ideology, on practicality, according to egalitarian principles or on grounds of efficiency, to name only a few of the criteria.

In Central and Eastern Europe, starting from an initial condition of unchallenged state ownership and control of virtually all societal, economic and political processes, the trend has been decidedly toward reducing the influence of the state, and increasing the role of the private sector. But where should this process stop? Which tasks should remain in the hands of the public sector? And how much communication and feedback should there be between policy makers and those who are affected by the policy?

Outsourcing

Outsourcing, in our context, is a practice of delegating previously publicly provided services to the private sector, with the overall responsibility and oversight remaining with the public agency. Outsourcing has been embraced by the public sector on grounds of efficiency gains.

84% of interviewees reported that their institution has been engaged in outsourcing, while 16% reported not knowing of any outsourcing activities at their institution. In particular representatives of the Ministry of Social Affairs and the Ministry of Culture reported successful outsourcing experiences, with what can be called essential services. In many instances this represents handing over service provision and management to the local level, in collaboration with non-governmental organizations (NGOs).

As to be expected, representatives of the Ministry of Foreign Affairs, which are principally engaged in "sovereign transactions," reported very limited incidence of outsourcing, or none at all. If outsourcing occurs it is reportedly limited to public relations campaigns, web-site construction and management, as well as educational services.

When asked whether *at their institution* there was too much outsourcing going on, 21% of interviewees reported "yes," and 79% reported "no." When asked whether their institution should do more outsourcing, relative to the current level, 16% answered in the affirmative, while 84% responded with "no." So the majority of respondents expressed satisfaction with the level of outsourcing occurring at their institution.

A similar pattern of responses is observed, when interviewees were asked, whether in general, *in their country*, more tasks should be transferred from the public sector to the private sector. 14% of respondents voiced the opinion that more tasks should be shifted to the private sector, while 75% said there should be no more transfers to the private sector, and 11% were unsure.

The interesting thing is what lies behind the differentiated responses.

Outsourcing and Efficiency?

The most frequently heard argument in favor of transferring tasks to the private sector is efficiency. Some schools of thought in public administration, in particular "New Public Management," consider private management to be categorically superior to public management. The main reason for their judgment is the perceived higher efficiency of private management relative to public management. The focus of these schools of thought on the issue of efficiency is so strong that it sometimes has led to mistaking efficiency for a goal, rather than recognizing it as an attribute of the means for reaching a goal.

When asked whether there are efficiency gains from outsourcing to the private sector only 27% of interviewees responded with "yes," while a surprising 73% responded with "no." After probing for the reasons behind the answers the following picture emerges.

The majority of the 73%, who responded that there were no efficiency gains from outsourcing, reported that they had come to this opinion relatively recently, and a few years earlier would have voiced a more favorable opinion about efficiency and outsourcing. Reportedly, there were initial efficiency gains through outsourcing in the sense of providing services at lower cost. But these gains were short-lived. Soon the contracted private service providers ran into budget problems. These budget problems were dealt with by either raising the prices they charged for the services, or by eliminating a number of services, and often both.

This means that in the end fewer services were available, many of them at higher prices (relative to the imputed prices of the initially publicly provided services). Some respondents went so far as to voice a sense of "betrayal." A high incidence of private companies invoking escape clauses, built into their outsourcing contract, is observed—an event, which had appeared very remote, at the time of the signing of the contract.

Of the 27% who reported efficiency gains from passing on services to the private sector, there were representatives from the Ministry of Social Affairs and Ministry of Culture, who, as mentioned above, had successful outsourcing experiences to private service providers and NGOs. This group also included those, whose institutions had outsourced only non-essential services, such as website construction, or preparation of public relations brochures, i.e., tasks, for which there was no dedicated in-house expertise. Among the 27% reporting efficiency gains was also a group, which operated with a peculiar definition of efficiency, which can be summarized as: "Efficient is that which reduces the public institution's budget." This is not the economists' definition of efficiency. This last point deserves some attention, as there seems to be considerable confusion about the meaning of efficiency in the public administration environment.

The following serves as our working definition of economic *efficiency*:
We say that practice A is more efficient than practice B if

1. Practice A provides the same output (qualitative and quantitative) of services as practice B, but practice A uses less (or less costly) inputs than practice B or
2. Practice A provides more output (qualitative and/or quantitative) of services as practice B, while using the same amount of (or value of) inputs.

Some of the respondents looked only at the input side, saying that private services are more efficient because they use less inputs. But they forgot to look at the simultaneous reduction in output (services). At the other extreme were some respondents, who looked only at the outputs, claiming to observe a reduction in services (outputs) after outsourcing, while neglecting to look at the input side, which had also been reduced.

The assessment of efficiency of transferring tasks to the private sector is complicated by a number of factors. Outsourcing may reduce public sector budgets. But if quantity and/or quality of services are also reduced—how do we evaluate that? Reduction of the public sector budget by itself certainly is not a proof of efficiency.

This does not mean that it is bad to evaluate the need for given services. As societies change, so changes the mix of desired service. Identifying obsolete and redundant services, as well as discovering new needs, should be an ongoing process in any system of public administration. So, reduction in services, by itself, also is difficult to judge.

The question is whether or not, or to what extent the market is the best forum to decide which needs are important and which are not. Important to whom? Different societies have passed judgment on this in different ways.

Private Sector Participation in the Public Policy Process

Central and east European countries reportedly suffer from a lack of constructive dialog between the public sector and the citizenry. Or, put in a different way, there is little communication between policy makers and those who are affected by the policy, *before* a policy is implemented. 72% of interviewees listed the lack of dialog as a serious concern.[8]

There are exceptions, such as some of the Ministries of Agriculture, which may reportedly have gone too far in the opposite direction, and may run the risk of being "captured" by special interests. Of course the ministry of agriculture, in many countries, is cast into the dual role of cheerleader for the industry, while at the same time performing the role of policeman through its various regulatory programs.

But in general, there is a reported need for public hearings and comment periods, during which segments of the population that will be affected by a proposed policy have the opportunity to voice their concerns. In the absence of an early comment period, the population's outlet for opinion is typically in the form of complaints after the policy is in force. Improvement in the quality of policies, and a reduction in implementation problems are expected from such a participatory approach. In particular, timely communication is expected to reduce the above mentioned incidences of abrupt policy reversals, and aborted policies, thereby promising to lift the image of public administration professionalism. Both sides are bound to win.

12.3.4.2   Relations Between Civil Servants and Politicians

The reform of public administration is facing formidable obstacles. Owing to a history of political control over civil service people had grown accustomed to seeing civil service in an ancillary position relative to political power (Verheijen and Coombes 1998, pp. 207–219, Hesse 1993, pp. 65–74). This former "feudal" culture of patronage-based relations conditioned people to accept loyalty to the patron, rather than professionalism, as the most important attribute of a successful civil servant. Turning around this role perception, and transforming civil servants into creative policy designers, who take responsibility for their own decisions, is a task that is by no means completed.

The urgency of de-politicizing civil service is not only perceived by observers and analysts, but, as the interviews show, also by civil servants themselves, as well as by the politicians participating in this research project. 100% of interviewees

---

[8] See for example (UNDP/BRC) (2007) for an assessment of the sorry state of ex-ante policy impact assessment in South-Eastern Europe.

expressed an opinion on this issue. The opinion was unanimous: Civil Service career positions should be kept out of the direct influence of politicians. Furthermore, 100% of interviewees reported that civil service and politics were at present NOT kept sufficiently separate in their country. (See Nistotskaya 2009 for more on this issue for the case of Russia).

One of the consequences of high politicization of civil service is an observed high turnover rate in senior civil service positions, stemming from frequent changes in the composition of government. This high turnover is on collision course with the desire for greater administrative stability and stronger administrative capacity. Interviewees expressed strong opinions in these matters.

98% of interviewees considered it very important to shield civil service from direct political interference, 95% of interviewees considered it very important to establish a culture of civil service professionalism, and 91% considered it very important to achieve administrative stability.

High Turnover of Civil Servants

94% of interviewees reported to have observed civil servants replaced after formation of a new government. The allegedly politically motivated replacements typically occur in the highest civil service positions. However, there is significant variation in the affected levels of the ministerial hierarchy. Occasionally, politically motivated replacements were reported to include the level of department directors.[9] But, regardless of the point of incidence within the administrative hierarchy, the practice of politically motivated replacements of senior officials increases personnel turnover. It also tends to drain expertise from the system, as, frequently, more experienced people are replaced by less experienced people. Whether politically motivated or not, high turnover in civil service presents a serious obstacle to the building of administrative capacity.

One might think that politicians like to see civil service under the control of political power. However, the politicians interviewed for this research expressed a preference for a civil service that is independent of direct political interference.[10] They were found to value a stable and professional civil service, because without it policy implementation does not function well.

There is also a cynical point of view: After politicians of the governing party or coalition have filled key civil service positions with people loyal to their cause, of course they are for stability and continuity of civil service, so that their people stay in place, even if the opposition wins the next elections.

---

[9] For example, this was reported to have happened at the Estonian Ministry of Agriculture.

[10] We recall that 100% of interviewees expressed the view that civil service and politics should be kept separate. This includes politicians, which constituted 15% of all interviewees.

Adverse Consequences of Politicization

Politicization of civil service is known to have a number of adverse consequences. First of all it hampers the building of high administrative capacity. Given the frequent changes in government, civil servants, who only last as long as the current government, simply do not stay in their jobs long enough to accumulate experience. 93% of respondents reported the adverse effect of high turnover on administrative capacity and professionalism as a very serious situation.

High turnover in civil service positions destroys continuity of the policy-making and policy-implementing process. 88% of respondents reported incidences of aborted policies or abrupt policy reversals. Thereof 69% saw a direct link to personnel changes in key civil service positions.

The negative impact of policy discontinuities is twofold. First there is the encumbered policy process itself, and the danger of serious mistakes. Second the perception of the public deserves attention. If policy makers are perceived to be erratic, unpredictable and willful, this will promote neither dialog nor trust. Needless to say, an erratic policy behavior is a serious obstacle to the creation of a professional administrative culture.

Civil Service Legislation

At the time of the interviews, civil service laws were in place (among the target countries of this research) in Poland, Lithuania and Estonia, while in the Czech Republic comprehensive civil service legislation was still awaiting parliamentary approval. These laws typically explain the rights and duties of civil servants. They also draw the line between civil service positions and political positions, and usually state that the incumbents of civil service positions should not be replaced due to political reasons.

It is not surprising to see a marked difference between what the civil service laws prescribe, and what is practiced—the typical implementation problem.

More disturbingly, civil service laws have taken on a "proprietary" character. A particular civil service law is "our" civil service law, or "their" civil service law, depending on whether we take the perspective of the current government or its political opposition. Particularly in Poland and Lithuania, it was reported that an incoming government will want to quickly rid itself of "their" law, and put in its place the "own" law. In this way civil service laws are, reportedly, used as political tools, to facilitate the placement of party-loyal staff into key positions, whenever there is a new edition of civil service law.

This also points to immature political and administrative processes, in particular, a serious weakness in current coalition politics. The idea that a parliamentary majority should share governance with the parliamentary minority is ill understood. Consequently, the opinions of the opposition parties, with regard to appointments to key civil service positions, are typically ignored. Opposition parties, resentfully, wait until it is their turn at the government table. Then it is their turn to ignore the opinions of the parliamentary minority.

12.4 Policy Implications

The interviews that form the basis for this research clearly reflect a number of high priority policy goals, as well as preferences and criteria for the means by which the goals are to be pursued.

First and foremost the need for de-politicization of civil service can hardly be overemphasized. The political dominance over civil service, together with significant remnants of the "feudal" culture of administrative relations, often referred to as the "patronage system," form the principal retarding element to the building of high administrative capacity. The fallout of politicization comes partly in the form of high turnover of senior civil servants. This prevents senior civil servants from accumulating the necessary experience to be effective. Moreover, it sets incentives to reward the wrong people for the wrong reasons.

Interview results clearly reflect an understanding of this issue among civil servants. As a matter of fact there was consensus about the high priority of creating a professional civil service, independent from political control.

The key policy question is: What mechanism will de-politicize civil service and lead to a professional civil service corps?

Two competing schools of thought are vying for attention. *New Public Management*[11] *(NPM)* emphasizes "market-like" structures, including remuneration schemes that consist of a base salary plus substantial bonuses and commissions, as well as vigorous outsourcing to the private sector. The philosophy is that self-interest is a powerful motivator. The energies released by self-interested behavior are to be harnesses by reward schemes, and bundled into market-like competitive structures with high output and high efficiency.

However, applications of this model, have shown a tendency to re-establish political control over civil service—exactly the opposite of what 100% of interviewees of this study considered desirable for their country.[12] So, in the important aspect of relations between civil servants and politicians, the NPM approach appears to be unsuitable, given the current needs.

Given that 98% of interviewees considered the shielding of civil service from direct political interference to be very important, 95% considered it very important to establish a culture of civil service professionalism, and 91% of interviewees considered it very important to achieve high administrative capacity; this points to the *classical model*[13] of public administration as a suitable candidate. The so-called classical model of public administration displays the features of

---

[11] Examples of public administration systems that adhere to this school of thought are England, New Zealand, and Australia.

[12] We recall that 100% of Interviewees expressed the opinion that civil service and politics should be separate, while at the same time they reported that currently civil service and politics are not sufficiently separate.

[13] Examples are France and Germany.

self-management of public administration, clear separation between civil service and politics with strict rules of non-interference by politicians in civil service matters, high job security for civil servants, and a career system that relies on merit and seniority.

The perceived inefficiencies of the classical system may be a small price to pay, if in return we get a professional civil service corps that understands whom it is to serve.

These considerations, together with the interview results reported in the preceding chapters, lead to the following principal policy implications.

- Given the current state of civil service and its relation to politics, the market-like incentive structures associated with *New Public Management* appear to be ill advised.
- Sequencing is important: Only after the steps of de-politicization have been completed, and after the vicious circle of patron-client relations has been broken, and a sufficient level of transparency and accountability have been reached, does it make sense to consider pay for performance, bonuses, and other incentive structures.
- Prematurely implemented market-like structures are a retarding element for public administration reform and are to be avoided. They tend to reward the wrong people for the wrong reasons. More destructively, they tend to preserve and nurture old structures of patron-client thinking. This puts them on direct collision course with the goals of public administration reform.
- The *classical model* of public administration presents itself as a suitable system, given the current needs. Market-like incentive schemes may be introduced in the future, after a stable and professional civil service has been established.

Furthermore, interview results point to the following subsidiary, and more specific, policy implications:

- Personnel departments need to be strengthened. They must learn to aggressively compete for talent in the labor market. At the same time personnel departments should provide professional career counseling in order to retain and nurture good employees. The idea of alternative career paths needs to be developed.
- Performance evaluation and tracking systems, as well as general accountability systems need to be designed and implemented. This, first, requires an understanding of what appropriate criteria for good performance are. There should be criteria for individual performance, as well as group performance.
- After accountability systems and performance criteria are in place, motivation systems linking promotion and remuneration to performance should be designed.
- Outsourcing to the private sector should be carefully considered.
- Participation of the public in the policy-making process should be encouraged. In particular, it should become more common practice to conduct hearings before implementation of a policy. This allows for comments particularly by segments of the population that will be most affected by the policy.

12.5   Conclusion

Public administration reform in the countries of Central and Eastern Europe has had successes as well as failures. On the whole, the target countries of this research are pursuing similar goals along similar trajectories. This seeming convergence originates from the necessary compliance with EU criteria that was required as a precondition to their 2004 entry into the European Union. By imposing a common set of qualification criteria, including criteria for public administration capacity, the European Commission focused the reform efforts of East European countries on a common set of goals and objectives.

Of the three types of relations examined in this report, (public–private sector relations, civil service and politics, and employment relations) the relation between civil service and politics emerges as the most crucial and consequential. The other two relations are seriously affected by it. This is given recognition by the fact that 100% of respondents perceived this relation to be flawed, in that politicians wield too much direct influence over civil servants. The related high turnover rate in civil service retards the raising of the level of administrative capacity, as well as the stabilization of civil service. As 95% of interviewees considered the establishment of a culture of civil service professionalism to be very important, and 91% considered administrative stability to be very important, de-politicization of civil service appears to hold a central position in the reform process, as it is a pre-condition for other reform processes to be effective.

The sequencing of reform steps appears to be crucial. Market-like incentive schemes for civil servants are ill advised, before civil service has been sufficiently de-politicized, and before a credible accountability, and performance evaluation system is in place. So, reducing political influence on civil service will also benefit internal employment relations.

Judging from the interview responses, and considering the features of some of the dominant public administration paradigms, a public administration system that preserves the major features of the "classical model of public administration" appears advisable.

A competing paradigm, known as "New Public Management" (NPM), which has attracted attention through its emphasis on efficiency and "market-like" competitive structures, has also shown a tendency to re-introduce political control over civil service, which is exactly the opposite of what 100% of interviewees of this study considered desirable for their countries.

There is much unfinished business in public administration reform. The task of *simultaneously* building markets, political institutions, and civil service structures has put enormous pressure on resources of all kinds.

An encouraging sign is the high awareness among civil servants of the major problem areas. A particularly positive signal is the pragmatism that characterizes many reform efforts in Eastern Europe. In a rather eclectic way, many designers of public administration systems are focusing on "what works," given the country's priorities and goals. They are refreshingly disinclined to attach themselves to particular ideologies. Unfortunately, sometimes they had to learn this "the hard way," after detrimental results owing to misguided trust in western advisors, who arrived as salesmen of their own favored ideologies.

References

Hesse JJ (ed) (1993) Administrative transformation in central and eastern Europe. Blackwell, Oxford
Ioniță A-L (2006) The EU's impact on reform in Romania: the case of the civil service. Paper presented at the 14th NISPAceel conference public administration and public policy in emerging Europe and Eurasia: for professionalism, impartiality and transparency, Ljubljana, Slovenia, 11–13 May 2006
Keris M, Jako S (2006) The role patterns of ministers' personal advisors in politico-administrative dichotomy. Comparative case study of two Estonian ministries. Paper presented at the 14th NISPAcee annual conference, public administration and public policy in emerging Europe and Eurasia: for professionalism, impartiality and transparency, Ljubljana, Slovenia, 11–13 May 2006
Majcherkiewicz T (2006) Between the pool of spoils and shallow professionalism—the role and cadres of the political cabinets of ministers and prime ministers of Poland in the period 1997–2006. Paper presented at the 14th NISPAcee annual conference, public administration and public policy in emerging Europe and Eurasia: for professionalism, impartiality and transparency, Ljubljana, Slovenia, 11–13 May 2006
Meyer-Sahling J-H (2004) Civil service reform in post-communist Europe: the bumpy road to depoliticisation. West Eur Polit 27(1):71–103
Meyer-Sahling J-H (2006) The institutionalization of political discretion in post-communist civil service systems: the case of Hungary. Public Adm 84(3):693–716
Nistotskaya M (2009) Organizational design of welfare-enhancing public bureaucracy: a comparative analysis of Russia's regions. PhD Dissertation, Central European University, Department of Political Science, Budapest
Rabrenovic A, Verheijen T (2005) Politicians and top civil servants in former Yugoslav states: back to discarded traditions? Paper presented at the 14th NISPAcee annual conference, democratic governance for the 21st century: challenges and responses in CEE countries, Moscow, Russia, 19–21 May 2005
(UNDP/BRC) (2007) United Nations Development Programme's Bratislava Regional Centre. Mapping of ex-ante Policy Impact Assessment Experiences and Tools in Europe: Based on a Literature Survey and Case Studies from Southeast Europe. http://europeandcis.undp.org/home/show/4D531880-F203-1EE9-B16CA90EB5DEFCD3
UNDP/RCPAR (2011) United Nations Development Project/Regional Centre for Public Administration Reform. Mid-Term Review and Evaluation Report. http://www.rcpar.org/mediaupload/publications/2011/20110215_RCPAR_MidTerm_REVIEW__EVALUATION_REPORT_FINAL.pdf
Verheijen T, Coombes D (eds) (1998) Innovations in public management. Edward Elgar, Cheltenham

Chapter 13
A New Methodological Approach of Job Requirement Assessment

George M. Korres, Constantinos Tsamadias, Panagiotis Liargovas, George O. Tsobanoglou, and Aikaterini Kokkinou

13.1 Introduction

Human capital accumulation, education and training skills, is one of the main determinants of individuals' earning capacity and employment prospects and therefore plays an important role in determining the level and distribution of income in

G.M. Korres (✉)
Centre of Urban and Regional Development Studies (CURDS),
University of Newcastle, Newcastle, UK

Department of Geography, University of Aegean,
Mytilene, Greece
e-mail: George.Korres@ncl.ac.uk; gkorres@hol.gr; gkorres@geo.aegean.gr

C. Tsamadias
Harokopio University, Athens, Greece
e-mail: ctsamad@hua.gr

P. Liargovas
Department of Economics, School of Economics and Management,
University of Peloponnese, End Karaiskaki Street,
22100 Tripolis, Greece
e-mail: liargova@uop.gr

G.O. Tsobanoglou
Centre of Urban and Regional Development Studies (CURDS),
University of Newcastle, Newcastle, UK

Department of Sociology, University of the Aegean,
Mitilene 81100, Lesvos, Greece
e-mail: George.Tsobanoglou@ncl.ac.uk; g.tsobanoglou@soc.aegean.gr

A. Kokkinou
Department of Economics, University of Glasgow,
Adam Smith Building, G12 8QQ Glasgow, Scotland, UK
e-mail: a.kokkinou.1@research.glasgow.ac.uk

E.G. Carayannis and G.M. Korres (eds.), *European Socio-Economic Integration*,
Innovation, Technology, and Knowledge Management 27,
DOI 10.1007/978-1-4614-5254-6_13, © Springer Science+Business Media New York 2013

society. Many countries seek to ensure that all young people enter working life with a minimum amount of human capital acquired during the years of compulsory education (Wende van der 2003). However, governments are also heavily involved in the financing and delivery of post-compulsory education and training where returns may to a larger extent accrue to the individual and where participation is by choice. An important motivation for individuals to invest in education is that the acquired knowledge and skills tend to raise their productivity and hence earnings potential. Education appears to provide not only an initial earnings advantage but also a wage premium that increases with time spent in the labour market. The strategic objectives for the European systems of education and training were grouped in three big categories that concern:

- The improvement of quality and the effectiveness of systems of education and professional training in the EU
- Facilitation of access to overall systems
- Opening of the systems in the third part world

At the level of initial and ongoing training, there is an effort to encourage business and organisations to invest in the development of workers, skills and promotion of high quality and flexibility in the training schemes. This chapter attempts to examine the job requirement assessment (JRA) in a research study through a questionnaire carried out by a project of OECD, and it attempts to measure the implications and the effects in Greece.

13.2 Job Requirement Assessment

13.2.1 Training Needs Assessment Process

A training needs assessment is the process of separating the job tasks into those for which training is needed and those for it is not and then developing an individual training plan for accomplishing the needed training. This does not merely mean selecting those knowledge, skills or abilities, which are critical to the job performance, but also means determining which the capabilities of the current job incumbents are. Worker skills and job requirements is a policy-oriented study on the skills mismatch debate, which is intended for academics, policymakers and the general public (Alba-Ramirez 1994). Figure 13.1 illustrates the training needs assessment model.

Assessment of the job requirement (skills and competencies) is imperative in the final selection of employees or training candidates. Every effort is made to objectively formulate exactly what the requirements in terms of skills and competencies are. The assessment and development of people forms a cornerstone of the strategic and operational management of human resources, for instance, human capital development and succession planning (Barron et al. 1989).

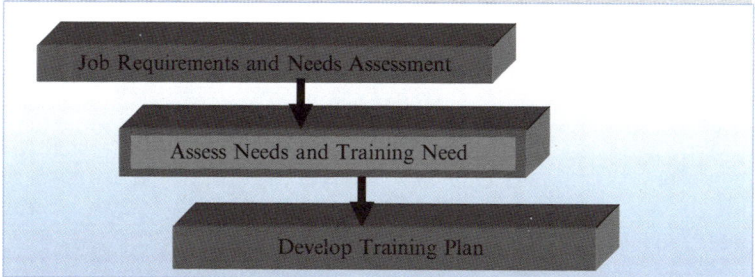

Fig. 13.1 Job requirement assessment

13.2.2 Factors Affecting the Job Requirement Assessment

Despite recent progress owing to positive actions and sensitization campaigns undertaken by governments, disparities in education and training still exist. The various factors which hinder education and training may be grouped into the following main categories (Freeman 1991):

- On the *demand side,* socio-economic and cultural factors which affect the behaviour and the choices (such as poverty budget constraints, structural adjustment programmes, direct costs of training, inconsistent educational and training policies, parents' low level of education, limited school/classroom space, sceptical attitudes towards the benefits, distance from info for education and training)
- On the *supply side,* political and institutional factors (such as insufficient public support, political instability, limited employment opportunities for graduates, lack of clear strategy for education and training, lack of public support for scientific activities)

There is an obvious need to measure the job requirement assessments and to carry out research on their interrelation with the social, economic and cultural characteristics of the countries and communities, as well as with the supply and quality of educational and training opportunities (Holzer et al. 1993).

13.3 Methods of Collection Variables Collected on Job Requirement Assessments

13.3.1 Methodology, Data Channels and Analysis

Data required for measuring the job requirement assessment can be collected from different sources using a variety of existing methods of collection. Essentially, the data sources may be categorised into (OECD 1997, 2008):

(a) Households and individual persons
(b) Teachers

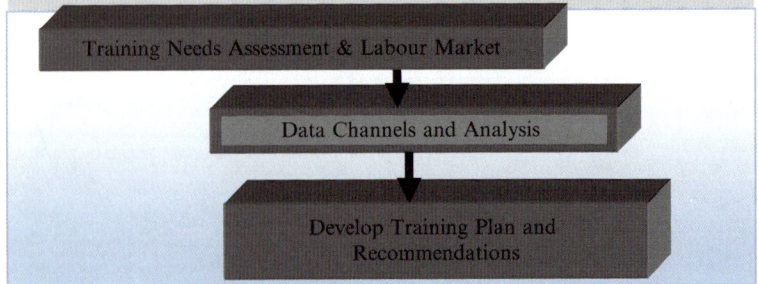

Fig. 13.2 The structure of research approach

The individual persons (households) in this respect refer not only to the students and teaching staff but can also include the parents, other members of the same family, employees, employers, etc. Moreover, the methods of collection may include the regular surveys and the household surveys. Each of these methods has proved to be effective for collecting specific types of education and training statistics.

In the JRA project for Greece, in order to overcome the problems of low budgeting, we have chosen to survey exclusively the Attica region. The estimated target population comprises 1,693,887 individuals, residents of the Attica region (islands excluded), and aged 18–64 years old and currently employed, who belong to 1,079,122 households. This estimation of the population was based on the data of the 2nd quarter of the year 2008 (the 2nd quarter was chosen as the most representative quarter of the year) of the labour force survey (LFS), conducted by the National Statistical Service of Greece (NSSG). The estimation of households is robust as it was based on a sample of 7,500 households, which were selected in a way that the sample was self-weighted (sampling fraction 0.55%). Figure 13.2 illustrates the structure of the research approach (GNSS 2008).

The addresses of the LFS sample of households were not available in electronic form (GNSS 2008). Therefore, the sampling households of the EU-SILC (European Union-Statistics on Income and Living Conditions) survey of the years 2003, 2004 and 2005, in which there were eligible individuals for the survey, were used as our sampling frame. The EU-SILC survey offered the advantage of having in electronic form all the necessary data for the survey such as all the personal information of the individuals (first name, surname, address, telephone) as well as information on the synthesis of the households and the employment status of the household members. The households of the sampling frame with eligible members are 1,608, while the individuals of these households that hold the characteristics of the target population sum up to 2,491. The research sample results can be classified in two main categories, for teachers and households. In the sample of households included the following categories: labourers in mining, construction, manufacturing and transport, sales and services; elementary occupations; drivers and mobile plant operators; machine operators and assemblers; stationary plant and related operators; other craft and related trades workers; precision, handicraft, craft printing and related trades workers; metal, machinery and related trades workers; extraction and building trades workers; skilled agricultural and fishery workers; models; salespersons and demonstrators; personal and protective services workers; customer services clerks; office clerks; other associate professionals; teaching associate professionals; life science and health associate professionals; physical and engineering science associate professionals; other professionals; teaching professionals; life science and health professionals; physical, mathematical and engineering science professionals; managers of small enterprises; corporate managers; legislators and senior officials; and armed forces.

Current data gathered from regular surveys and household surveys are essential for obtaining a general outlook of job requirement assessment. Specific additional data are necessary if one wants to study more in depth the reasons for inequalities in order to identify appropriate measures to reduce disparities. Similarly, information is needed about the aspects of the supply of education, for instance, public policies, resources allocation and school infrastructure. For this kind of information, ad hoc (sample) surveys are best suited, although cost considerations limit their use.

The two-phase sampling was adopted for the selection of household members. The sample size was defined at 709 individuals, according to the available financial resources.

At the first phase with the use of the LFS survey results (two-stage stratified sampling), we defined the distribution of the target population per classes (strata). The total sample of 709 individuals was distributed proportionally in every stratum (stratum = gender × age group) with sampling fraction (GNSS 2008):

$$f = \frac{sample\_size}{target\_population\_size} = \frac{709}{1,693,887} = 0.0004.$$

In order to select the sample of primary school teachers, we used a relatively reliable register of primary school teachers found in the Ministry of National Education and Religious Affairs. At first, we selected the primary school teachers belonging to the Attica region (islands excluded) and then we allocated them by sex, type of teacher and longevity, inserting at each one of them a number of ascending orders. Additionally, we should point out that primary school teachers are aged approximately from 22 to 60 years old.

The sample size distribution per stratum, h, is the following:

Stratum	Gender	Age group	Sample size
11	1 (male)	1 (18_24)	24
12	1 (male)	2 (25_34)	112
13	1 (male)	3 (35_44)	124
14	1 (male)	4 (45_54)	101
15	1 (male)	5 (55_64)	51
21	2 (female)	1 (18_24)	19
22	2 (female)	2 (25_34)	99
23	2 (female)	3 (35_44)	90
24	2 (female)	4 (45_54)	67
25	2 (female)	5 (55_64)	22

Source: GNSS (2008).

The second phase includes the selection of the survey units (GNSS 2008). The individuals comprising the sample were selected in every stratum using as sampling frame the EU-SILC survey data described above. The sampling units' selection was based on equal probabilities and systematic sampling while the sampling frame used had been previously sorted per municipality. During the individuals' selection, in case a second member of the same household was about to be selected, an individual of a different household replaced him/her. So during the individuals' selection, great attention was paid in order to select only one individual per household.

With the implementation of two-phase sampling, the sampling fraction, f, is about 0.0004 ($f = (709/16,93,887) = 0.0004$), and since both LFS and EU-SILC surveys have self-weighting estimators, the selection probability of the sampling units almost coincides with $1/f$ (design weight). Furthermore, since we also have non-response in the survey, in order to properly calculate the extrapolation factors, the initial weights were corrected by being multiplied with the inverse of the response rate in every stratum, thus somehow abolishing self-weighting (GNSS 2008).

The structure and the tasks of questionnaire for the job recruitment assessment were organised into the following activity areas: gender, age and sexual orientation; education and training; litigation and compliance; description classification; personnel information; development of personnel selection procedures; administration/implementation of personnel selection procedures; empirical validation research; training programme development and evaluation; general supervisory/management; personal/professional growth/development/service/continuing education; and general activities applying to multiple categories.

Moreover, the questionnaire for skill domain and underlying skill requirements includes the following categories:

1. *Cognitive skills*: Such as literacy, numeracy, scientific knowledge, problem solving and computing
2. *Interaction/social skills*: Such as influence, managerial skills, self-direction, interaction/social, horizontal interaction and client interaction
3. Physical: Such as strength, manual skill
4. Broad: Such as occupational knowledge and ongoing learning requirement

13.3.2   Results and Implications

The fieldwork has been based on questionnaire formation and interviewing on the questionnaire formatted. The method used was the personal interviewing (GNSS 2008). The questionnaires have been answered by a statistical sample consisted of one hundred eighteen (118) primary school teachers and four hundred and seventy-eight (478) households, located in Athens Prefecture, Greece. The sampling method, as well as the corresponding sample selection, has been executed by the Greek National Statistics Service, Athens, Greece. The draft questionnaire supplied to Greek participating authorities by OECD was translated twice in order to acquire its final form, regarding the Greek language (GNSS 2008).

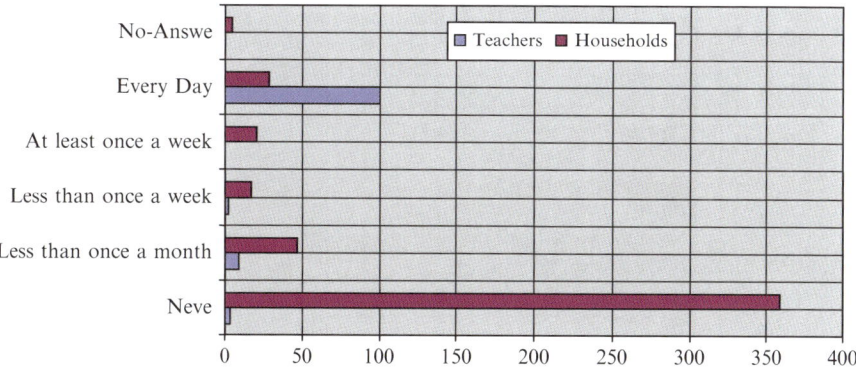

Fig. 13.3 The impact of training in the job

The sample was selected and interviewed by the Greek National Statistics Service. The questionnaire interviews resulted in interviewing one hundred eighteen (118) primary school teachers and four hundred and seventy-eight (478) households in Attica Prefecture, Greece. The data collected have been controlled and confirmed by the Greek National Statistics Service and the General Secretariat of Adult Education (Ministry of Education). Gross response rate (GRR) and net response rate (NRR) coincide in our survey, and they are depicted in the following table (GNSS 2008):

Stratum	Gender	Age group	GRR_NRR (%)
11	1	1	29
12	1	2	83
13	1	3	80
14	1	4	54
15	1	5	39
21	2	1	37
22	2	2	100
23	2	3	62
24	2	4	52
25	2	5	32

Source: GNSS (2008).

The following Figs. 13.3, 13.4 and 13.5 illustrate some of the main findings.

The role of education and training is more and more designated as a major factor of survival and progress of the societies. The current social needs due to their nature place emphasis on knowledge, adaptability and inventiveness. The educational and training system, basic structural element of formation of the future human potential, needs to move gradually so as to meet the new needs and challenges.

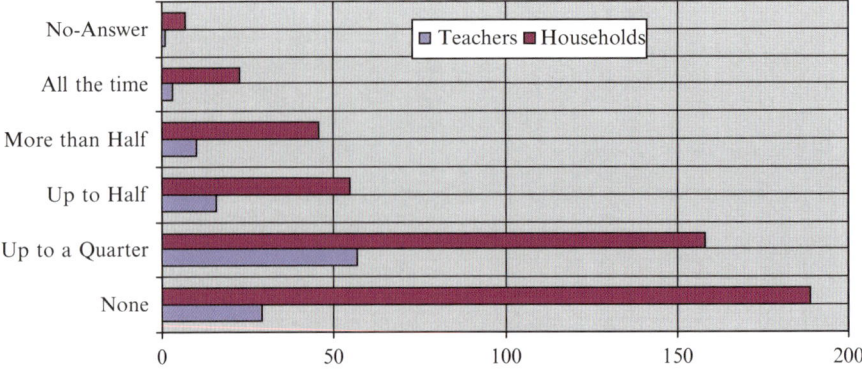

Fig. 13.4 Scientific knowledge: time using scientific knowledge

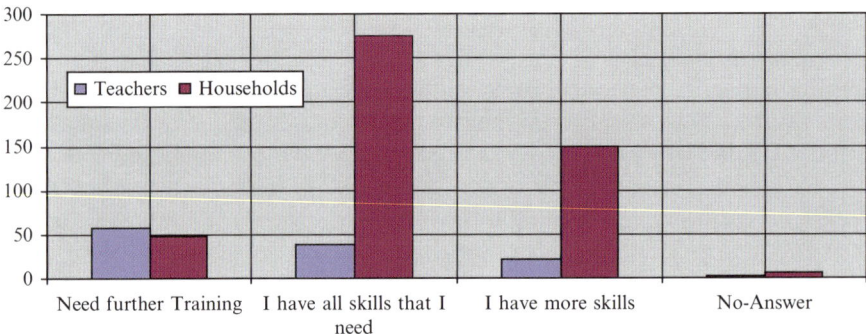

Fig. 13.5 Skills at the work

The main results can be summarised as follows:

- Limited access to training
- Low skills
- Low female participation in scientific and technical fields
- High proportion of illiterate and training
- Scarce or low-scale employment opportunities
- Reduced contribution to national economic and social development
- Limited bargaining power
- Absence from the political decision-making processes

13.4 Summary Conclusions

The Greek national policy in the past for the education and training in relation to employability and vocational training has been emphasised towards the following points:

- Prevention of the unemployment through personalised interventions
- Promotion of the opportunities of access to the labour market
- Empowerment and upgrading of effectiveness and the quality of the interventions in the labour market
- Promotion of entrepreneurship and adaptability of the human resources
- Improvement of the access and participation of women in the labour market

Following our results from the above analysis, in order to ensure the active participation of all in the knowledge society and to improve the position of Greece within the EU and towards the future strategy for the job requirement, assessments have to be emphasised in the following main objectives:

- Teaching of the new ICT as a basic subject, through the use of the new technologies
- Training of the teaching staff
- Improvement of the infrastructure and the communication network in schools, universities and research institutes
- Empowerment of the production and dissemination
- Empowerment of the research, tapping of the new technologies in the research and dissemination of the scientific results

Acknowledgment   The OECD research project entitled "Job Requirement Assessment" was co-funded in Greece by General Secretariat of Adult Education (currently, General Secretariat of Life Long Learning) and IDEKE, Greece. In this project, the participants were the General Secretariat of Adult Education (National Ministry of Education), National Statistical Services of Greece, National Ministry of Employment, National Centre of Public Administration, National Centre for Social Studies and Hellenic Open University.

References

Alba-Ramirez A (1994) Formal training, temporary contracts, productivity and wages in Spain. Oxford Bull Econ Stat 56 p. 151-170.
Barron JM, Black DA, Loewnstein MA (1989) Job matching and on-the-job training. J Labour Econ 7 1-19.
Freeman R (1991) Labour market tightness and the mismatch between demand and supply of less-educated young men in the United States in the 1980s. In: Schioppa FP (ed) Mismatch and labour mobility. Cambridge University Press, Cambridge
Holzer H, Block R, Cheatham M, Knott J (1993) Are training subsidies for firms effective? The Michigan experience. Ind Labor Relations Rev 46 625-636.
GNSS (Greek National Statistical Service) (2008) Report for Job Requirements Approach (JRA) Pilot Survey: specification for National Technical Reports, Programme for the International Assessment of Adult Competencies (PIAAC), Athens, Greece
OECD (1997) Implementing the OECD jobs strategy—member countries experience. OECD, Paris
OECD (2008) Job Requirements Approach (JRA) pilot survey: specification for National Technical Reports, Programme for the International Assessment of Adult Competencies (PIAAC), OECD based in OECD' research project job requirement assessment. In: collaboration with General Secretariat of Adult Education, General Secretariat of Life Long Learning, OECD conference, Paris, 1-2 December 2008.
van der Wende M (2003) European higher education policy: the EU's continuing impact. Int High Educ 32:15–18

Chapter 14
Critical Evaluation of the Greek Tourism Policy

Paris A. Tsartas and Dimitrios G. Lagos

14.1 Introduction

Tourism is an important economic activity for Greece that accounts for about 17.20% of the GDP and creates 20.89% of the employment positions (WTTC 2009). In 2008, the sector of hotels and restaurants accounted for a 7.1% of the country's GDP. At the same time, approximately 963,000 employees, a great percentage of whom live in some periphery, are either directly or indirectly involved in tourism. Greece as a tourist destination holds the seventh position on the scale of tourism profitability (4.6% of the total of the 25 EU member states). Additionally, during the post-war period tourism development had been impressive, since the average annual increase of foreign tourism revenues in dollars for the years 1960–2005 amounted to 13.3%.

If the worldwide estimations (WTO 2000) are confirmed and taking for granted that there will be a travel increase by European citizens, who form the vast majority of the tourists visiting Greek destinations, it is anticipated that in 2016 tourism and travel activities will account for 15.6% of the GDP (i.e. 52.5 billion euro).

In general, during the last years in Greece, the growth of figures relating to tourism can be considered positive. The main reasons for this growth are the country's natural advantages, namely its magnificent Mediterranean landscape along with its mild climate. However, despite the overall good statistics of the Greek tourism in comparison to the international figures and despite its potential, in the recent years tourism industry has presented some signs of fatigue. Greece has been considered a country that hosts low and middle income tourists. Its tourism product is of simple

P.A. Tsartas (✉) • D.G. Lagos
Department of Business Administration, University of the Aegean,
Michalon 8 82100, Chios, Greece
e-mail: ptsar@aegean.gr; d.lagos@aegean.gr

E.G. Carayannis and G.M. Korres (eds.), *European Socio-Economic Integration,*
Innovation, Technology, and Knowledge Management 27,
DOI 10.1007/978-1-4614-5254-6_14, © Springer Science+Business Media New York 2013

form and moderate quality. Consequently, price is the most important factor for the attraction of tourists, which means that its demand will turn to rather less developed countries with a lower labour cost (e.g. Turkey). The indications up to now show that the quality of tourism services rendered is not improving, despite the increasing figures of tourist flow. This is mainly due to the ever-lasting problems of tourism industry, which are endogenous and structural.

This article provides a critical analysis of both the logic and the contents of the Greek tourism policy in order to shape a framework of strategic directions aligned with the international tendencies and tourism industry evolutions. This framework will correspond to the targets of the European integration and will exploit Greece's comparative advantages as a tourism destination.

With regards to the methodological approach, the above objectives could be achieved by means of a PEST analysis in Greece that would define the factors that affect the shaping of both tourism development and policy within the framework of global developments in tourism market, and by means of a SWOT analysis that would define some more specialised internal factors that affect tourism policy and determine the general framework of strategic development for the coming years.

14.2   Review of the International Framework for Tourism Development and Policy

For the first time researchers and literature began referring to tourism development and policy issues in the 1950s. At the beginning, they focussed on development models of tourist destinations by means of which they examined the role that tourism industry plays among tourists-consumers at the place of their origin and tourism product at their destination place.

During the 1970s and 1980s various tourism development models were created (geographical models, spatial planning models, travel and tourism models, origin-destination models, core tourism industry models, economic models, psychological and social models).

Nowadays there are two basic issues found in the international literature concerning tourism development and policy. On one hand they deal with the impact of tourism development and policy on the economy, society, culture and environment of the various tourist destinations and on the other hand with the problematic on whether the tourism development of a location takes place evolutionary or stage by stage (Fennel 1991; Getz 1992; Lagos 2005).

In terms of the aforementioned problematic below follows a brief presentation of the most important tourism development models that have been designed worldwide (Stabler 1997; Sinclair and Stabler 1991; Pearce 1992; Dredge 1999).

Travel models, which were designed based mainly on researches in North American areas, where the journeys by car are the most common ones. Those models describe flows among various tourist destinations, pleasure trips from metropolitan areas (Campbell 1967), tourism flows from urban cores (Rajiotte 1975;

Pearce 1995) and multiple destination trips (Lue et al. 1993). The models under consideration cannot be implemented widely for other tourism destinations, since they are closely related to natural characteristics of particular locations, costs, distances and conditions applying to the routes between places of interest for tourists.

Structural models, which describe the recreation business zones (Stansfield and Rickert 1970) and the spatial planning evolution of coastal resorts due to changes taking place in the natural structure of many coastal resorts (Smith 1992), the attraction of tourists to some locations or destination zones (Gunn 1965, 1993). These models reflect the current situation, are operative and their natural structure has been simplified to interpret some particular phenomena.

Evolutionary models, which take into account the various aspects of development for tourism destinations. Most important among these, Plog's (1973, 1991) *allocentric—psychocentric* model, examining tourism development at a tourist destination based on the succession of tourist personality types, Miossec (1976, 1977) model describing the evolution of tourism destinations in time and space, Opperman's (1993) model describing spatial allocation and the role different groups play in the destinations' evolution, Leiper's (1995) model describing the characteristics and conditions that shape tourism evolution, Butler's (1980) "Tourist Area Life Cycle" model, describing the six stages of tourism evolution, Gartner's (2001) model referring to a three-stage evolutionary process and Papatheodorou's (2004) economic—geographic model that complements Butler's model, emphasising on the evolution of economies where duality (sub-culture) phenomena are observed, in the market and in spatial allocation. These models constitute widely accepted but also significantly criticised paradigms Leiper 1995; Pearce 1995; Lagos 1998).

The *mass tourism model* that constitutes the dominant post-war model for tourism development for many developing countries (Turner and Ash 1975:129–254; Cazes 1989:101–315; Pearce 1992:59–62), the main forms of which are heliotropic-beach tourism and winter-mountain tourism. The seventies crash, with the negative economic, social and environmental consequences brought upon many developing countries, this organised mass tourism model being questioned, due to the "monoculture" phenomena which it created (EC 1993; UNESCO 1976; Vanhove 1997; Fennel 2001).

The *sustainable tourism development model* (Clarke 1997; Hunter 1997; Butler 1999) adopted since the Rio Summit and the fifth EU Action Plan and more specifically by the implementation of Agenda 21. This model, based on innate tourism development, promotes special forms of tourism on a local and regional level since these are considered the basis of development for many areas that are in the initial stages of their development. The implementation of Agenda 21 locally in the Calvia Municipality, Mallorca, Spain is a characteristic example.

In the framework of the aforementioned tourism activity development models, corresponding tourism policies have been developed (Hall and Jenkins 1995; Pridham 1999; Andriotis 2001; Farsari and Prastacos 2004:92–93). Specifically, the tourism policies refer to the guidelines set by international organisations (WTO,

IATA, EU), to the effective functioning of the tourism market (Tremblay 1998; Shaw and Williams 1998), to tourism planning (Inskeep 1994; Hall 1999; Ivars Baidal 2004) and sustainable tourism development (WTO 1993; Weiler and Hall 1992; Stabler 1997). More specifically, the European Union aims at influencing the tourism development of tourist destinations within its member states with a broad array of measures touching various issues (e.g. sustainable development, competition, cultural heritage, transportation, quality, professional education and training, environment), even though tourism policy remains under the authority of the various governments.

The different views represented by the various tourism development models developed post-war reflect at the same time also the different perspectives of the scientific branches from which these have evolved. Most models arose from experience and through observation of existing tourism areas. An analysis of the existing models, despite criticism and any weaknesses these present when applied widely, leads to important conclusions, useful to the study and planning of tourism destinations. However, despite individual disagreements and variance of opinion, the common assessment is that the growth of tourism areas takes place at different phases and it is looked at as a natural change procedure (Miossec 1997; WTTC (World Tourism & Travel Council)/OEF 2005).

Tourism is based on the comparative advantage theory, usually being a labour- rather than capital-intensive activity during the first stages of its development. Later on, it requires large scale investments in infrastructure, highly specialised staff and the use of new technology. This is positive for low to middle growth level countries, where capital is rare and labour abundant. The case of Greece is a characteristic case of implementation of the mass tourism and beach tourism models (Ministry of Development 2006).

14.3 Post-war Greek Tourism Policy Review

After the international economic crisis during the 1970s, which mainly affected the industrial sector, the tertiary sector—and more specifically tourism—rose in importance on a global level, primarily in countries representing an intermediate development level. In this framework, tourism in Greece was considered an alternative strategic choice for development that could contribute to the transformation of the traditional agricultural economies into developed ones, since the peculiar tourism activity structure spreads to the whole spectrum of the economy and can carry other sectors along too, especially those producing consumer goods. Economic development via tourism is considered feasible mainly because the productive resources required for tourism development are usually internally available and do not require import (Dritsakis 1995:1). Moreover, tourism as a par excellence export activity assures the influx of foreign capital and functions as a form of export substitute. Plus, the nature of tourism activity does not require the achievement of economies of scale, as emphasis is placed on the quality of services offered.

In Greece, tourism has always been of great importance for the support of the less favoured or disadvantageous areas. To be able to document the above claim, a diachronic examination is required of both tourism policy and its impact on tourism development. For this reason, the post-war Greek tourism policy can be distinguished into three eras (Tsartas and Lagos 2006:733–761):

- The era of small industry tourism (1950–1966)
- The era of transition to industrialised tourism (1967–1991)
- The era of the political quest for a way out of the crisis (1991–2006)

14.3.1 The Small Industry Tourism Era (1950–1966)

During the period 1948–1966 13 programmes for financial and social development were elaborated and the systematic promotion of tourism activity began by means of adopting strategic objectives and policy proposals. The contents of the various programmes of that era indicate that they were rather occasional and aimed at ensuring as many exchange resources as possible in form of financial and technical aid and not in form of support for the production base of economy, wherein tourism activity could also be included (Sakkas 1994:72). The targets or objectives of tourism policy were general references that most of the times were not accompanied by particular policy measures, the implementation of which would lead to promoting tourism development.

The tourism sector structure of this era can be characterised as that of a small industry, due to the number and the size of tourism enterprises (hotels had an average capacity of 40 beds) as well as due to the organisation of the sector (a small number of non organised travellers, lack of staff qualification, lack of administration methods and product promoting methods).

The post-war acceptance of the liberal concept for the recommended way for economic development of the financially dependent countries mostly formed the prerequisite for providing financial and technical aid by financially developed countries. The demand of US or other international credit institutions from the borrowing countries to elaborate economic programmes aimed at both ensuring a rational utilisation of the provided credits and supervising the economic policy of those countries. In terms of this development logic, the activity of tourism was not the first priority although many international organisations and primarily the World Tourism Organization (WTO) were urging for its systematic promotion.

The critical evaluation of tourism policy, as this is formulated in terms of development programmes, leads to a general questioning as regards the effectiveness of the objectives and aims concerning both the implementation of such tourism programmes and the ability of private tourism entrepreneurship to reconstruct its powers in order to improve the quality of tourism industry.

14.3.2   The Era of Industrialised Tourism (1967–1991)

As regards the programmes of the period 1967–1970, the implemented tourism policy played a significant role for the size and the way of development of tourism industry. The phrasing of those programmes reinforce the logic of promoting tourism by utilising the country's natural and cultural resources and by applying particular policy measures that had clear targets and objectives. These had a rather general character and aimed at achieving high rates of income growth.

More particularly, until 1973 tourism policy aimed at a fast development of the sector intending to maximise foreign exchange revenues to cover the trade deficit of the balance of payments on a current account. Later on, by means of the contents of those programmes until 1980, an attempt was made to rationalise tourism activity development through the enforcement of development laws (L.1313/72 and L.1378/73) in combination with the achievement of regional policy targets (L.289/76) and the reinforcement of less favoured areas (L.849/780). Yet, the results were the exact opposite of what was anticipated due to motive ineffectiveness, not fulfilling the requirements for self-financing as well as various administrative and institutional inadequacies (Mylonas 1997:608).

Private investors remained sceptical towards tourism until 1965. After this year and during the dictatorship (1967–1974) the situation changed, since both the investment motives and the tourism demand were increased, reducing this way the risk of private capitals to a minimum. The greatest part of those investments was directed to big resorts at the coastal zones of tourism destinations that were already known to the international tourism market, such as Rhodes and Corfu, to benefit from the already existing foreign economies, and to new destinations, such as Crete and Chalkidiki. In this era, tour-operators started intervening in the organisation and spatial expansion of the activity, either by promoting some areas or by financing private investments within zones of high demand (Leontidou 1991:88–90).

In the development programmes of the 1980s a new motive system is established (L. 1116/81 and L.1262/82) that aims at decentralisation and creation of small hotel units. However, the investing interest focused again on 5–6 already developed tourism destinations, a fact that led to an oversupply of beds. The rest of them did not have the appropriate social–financial infrastructure and substructure, since the financial resources disposed by the Public Investment Program were insufficient. Therefore, the interest of private initiative was turned to providing illegal accommodation.

The policy of providing motives for investments continues with the same intensity until 1990. The growth rate of the number of beds remains unaltered and the concentration remains very limited despite the differentiation of the percentages of investments and constructing programmes to the benefit of less developed areas. Parallel, a great increase of illegal constructions is noted due to the high demand for accommodation and due to a deeper, fully new speculation on earth, mostly in tourist destinations. This period is characterised by the introduction of the relevant production and organisation methods to the sector, which had been applied in the industry sector.

14.3.3   The Crisis Era (1991–2006)

The drawn tourism policy of this era is described in the Community Support Frameworks. The development programmes of the 1990s (mainly the first and the second CSFs) end up—because of the inexistence of a more comprehensive strategic plan for regional development—to a segmental and fragmented intervention at a regional level, with a doubtful contribution to regional development (Petrakos—Psycharis 2005:396) and consequently to tourism development. However, both the first and the second CSF followed a shallow approach to the tourism sector, which led to lack of attracting motives as well as to the existence of a series of countermotives for the attraction of investors. Furthermore, an unsuitable distribution of the financial resources provided by the Mediterranean Integrated Programs and the First Community Support Framework (CSF) resulted to a maximisation of black economy and the accumulation of problems that limited the country's tourism development. The largest part of the resources is directed to sectorial policies that have a regional dimension and by nature premise the criterion of effectiveness rather than that of interregional equality (Petrakos 2005:104).

In the development programmes of the 2000s, the European Integration results to the country's tourism policy being shaped on a new basis in order to face the new challenges of globalisation, to exploit its comparative advantages and improve its infrastructure, whereas at the same time to attract higher income tourists (Ministry of Development 2003:4). Therefore, the third CSF (2000–2006), which is still in force, has an integrated character and sets targets that serve the European strategy of economic and social integrity and the fulfilment of the prerequisites for a country's accession to the Economic and Monetary Union, which is expected to shape those financial and currency conditions that will favour intra-European tourism and consequently also the Mediterranean tourism.

14.4   Critical Evaluation of Post-war Greek Tourism Policy

The development of Greek tourism began with a significant time delay and evolved in an anarchic and unplanned fashion, a fact that can be proven by the spatial distribution of tourism activity. Specifically, the anarchic tourism development led to the degradation of the environment and the quality of life, which finally caused the loss of comparative advantage for many regions of Greece (Pavlopoulos 1999:121). The influx of tourism currency proved to be especially vulnerable to exterior variations, like wars in the wider area, terrorist attacks, travel guidelines unfavourable for Greece, etc., but the long-term trend has remained upward. Structural problems, such as black economy, seasonality and the inability to attract high-income tourists, remain to a great extent even today. However, the role incoming currency played in the development of the Greek economy cannot be questioned. It has been empirically proven that in the case of post-war Greece, the engine that pulled the Greek economy towards the road to development was the tertiary sector and especially tourism (Delivani 1991).

This can be interpreted by the fact that Greece constitutes an alluring tourist destination internationally, owing to its very long coastline, the great number of island complexes, the good climate combined with the sun—sea diptych, as well as the vast richness of its archaeological sites and museums. This comparative advantage constitutes a characteristic criterion for the preference shown to Greece as a tourist destination, something indicated by the increase in total arrivals by 2.4% on average during the 1960–2000 period (Dritsakis 2004). As a result, in the period mentioned, the share of tourism in the GDP rose from 2.5% to about 15%. Moreover, the successful organisation of the 2004 Olympic Games meant that Greece's recognisability as a tourist destination was greatly elevated, whereas it also had other positive results (increase in international arrivals and income for 2005 and 2006). The utilisation of the Olympic Games infrastructure and installations for various purposes provides also the possibility to improve the efficiency of tourism-related authorities, following the model set by Barcelona, and could prove uselful for entering into new tourism markets (e.g. Russia, China) and increasing the share it enjoys in the existing ones, ultimately aiming at improving the competitiveness of the Greek tourism product.

However, despite the good general image Greek tourism enjoys, the basic synthesis of the advantages it enjoys is not substantially differentiated since the 1950s and remains the same (Tsartas and Tsartas 2000; Apostolopoulos and Sonmez 2001; Farsari and Prastacos 2004). The European countries constitute 90% of the countries of origin for tourists in Greece and this creates a great dependence on specific market-countries abroad. This can be understood if we consider the empirical application of Butler's (1980, 2006) Tourism Area Life Cycle (TALC) theory concerning evaluating the maturity of the main competitive tourism destinations in Greece based on the population/arrivals index for a tourism destination. It is estimated that the relevant index has the approximate same value for Spain, Greece and Portugal (0.82, 0.84 and 0.85 respectively), while it stands at 6.17 for Turkey, having shown the greatest variation in the last years. Should these variations continue at the same pace for the following years, then Turkey will be almost at the same levels as the other three countries, that is to say, at the maturity stage (SETE 2005:39). Moreover, taking the assessment of the six competitiveness indexes into account (related to infrastructure, the environment, technology, human resources and freedom of access) conducted by WTTC in the Mediterranean, we have a different evaluation of the current tourism competitiveness (Fig. 14.1). We can see that Spain is the most competitive country, followed by Cyprus, Portugal, Greece, Egypt, Croatia and Turkey (SETE 2005:21). This assessment is based on a series of socio-economic macro-variables in each country and it ignores each country's tourism market's conditions and trends at any specific point in time.

Of course, the authorities exercising tourism policy in Greece did not pay the required attention to the above, since currency influx continued to rise over time. However, the rapid development of other competitive tourism destinations, such as Turkey, Tunisia, Morocco, Egypt and others, offering a similar tourism product has

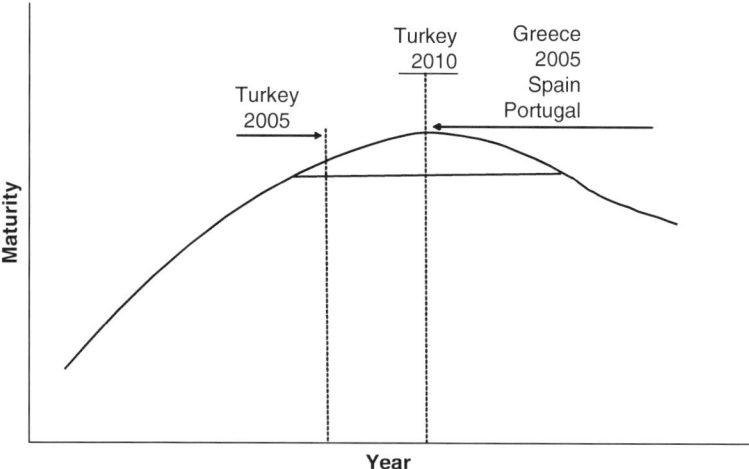

Fig. 14.1 Tourism area life cycle. *Source*: SETE 2005:39

created an intense competitiveness problem, since competition remains at the same level and there is no essential differentiating element between the Greek tourism product and these competitor countries. On the other side, there exists a series of important inhibitory factors restraining entrepreneurial activities with Greek tourism, namely the strict regulatory environment, the obstacles to foreign investment and restrictions to foreign nationals acquiring property in Greece.

The general ascertainment arising form the above is that during the whole postwar period tourism has played an important role in economic development, mainly as a foreign currency source, but also as an additional income source. However, there are some indications that the size of tourism flow is decreasing, the used capacity of the existing facilities is being limited, the qualitative level of the rendered services is not being improved and the tourist season covers a few months only. Moreover, the logic of tourism policy is based on the argument that tourism is an important wealth-bringing source that contributes in a positive way to the country's social-economic development. This policy that remained unchanged over the years was based on the prevailing model of organised mass tourism and that of the standardised package, which used to express the international tourism demand. Since the 1980s, the issue of creating special forms of tourism arose. However, Greece's lag in areas of specialised tourism infrastructure (marinas, golf courts, conference centres, thalassotherapy centres, etc.) compared to its main competitors constitutes a negative element to the modernisation and upgrading of the tourism offer, but also to the differentiation of the qualitative composition of the Greek tourism product. Countries such as Switzerland, France and Italy dispose of a developed internal tourism and a comparatively small Tour Operator penetration, while more and more people turn to special forms of tourism.

In general, the logic of the post-war tourism policy was expressed by an excessive love for figures (arrivals or tourist currency or new jobs), regardless of their real impact on economy and society. All the aforementioned tend to make tourism a problematic sector, whereas in fact Greece has some very essential comparative advantages in relation to the other competitive countries.

14.5   Analysis of the External Environment Affecting Greek Tourism Policy

Variations in tourist flow have been noted during the last years, which lead to changes in the receiving countries' participation ratios out of the total international tourism. Europe and America see their share in international tourist flow falling, while East Asia and Africa notice an increase in theirs. The main factors to contribute to these developments are the transit fee reductions because of the intense competition in international air transport, as well as the development of mass tourism.

The countries of the Mediterranean are divided in two categories depending on the emphasis placed on tourism product (Patsouratis 2002:110–111). Greece, Spain, Portugal and Turkey as well as Italy, to a lesser degree, are included in the first category, offering recreational tourism based on sun and sea. The second category contains France and Italy that offer vacation tourism with a great variety of traditional and modern culture. Over the last few years, the countries in the second category have begun to orient themselves to special forms of tourism, which are the new international trends in tourism development in order to hold on to and increase their shares of the global tourism market.

The share held by the Greek tourism compared to the European and international competition has shown a downward movement over the last few years. Explaining this course lies with the factors that define cost and quality in general for the tourism product offered to the international tourism market. The factors refer to the production sector (cost, productivity), the organisation of production and distribution, the macro-economic environment (e.g. currency policies) within which the sector operates and even to the practices and policies adopted by other tourist destinations in order to attract tourists.

The *factors* affecting tourism activity in Greece are both internal and external and are the following (Mylonas 1997:575–615; Lagos 1998; Patsouratis 2002:196–198; Tsartas 2004:79)

- Globalisation of tourism development
- Development of large verticalised and internationalised tourism enterprises
- The new economy
- The Knowledge Society (a shift in the relation of work, rest and education)
- The structure and the role of the State
- Local authorities

- The structure of the market and more particularly that of the tourism market
- The quality of the tourism product
- The ageing of population
- The change in consumer conditions and living conditions
- The circles of life (education–work–pension)
- The environment
- The culture
- Sports
- Transports
- New technologies and especially the internet

The aforementioned factors affect both the side of tourism product supply and demand and the side of the philosophy and structure of the tourism model itself as well as the role of tourism in the financial life of the country and its citizens.

Beyond the above, other factors exist that affect the development of tourism on an international level and as a consequence the structure of tourism demand and offer.

Under the light shed by the factors mentioned above and that of international tourism characteristics, it is obvious that the external environment affects tourism policy in every country that is receiving tourists. The tourism policy authorities take these factors into account; factors affecting and defining policy in quantity and quality.

14.6   Factors that Will Affect Tourism Policy in the Next Years

Obviously, for the shaping of a framework for future tourism policy it is essential to detect and examine the main *characteristics* and *problems* of the Greek tourism that affect the operation of the country's tourism system.

The main characteristics of the Greek tourism development model can be localised in the following points (Tsartas and Tsartas 2000:189–211; Patsouratis 2002:15–32)

- Increasing arrivals of foreign tourists (foreigners account for approximately 75% of the total overnight stays in hotels).
- Dependence of many areas on organised tourism taking place in the summer season.
- Most frequent is the mass tourism of low and middle income classes.
- Reduction of the tourism expenditure per capita in steady values.
- Increase of the share of visitors from Europe.
- Great reduction in the share of American tourists.
- Increase of tourists coming from Eastern Europe.
- Increasing share of domestic tourism.
- Increased seasonality of Greek tourism.

- Small number of tourism enterprises other than hotels.
- One-dimensional tourism product: "Sun and sea".
- The comparative advantages of the Greek tourism are mostly inherited ones (natural environment, cultural heritage).
- High geographic concentration of tourism infrastructure.
- Oligopsonic structure of tourism demand with just a few tour-operators.
- Hotel units/accommodations:
- Of small size and moderate/low quality
- Of a small degree of concentration and a very small verticalization
- Facing administrative hindrances as regards the entrance of new hotel enterprises in developed tourist destinations (saturation).

The most important *problems* that the Greek tourism faces today are mostly structural ones and can be summarised in the following points (Lagos 1990; Leondidou 1991:84–106; Aggelidis 1995:63–68)

- The great dependence of Greek tourism on tour-operators and consequently on their volition and interests.
- Greece was deprived of its comparative advantage of low-priced tourism product as a result of the tourism engagement of countries with low labour costs.
- Lack of existence of a special tourism infrastructure.
- Low degree of development of special forms of tourism.
- Many illegal accommodations causing various problems.
- Great seasonality of tourism activity.
- Interregional and intraregional inequalities of tourism development.
- Dominance of low class accommodations and uneven spatial distribution of hotels within the country.
- Environmental pollution problems and noise pollution noted in many tourist destinations.
- Mass tourism orientation as a model for tourism development as well as an old-fashioned institutional framework.

According to the above characteristics, problems and defining factors of the Greek tourism as well as the conclusions that arose from the critical evaluation of the post-war programmes for financial development concerning tourism development, a SWOT analysis is carried out for the shaping of a new tourism policy and strategy for the coming years (Konsolas 2002:110–130). This analysis aims at strengthening and presenting advantages, limiting disadvantages, maximising the seizing of opportunities and minimising the risks of tourism activity in Greece.

More particularly, this analysis comprises of the following points (Table 14.1).

According to the above data, the solution of the problem lies in offering high quality tourism services, which will create the prerequisites for supplying a competitive tourism product in the international tourism markets. This can be achieved by utilising the cultural heritage and the historical monuments of Greece, which form its competitive advantage, as well as by enriching and differentiating its tourism product.

Table 14.1 SWOT analysis of Greek regions

Strengths	Weaknesses	Opportunities	Threats
• A mild climate for a long period annually • A differentiated and of high quality natural environment • A great cultural heritage • Existence of many SMEs, which account for a "person-alised hospitality" • A powerful "cultural" image of the country • An intense insular character • A high degree of security feeling for tourists in comparison to other competi-tive destinations	• A low tourism expenditure due to the attraction of low income tourists • A low quality of tourism infrastructures and private services rendered • A restricted utilisation of natural and cultural resources • Lack of special tourism infrastructures, additional activities as well as activities for people with special interests • Mediocre training of man-power (both entrepreneurs and employees) • Great concentration of accommodations and tourists in some areas (mostly islands) • Lack of complex tourism products to attract tourists with special Interests	• Differentiation of supply by the consumers who create new potential markets besides the ones of mass sun/tropical tourism • Unification of the internal European market by means of the euro currency • Promotion of the country through the 2004 Olympic Games • Increase of the ability to access the consumer directly through the internet • Opportunity to exploit local/traditional products by the tourism network in order to upgrade and differentiate it	• Increasing concentration of tour-operators • Increasing competition abroad by cheaper countries (Mediterranean, East Europe, Middle East) • Increasing competition among countries with tourism products of high quality and differentiation

14.7 Tourism Policy During the New 5 Years Planning Period 2007–2013

The basic target of the interventions in the tourism sector for the next planning period of the community programmes 2007–2013 (National Strategic Reference Framework—NSRF) is the increase of demand for an overall qualitative improvement of the Greek tourism product and the rendered services at all levels. This basic development target can be analysed into the following partial strategic targets:

• Utilisation of the country's natural and cultural resources for the reinforcement of the tourism product.
• Tourism product differentiation combined with a dynamic development of special forms of tourism.

- Construction or upgrading of hotel infrastructure, but also of special tourism infrastructure required for the development of special forms of tourism.
- Upgrading the qualifications and skills of the man-power engaging in the tourism sector.
- Reinforcing the international promotion of Greece as a safe and attractive destination.
- Extanding the tourism season and decreasing seasonality by means of an increased arrival of foreign visitors and the parallel reinforcement of domestic tourism.
- Rational settlement of spatial problems and promoting of legislative and institutional issues required for the dynamic development of all forms of tourism within the framework of sustainable development that respects the environment and the cultural heredity on a national and regional level.
- Encouraging innovative actions by means of using the achievements and tools provided by the society of knowledge, modern information technologies and communications as well as modern financial tools.

The above strategic targets arise from the imperative need to face main issues regarding tourism industry, which focus on the following points:

- Reinforcing entrepreneurship and tourism investments for the expansion and upgrading of the tourism product.
- Developing special forms of tourism in order to expand the tourism product, stretch tourism development geographically and reduce seasonality.
- Reinforcing synergies, innovations and utilisation of knowledge in tourism entrepreneurship.
- Upgrading, proposing and promoting tourist destinations with special actions for developing or developed special tourist destinations.
- Reinforcing competitiveness and extraversion of the Greek tourism by developing ways for its support and making them operative.

The aforementioned tourism policy refers to all aspects of tourism in Greece. It relates to both demand and supply. It strengthens the development model of a small/medium tourism enterprise of family type. Perhaps the main disadvantage of this policy lies in the fact that it is quite general and aims at covering everything without setting any priorities and without a systematic planning. It does not provide answers to the main questions whether and to what extent the mass tourism model will remain the prevailing model in Greece, how could the influence of tour-operators be limited—if, of course, it can be limited—whether special tourism infrastructures can develop correctly, and, more generally, whether the development of tourism will or will not respect the natural environment. Additionally, there is no clear strategy for the development of tourism on a 12-month basis, the elaboration of the Special Spatial Plan for tourism has not been completed yet, there is no scientific support of tourism, since there is a deficit in university education and no Satellite Tourism Accounts have been created and finally there is no framework for the restoration of the good market operation that would create competitive conditions for the improvement of tourism product quality (Kourtis 2004:77–82).

Consequently, the current policy should be re-evaluated and in the future it should be based on new management criteria, accompanied parallel by a clear positioning strategy for the Greek tourism product. The objective should be to materialise both short- and long-term goals such as upgrading the quality of all services provided by every tourism authority, facing present problems and increasing the tourism industry's competitiveness and productivity. This requires the establishment of an integrated long-term tourism plan with the aid of modern marketing tools that will aim for specific quantity and quality goals, such as softening seasonality, exploitation of comparative advantages, development of special forms of tourism and connecting tourism activity to the productive process. This policy should contain separate policies which will be connected to the model of integrated innate local tourism development and will also take into account the principles of sustainable development.

14.8   Conclusions and Implications

The above critical review of the Greek tourism policy shows that in the post-war era the Greek tourism industry was based as a tourist destination on an almost granted composition of the country's comparative advantages. This composition included the natural attractions, the mild climate and the monuments, which led the tourism market to organise the entrepreneurial activity with the orientation from "demand to supply". This model functioned sufficiently during the 1960s and the 1970s, but the tourism industry continues in its vast majority to apply the same model even today. The basic composition of the advantages of the Greek tourism remains the same. The large part of the visitors supporting the tourism industry comes to Greece to enjoy the sun, the sea, the ancient monuments, the environment, the hospitality and the originality of the people.

More particularly, the overall estimation is that during the whole post-war era there was an inability to plan a steady, long-term tourism policy. This is also obvious from the incomplete planning attempts of some specialised fields of tourism development (e.g. spatial distribution, environment, decentralisation, regional development, legislation on motives, advertisement). On the contrary, Community Support Frameworks, regardless of the criticism on whether or not the distribution of the available financial resources is rational, shape a new framework of tourism policy that attempts to enrich and differentiate the Greek tourism product. However, the prevailing opinion that in Greece the logic of elaborating measures for tourism development is just mere empiricism resulted in tourism development following a distorted spatial planning that led to excessive concentration of tourism supply in some areas, to uncalculated pollution of the natural environment, saturation and degradation of some areas. The consequence of the above was that the Greek tourism product is not competitive and there are many structural tourism problems that obstruct the effectiveness of tourism policy measures.

Moreover, the above review leads to the general conclusion that tourism in Greece is and will remain a healthy dynamic sector that will bring revenues, contribute to the GDP increase, encourage investments and vitalise employment. Therefore, it is anticipated that it will form an essential element and an important parameter of the Greek tourism development. However, the existing model of tourism development in Greece exploits only very few comparative advantages of the ones that the country has to offer as a tourist destination and focuses mostly on insular and coastal areas and utilises solely the good climate and the close relation to the sea. Thus, the suggested tourism policy framework for Greece should focus on the high international competitiveness and the effective operation of its tourism industry in terms of the sustainable tourism development (WTO 1993). For this reason it should draw an integrated tourism development programme on a national and regional level with main axes the strong points of the Greek tourism and the opportunities emerging in the international tourism market, whereas at the same time it should limit its disadvantages and weaknesses. This programme must be accompanied by a specialised tourism policy and strategy that will cover all aspects of tourism industry and will form a complex "grid" of all individual policies of the central state with a regional dimension (Zacharatos 2002; PNUE/PAM 2005:68). Furthermore, it will also take into consideration the specialised issues that will be determined by the Special Spatial Plan of tourism. It is estimated that this will gradually direct the Greek tourism from mass tourism to selective—customer oriented tourism. In that way, it will manage to escape from "monoculture" and will be led to pluralism, quality and sustainability of the tourism product, which will be orientated towards the demands and the interests of modern tourists-consumers.

References

Aggelidis M (1995) Locating tourism in Greece. Problems of development, location and environment. Proposal in the day congress "Tourism and Environment", Technical chamber of Greece. Vol 5 J Technika Chronika 63–68, Athens (in Greek)

Andriotis K (2001) Tourism planning and development in crete: recent tourism policies and their efficacy. J Sustain Tourism 9(4):298–316

Apostolopoulos Y, Sonmez S (2001) Greek tourism on the Brink: restructuring or stagnation and decline. In: Apostolopoulos Y, Loukissas P, Leontidou L (eds) Mediterranean tourism; facets of socioeconomic development and cultural change. Routledge, London, pp 72–88

Butler RW (1980) The concept of tourism area cycle of evolution: implications for management of resources. Can Geogr 24(1):5–12

Butler RW (1999) Sustainable tourism—a state of the art review. Tourism Geogr 1:7–25

Butler RW (2006) The origins of the Tourism Area Life Cycle. In: The Tourism Area Life Cycle, vol 1, Aspects of tourism 28. Channel View Publications, Toronto, pp 13–26

Campbell CK (1967) An approach to research in recreational geography. In Occasional Papers No. 7. Department of Geography, University of British Columbia, Vancouver

Cazes G (1989) Les nouvelles colonies de vacances? L'Harmattan, Paris

Clarke J (1997) A framework of approaches to sustainable tourism. J Sustain Tourism 5(3):224–233

Delivani E (1991) Tourism as an alternative engine of growth: the case of Greece. Unpublished Ph.D., York University, UK

Dredge D (1999) Destination place planning and design. Ann Tourism Res 26(4):772–794

Dritsakis N (2004) Cointegration analysis of German and British tourism demand for Greece. *Tourism Management* 25, 111-119.

Dritsakis N (1995) An economic analysis of foreign tourism to Greece. Sakkoulas, Thessaloniki

EC (1993) Taking account of environment in tourism development. Study prepared by ECONSTAT EC DG XXIII. European Commission, Brussels

Farsari Y, Prastacos P (2004) Conceptualising tourism policies in north Mediterranean mass destinations. Tourism Today Fall:89–102

Fennel DA (2001) A Content Analysis of Ecotourism Definitions. *Current Issuesin Tourism* Vol 4, No 5, Department of Recreation and Leisure Studies,Brock University, St Catharines Ontario L2S 3A1. Canada.

Fennel D (1991) Ecotourism: an introduction. Routledge, London

Gartner WC (2001) "Issues of Sustainable Development in a Developing Country Context" in *Tourism in the Age of Globalisation,* edited by Salah Wahab and Chris Cooper, 2001:306-318, London: Routledge.

Getz D (1992) Tourism and destination life cycle. Ann Tourism Res 19:752–770

Gunn C (1965) A concept for design of tourism recreation region. BJ Press, Mason, MI

Gunn C (1993) Tourism planning: basics, concepts and cases. Francis and Taylor, Washington, DC

Hall CM (1999) Tourism planning: policies, processes and relationships. Prentice Hall, Harlow

Hall CM, Jenkins JM (1995) Tourism and public policy. Routledge, London

Hunter C (1997) Sustainable tourism as an adaptive paradigm. Ann Tourism Res 24(4):850–867

Inskeep E (1994) National and regional planning. Routledge/World Tourism Organization, London

Ivars Baidal JA (2004) Tourism planning in spain: evolution and perspectives. Ann Tourism Res 31(2):313–333

Konsolas I (2002) The competitive advantage of Greece: an application of Porter's diamond. Ashgate, Burlington, VT

Kourtis P (2004) Strategy and competitiveness in tourism within the framework of regional development. Doctoral dissertation (unpublished), Harokopio University, Athens (in Greek)

Lagos D (1990) Structural problems of the Greek tourism. J Tourismos kai Econ 136, Athens (in Greek)

Lagos D (1998) Tourism as a factor for promoting regional development. Rev Urban Region Stud TOPOS 14:47–65, Athens (in Greek)

Lagos D (2005) Tourism economics. Kritiki Press, Athens (in Greek)

Leiper N (1995) Tourism management. RMIT Press, Melbourne

Leontidou L (1991) Greece: prospects and contradictions of tourism in the 1980s. In: Williams AM, Shaw G (eds) Tourism & economic development. Belhaven Press, London

Lue C, Crompton J, Fesenmaier D (1993) Conceptualization of multidestination pleasure trips. Ann Tourism Res 20:289–301

Ministry of Development (2003) Strategic development plan of the Greek tourism 2004–2010. Ministry of Development, Athens

Ministry of Development (2006) Text for planning the interventions of the planning period 2007–2013 in the tourism sector. Ministry of Development, Athens

Miossec J.M., (1977) Un modele de l' espace touristique, L' *espace Geographique,* 6(1), 41-8.

Miossec JM (1976) Elements pour une Theorie de L' Espace Touristique. Les Cahiers du Tourisme. CHET, C-36 CHET, Aix-en-Provence

Miossec JM (1997) Une modele de l' espace touristique. *L' Espace Geographique* 6(1):41–48

Mylonas A (1997) Tourism as country's power. Minutes of the conference of the Athens University of Economics and Business titled: "The present and the future of the Greek Economy", vol 1. Press: Athens University of Economics and Business, Athens, p 595–615 (in Greek)

Opperman M (1993) Tourism space in developing countries. Ann Tourism Res 20:535–560

Papatheodorou A (2004) Exploring the evolution of tourism resorts. Ann Tourism Res 31(1): 219–234

Patsouratis B (2002) Greek tourism sector competitiveness. Institute of Tourism Research and Forecasting (ITEP), Athens (in Greek)

Pavlopoulos P (1999) Tourism sector: size and dynamics. Papazisis Publications, Athens (in Greek)

Pearce D (1992) Tourist development. Longman Scientific and Technical, Essex

Pearce D (1995) Tourism today: a geographical analysis, 2nd edn. Longman, New York, NY

Petrakos G (2005) Regional inequalities and regional policy in Greece. Minutes of the Day Congress titled: "Regional Development in Greece: Tendencies and Perspectives" (Editing Ch. Kokkosis – I. Psycharis). Press: Greek Department of the European Regional Science Association (ERSA), Volos, p 89–110 (in Greek)

Plog S (1973) Why destinations rise and fall in popularity. Cornell Hotel Restaur Admin Quart 14(4):13–16

Plog S (1991) Leisure travel: making it a growth market again. Wiley, New York, NY

PNUE/PAM (Programme des nations unies pour l'environment. Plan d' action pour la Méditerranée) (2005) Dossier on tourism and sustainable development in the Mediterranean. MAP Technical Reports Series 159, Athens

Pridham G (1999) Towards sustainable tourism in the Mediterranean? Policy and practice in Italy, Spain and Greece. Environ Polit 8(2):97–116

Psycharis I (2005) Regional programs of the community support frameworks. Scientific Studies in honor of Professor N. Konsolas of the University of Social and Political Studies, Athens, pp 375–399 (in Greek)

Rajiotte F (1975) The different travel patterns and spatial framework of recreation and tourism. In: Tourism as a factor in national and regional development, Occasional Paper 4. Dept of Geography, Trent University, Peterborough, ON, p 43–52

Sakkas D (1994) The regional programs of the period 1947-1966 and their relation with suggestive programming. Collective Volume "The Greek society during the first post-war era (1945–1967)", Athens, p 59–76 (in Greek)

SETE (Association of Greek Tourist Enterprises) (2005) The challenge of competitiveness and the need for readjusting the Greek tourism product. SETE, Athens (in Greek)

Shaw G, Williams AM (1998) Entrepreneurship, small business culture and tourism development. In: Ioannides D, Debbage KG (eds) The economic geography of the tourist industry. Routledge, London, pp 235–255

Sinclair MT, Stabler JM (1991) The tourism industry. an international analysis. Cab International, Oxon

Smith RA (1992) Beach resort evolution: implications for planning. Ann Tourism Res 19(2): 304–322

Stabler MJ (1997) Tourism and sustainability. Principles to practice. Cab International, Oxon

Stansfield CA, Rickert JE (1970) The recreational business district. J Leisure Res 2:213–225

WTTC (World Travel & Tourism Council) (2009) Travel & tourism's economic perspective. Brussels

WTTC (World Tourism & Travel Council)/OEF (2005) Travel & tourism simulated satellite accounts. Brussels

Tremblay P (1998) The economic organization of tourism. Ann Tourism Res 25:837–859

Tsartas P (2000) Critical evaluation of the parameters composing the characteristics of the post-war tourism development. In: Avgerinou-Kolonia S, Zacharatos Ger et al (eds) (Editing: P. Tsartas) Tourism development: multiscientific approaches. Exantas Press, Athens, p 189–211 (in Greek)

Tsartas P (2004) Tourism development in Greek insular and coastal areas: sociocultural changes and crucial policy issues. In: Bramwell B (ed) Coastal mass tourism: diversification and sustainable development in southern Europe. Channel View Publications, UK, pp 68–84

Tsartas P, Lagos D (2006) The policy of the Greek tourism through development programs, Collective Volume "Economic systems, development policies and strategies of enterprises in the era of globalization". Studies in honor of Professor Stergios Mpampanasis of the University of the Aegean (Editing: B. Aggelis–L. Maroudas). Papazisis Press, Athens, p 733–761 (in Greek)

Turner L, Ash J (1975) The golden Hordes: international tourism and the pleasure periphery. Constable, London

UNESCO (1976) The effects of tourism on socio-cultural values. Ann Tourism Res 4:74–105

Vanhove N (1997) Mass tourism: benefits and costs. In: Wahab S, Pigram JJ (eds) Tourism development and growth—the challenge of sustainability. Routledge, London

Weiler B, Hall CM (eds) (1992) Special interest tourism. Belhaven Press, London

WTO (1993) Sustainable tourism development: a guide for local planners. WTO, Madrid

WTO (2000) Tourism vision 2020, vol 1–6. WTO, Madrid

Zacharatos G (2002). Let us finally see tourism as an industry. J Economikos Tachydromos 38–41, 5.1.2002 Athens (in Greek)

Index

Printed by Printforce, the Netherlands